W*HAT* J*ESUS* B*ELIEVES*

"You have entered the Revelation Zone.

Your journey begins here."

Holy Spirit

WHAT JESUS BELIEVES

Thank You...

How can I express in words what my heart is feeling towards all of you who encouraged me and believed in the testimony behind What Jesus Believes? There are simply not words to accomplish that. You all know who you are...

...and so does *the ONE I LOVE.*

I love you all,
Jean

All blank pages, empty SPACE, including margins and space between paragraphs and / or headings and title or subtitle are available for Your Revelation Notes. Feel free to write everywhere and make your WJB book your new journal. Using different colored pens helps separate your notes. GOD bless you on your Journey.
You are loved.

What Jesus Believes

Jean Vandeman Fahey

Shining Lighthouse Books

Copyright © 1998-2016 Jean Vandeman Fahey

ISBN: 978-0-9977862-0-0

Dedication

While driving one night, I received a message from the LORD:

"I want you to write a book for Me."

When He told me the name of the book, *What Jesus Believes*, I was so afraid; I didn't want to mess up His book. In my mind, I thought about the Bible and how cherished every word is to me and to millions of others. I knew without a doubt that it was GOD, Who was speaking directly to me. It was so loud and so clear that it could not have been any clearer if it had been audible to my natural ears. I remember actually shaking at times while I would write the words He was speaking to me. At other times, I would laugh or cry; it was an experience unlike any other I had ever had. Isn't that just so like Him? We think, *Oh, I know GOD!* And, then, it's like He turns Himself a little bit so that you see another facet on an immeasurable diamond and you say, *Ah, LORD! I am completely undone! I spoke words that I did not know or understand!* I could so relate to *Job and to what he had felt when GOD spoke to him in Chapters 38-41*. His love patiently saw me through typing the Words I heard Him speak and the *many* questions I had as to what I was hearing. Over and over again, I would ask, *"Where is that in the WORD, LORD?"* Over and over again, He would give me my answers through His Scripture, and WJB would grow page by page, chapter by chapter until it was finally completed.

Holy Spirit is the wisest, most amazing, sweet, kind, holy and completely pure, perfect love and full of grace *person I* have ever met. He led me to know the GOD I serve and His Son, Jesus, in depths yet unknown to me when I started writing this book.

This book is dedicated to Him.

My ABBA
(GOD the Father)
My Y'SHUA HaMashiach
(GOD the Son, Jesus the Christ)
Holy Spirit
(The Spirit of GOD, the Spirit of Jesus Christ).
Who is and will forever be my Best friend.
He IS
THE ONE I LOVE.
I am eternally thankful to be His daughter, His sister, and part of His Beautiful Bride!

CONTENTS

GOD is Love. 8

INTRODUCTION 9

PART ONE 15

A Look at the Glory 15

1 16

A Look at the Book of John...16

2 28

"Everything That the Father Has Is Mine" 28

3 48

The Anointing 48

PART TWO 79

Walking in the Glory 79

4 80

The Disciples 80

WHAT JESUS BELIEVES

5 98

Follow by Example 98

6 112

Worship: Getting Intimate with GOD............................112

7 160

Sharing the Vision 160

8 194

On Whom You Can Depend..194

Edited by: Mary Montgomery

NOTE: I have taken the liberty of adding brackets [ ] and/or parentheses ( ) containing words to clarify, or definitions to help define or give explanation; and/or I have also utilized ALL CAPS, **bold**, *italics*, and/or underlining for emphasis].

GOD is Love.

I am eternally thankful for that.

Jean

INTRODUCTION

"Through the reading of this book, watch as scripture Divinely connects in ways you have not seen before."
Holy Spirit

"Most assuredly, I say to you, he who believes in Me, the works that I do he will do also; and greater works than these he will do, because I go to My Father" (John 14:12 NKJV).

"This is Truth."
Holy Spirit

"For GOD so loved the world, that He gave His only begotten Son, that whosoever believeth in Him should not perish, but have everlasting life" (John 3:16 KJV).

"I Love you this much."
Holy Spirit of Jesus Christ
(Holy Spirit is the Spirit of Jesus Christ)

GOD is inborn in us through Jesus His Son by the power of His precious Holy Spirit. Therefore, we are GOD and man because we have GOD in man. (See 2 Corinthians 6:16).

"We made you on purpose, We love you unconditionally and you are eternal. You are invited to spend Eternity with Us."
Holy Spirit

Jesus said, "That they" (The Church) "ALL may be ONE, as You, Father, are in Me, and I in You; that they also may be ONE in Us, that the world may believe that You sent Me. And the Glory which You gave

WHAT JESUS BELIEVES

Me I have given them, that they may be ONE just as We are ONE: I in them, and You in Me; that they may be made perfect in ONE, and that the world may know that You have sent Me, and have loved them as You have loved Me" (John 17:21-23 NKJV).

Are we (Christians) GOD? No. This is not saying that we are GOD, but that we are His children and "joint heirs with Christ" and we are to act (function, behave) like it. Verse 23 says, "...And have loved them as you have loved Me (Jesus)." Most of us easily believe that GOD loves Jesus His son, very, very much, but it seems *much* harder for us to believe that He really loves us as much as He loves Jesus. Once we have grasped that, a new fire is birthed in our souls! That new fire is the door to the Power, the Life, our <u>GOD</u> in Whom "we live and move and have our being;" all of which comes to us through the Holy Spirit of GOD. The red hot fire that opens this door is called "Faith"! The prophet Jeremiah said, "...but His word was in mine heart as a burning fire shut up in my bones..." (Jeremiah 20:9 KJV).

Faith is a key. Romans 10:17 NKJ promises, "So then faith comes by hearing, and hearing by the Word of GOD." Here we can clearly see GOD promising us that by believing in His Word, and speaking it aloud, He will impart to us Faith. Not just any faith, but His faith, the Power of the Holy Spirit! This is the same faith that Jesus walked in every day of His earthly life and it is the faith that He is still walking in up in Heaven today! This kind of faith comes only with knowing GOD the Father. This kind of faith comes only with the abidance of and a relationship with the Holy Spirit in us. We can't buy it; we can't earn it. All we need (to) do is *ask for It* because the "It" is a person, the person of the Holy Ghost (Spirit). He will come when He has been invited and He will never depart from us (willingly). There are keys in the Kingdom of Heaven. By evidence of the great miracles Jesus performed while He walked the Earth, we can be sure that this faith is a *key*. Faith is a Master key to everything including receiving GOD's Love! Faith is the key to living in Christ and believing what Jesus believes. (See Romans 1:16-17). Faith is available to everyone. Jesus paid the way for our faith, all that we need to do is to learn how to use it and that comes by listening to the Holy Spirit!

When we asked Jesus to be the Lord of our lives, the Holy Spirit came and took up residence within us. The Baptism of the Holy Spirit is the unleashing of this great POWER that resides within us. The Baptism of the Spirit is brought or ushered in by prayer and praise. (See Acts chapter 2). He is our key to great faith and the unleashing of **all** of our gifts in full force.

Jesus' ascension into Heaven. The Word tells us in John 16:7 (Amplified Bible), "However, I am telling you nothing but the truth when I say it is profitable (good, expedient, advantageous) for you that I go away. Because if I do not go away, the Comforter (Counselor, Helper, Advocate, Intercessor, Strengthener, Standby) will not come to you [into close fellowship with you]; but if I go away, I will send Him to you [to be in close fellowship with you]." Verse 12 of the same chapter goes on to say, "I have still many things to say to you, but you are not able to bear them or to take them upon you or to grasp them now." Since this was prior to Jesus' ascent into Heaven, the Holy Spirit, GOD's "Anointing Power," had not yet been released on the Earth to men. (See Luke 24:49). Jesus is telling us here, "Hey, guys, I still have a lot of things to tell you about and I need to explain many more of the Father's deep Truths to you, but you just couldn't understand it all without the Holy Spirit to explain it to you and give you full revelation knowledge!" Listen also to what verses 13–15 promise us, "But when He, the Spirit of Truth (the Truth-giving Spirit) comes, He will guide you into **all** the Truth **(the whole, full Truth)**. For He will not speak His own message [on His own authority]; **but He will tell whatever He hears [from the Father**; He will give the message that has been given to Him], and He will announce and declare to you the things that are to come [that will happen in the future]. He will honor and glorify Me, because He will take of (receive, draw upon) what is Mine and will reveal (declare, disclose, transmit) it to you. Everything that the Father has is Mine. That is what I meant when I

said that He [the Spirit] will take the things that are Mine and will reveal (declare, disclose, transmit) it to you."
GOD has created us with a destiny, a *Royal destiny*, to follow in the footsteps of Christ as "joint-heirs." Simply put, if we saw our 'Big Brother' and Lord and Savior do it, then GOD wants us, His children, the Body of Christ, doing it too. Jesus clearly delivered His power, which is His Anointing, to us when He sent the Holy Spirit to Earth to reside inside each of us, His Believers [His: disciples, children, brethren, followers, beloved, Bride]. The Bible tells us that those of us He knows, He foreordained and predestined to be children of the Most High GOD. (See Romans 8:30). This meant that He knew each of us ahead of time. Just imagine that, before the Earth was ever created, He knew us: every little idiosyncrasy, every mood swing, every sin of defeat, and every victory! He knew them all, and He loved us!

John 12:44–50 AMP tells us, "But Jesus loudly declared, the one who believes in Me does not [only] believe in and trust in and rely on Me, but [in believing in Me he believes] in Him Who sent Me. And whoever sees Me sees Him Who sent Me. I have come as a Light into the world, so that whoever believes in Me [whoever cleaves to and trusts in and relies on Me] may not continue to live in darkness. If anyone hears My teachings and fails to observe them [does not keep them, but disregards them], it is not I who judges him. For I have not come to judge and to condemn and to pass sentence and to inflict penalty on the world, but to save the world. Anyone who rejects Me and persistently sets Me at naught, refusing to accept My teachings, has his judge [however]; for the [very] message that I have spoken will itself judge and convict him at the last day. This is because I have never spoken on My own authority or of My own accord or as self-appointed, but the Father Who sent Me has Himself given Me orders [concerning] what to say and what to tell [Deut.18:18-19]. And I know that His commandment is (means) eternal life. So whatever I speak, I am saying [exactly] what My Father has told Me to say and in accordance with His instructions."

In verse 46, "I have come as a Light into the world, so that whoever believes in Me may not continue to live in darkness." Imagine a Lighthouse. See it brightly shining into the darkness so that ships can pass safely by all the obstacles on their way to Port. The LORD is that Lighthouse and He is our only Way to get safely through to Port. We live in the Light of His Truth. His Truth is Love which reveals to us His Revelation Knowledge, as such we are each His Shining Lighthouses filled with the Light of His Glorious Love and radiating (beaming) it out to a dark and dying world! The Lord is revealing to us that we now have the *ability* to "live" in the Light of Truth in all areas of our lives (See Philippians 4:13). **Not only is Jesus [our Lighthouse] our way to Salvation, but He is also our way to an array of other wonderful promises** including freedom from every curse as listed in the last half of the 28th chapter of Deuteronomy! It's true, if the Son has set us free, we are free indeed!

As Christians, we need to learn to act on these promises. I can tell someone for years and years that *I am going to cross the street*, but until I actually take the first step, I won't get any nearer to the other side of that street than I have ever been. We are going to see together how GOD led Jesus, yes, led Jesus, to walk in faith throughout His (Jesus') ministry on Earth. Jesus chose to come to Earth as a man, and as such, He was open to the frailties of the flesh just the same as you and I. (See Hebrews 4:15). The difference between Jesus' life on this planet, and yours and mine, is the submission He gave to the Father. It says "that in all things He submitted unto the will of the Father; even unto death, death on the cross" (See Philippians 2:1-11).

Both the Old and New Testaments are filled with the wonderful knowledge of GOD and His promises. Through the chapters of this book, my prayer for you is that the Lord will open your mind and grow your spirit to accept, understand, believe, and operate in His whole Word. My prayer for myself throughout the writing of this book will be the same and also the words Jesus spoke in John 12:50 (AMP), "And I know that His commandment is (means) eternal life. So whatever I speak" {write in my case}, "I am saying [exactly] what My Father has told Me to say and in accordance with His instructions." Now, believing, "... He hears the prayer of the righteous." (Proverbs 15:29 NIV). Let's look together at what the Word declares, because it is made clear to us in GOD's Word that this, and only this, is what Jesus believes!

"You came from GOD and He loves you."
Holy Spirit

WHAT JESUS BELIEVES

PART ONE

A Look at the Glory

1

A Look at the Book of John

Every book of the Bible is the inspired Word of GOD as written in 2 Timothy 3:16-17 AMP. "Every Scripture is GOD-breathed (given by His inspiration) and profitable for instruction, for reproof and conviction of sin, for correction of error and discipline in obedience, [and] for training in righteousness (in holy living, in conformity to GOD's will in thought, purpose, and action), so that the man of GOD may be complete and proficient, well fitted and thoroughly equipped for every good work," but the Gospel according to John is unique to itself in the fact that it contains only two of the miracles that are recorded in the Gospels of Matthew, Mark, and Luke. The additional five miracles that John reports are found *only here* in the book of John.

John reports the signs done by the Lord, usually referred to as miracles in the other Gospels. He has zeroed in on the Rhema Truth that Jesus is the One true, sent Christ (Anointed One), the World's only way to salvation, and the Son of the Most High GOD. The word "believe" (trust, adhere to, relying on; as given in definition in the Amplified Bible) is found a total of 98 times throughout the Gospel according to John. [You may want to take a special-colored highlighter pen and underline or highlight the words believe and faith every time you come across them while reading your Bible. It is a real faith builder assignment! They are also a big help when you are trying to find a special verse about faith and belief in GOD]. John was fervent in His belief that Jesus is the One and only true way to GOD, and that we, as believers, are to live our lives in the very Spirit of

Jesus. The knowledge that Jesus is the Son of GOD is reiterated in the Word again and again.

Let's start with the basic building blocks of our **Faith Facts**, as given from GOD through the apostle John in Chapter 1.

"IN THE beginning [before all time] was the Word (Christ), and the Word was with GOD, and the Word was GOD Himself. [See Isaiah 9:6]. He was present originally with GOD. All things were made and came into existence through Him; and without Him was not even one thing made that has come into being. In Him was Life, and the Life was the Light of men. And the Light shines on in the darkness, for the darkness has never overpowered it [put it out or absorbed it or appropriated it, and is unreceptive to it]" (John 1:1-5 AMP).

Now, when we flip over in our Bibles to Revelation 19:13 (AMP) [I encourage you to read *What Jesus Believes* with Bible, bookmarks, highlighter, and pen in hand, to take down any notes as you receive the prompting from the Holy Spirit], we read, "He is dressed in a robe dyed by dipping in blood" (some ancient manuscripts read "sprinkled with blood") "and the title by which He is called is *The Word of GOD*." Verse 16 goes on to say, "And on His garment (robe) and on His thigh He has a name (title) inscribed, King of Kings and Lord of Lords" [See Deut. 10:17; Dan. 2:47]. Now, let's look in Isaiah before we continue on in the Gospel according to John. Verse 6 of Isaiah 9 declares to us, "For to us a Child is born, to us a Son is given; and the government shall be upon His shoulder, and His name shall be called Wonderful Counselor, Mighty GOD, Everlasting Father [of Eternity], Prince of Peace" [See Isa. 25:1; 40:9-11; Matt. 28:18; Luke 2:11].

Okay, let's do that flip, back over to John 1:1–5 and we can put the name of Jesus over the words, "the Word," since we now know they are synonymous [one and the same] to help make these verses a little clearer to us. (Later in the book, I will suggest that you read the first bit of John and read the name Jesus in place of the word, "Word" or "the Word." As you do that be sure to meditate on it by reading it and re-reading it, with the help of the Holy Spirit). "In the beginning [before all time] was Jesus, and Jesus was with GOD, and Jesus was GOD [Himself]. [See Isaiah 9:6]. He was present originally with GOD. All things were made and came into existence through Him; and without Him was not even one thing made that has come into being. In Him was Life, and the Life was the Light of men. And the Light shines on in the darkness, for the darkness has never overpowered it [put it out or absorbed it or appropriated it, and is unreceptive to it]." Here we see that Jesus (Who is the [Eternal] Living Word of GOD [see also: Hebrews 4:12]) believes (and knows for certain) that He was in the beginning before all time with GOD and He was indeed even GOD Himself. For some of you, this may be new, but we can believe it without fear, having read it for ourselves in the very Word of GOD.

Let's keep going and see what is said a little further down in verses 9–11, "There it was – the true Light [the genuine, perfect, steadfast Light] [was then] coming into the world that illumines every person. [See Isa. 49:6]. He came into the world, and though the world was made through Him, the world did not recognize Him [did not know Him]. He came to that which belonged to Him [to His own – His domain, creation, things, world], and they who were His own did not receive Him and did not welcome Him." Can you imagine coming to visit your own children, whom you love with all your heart, after having been away for a long time, and upon opening the front door to your knocks, they look you in the face and say, "Go away! We don't want anything to do with you!"? I know I'd be devastated! And yet here in these verses, Jesus is telling us what He knows to be true and even knew to be true before He came down to His Earth as Messiah (Christ), the Anointed One, the Sacrifice, and the Savior of the World. That His people, the very creation He had created to commune with and love Him would turn their backs on Him and not receive Him; even to the point of hanging on the cross their own loving Creator. We may wag our heads and say, "Oh, I would never reject Jesus!" And I do not believe that any one of us would intentionally reject the Savior we love. Unfortunately, what we unintentionally do is still a form of rejecting Him. You may be asking, "How on earth do I do that?" Simple really. We don't receive the gifts He brought to Earth for us. We don't receive the gifts He bought for us with His blood and His life. "But I receive His salvation and forgiveness of sins!" And it is wonderful that you do, but it's more than that. It is so much more than that.

Just think back for a moment about the lives of Jesus' disciples. Think about all the really wonderful miracles performed through their hands, human hands, by GOD! If all that the Bible stated about the disciples of Jesus had been that they all received salvation, the New Testament would be quite a bit shorter! Thank GOD, it isn't! He used those great men of GOD to lead the multitudes to salvation and to teach. He also used them to heal the sick, cast out demons, raise the dead, and write down visions given to them by GOD for us, the latter generation!

"Oh, but I'm not one of them and I'm not one of the twelve great disciples. GOD would never use me to do such great things!" The wonderful news, and I mean truly wonderful news, to you and me, is that all of those men were ordinary people, just like you and me!

Before Jesus left the Earth to go back to the Father, He promised His little flock (His followers) that He would send down the Holy Spirit to them. Unlike what many have been taught and believe, the Holy Spirit is also a promise to us today: "for to you is the promise, and to your children, and to all those afar off, as many as the Lord our GOD shall call" (Acts 2:39 YLT98). Jesus spoke the words that through Him they (and we) would do "greater works" than what He had done (while upon the earth). (See John 14:12). The Bible, being the ever-living Word of GOD, and an ever-current word to us, teaches that we can know that these wonderful promises are applicable to us today! *Yes, you and I.* Not just to brother or sister so and so. Praise GOD! Now we are really starting to see the power of GOD that is available!

WHAT JESUS BELIEVES

Another way of unintentionally rejecting Jesus is the way we allow our lives to become too busy. Has anyone of you ever been guilty of that besides me? In this day and age, it's easy, far too easy, to get caught up in the "I have to" syndrome. You know the old recording in your brain that I am talking about. That old 'I have to do' list, the one that sometimes seems to play on endlessly in our minds? I know how often I get caught up in that in my own life, so I am not pointing a finger at anyone.

For a minute, let me wander off...I'm reminded of the story in the Bible of the adulteress who was brought to Jesus by the Scribes and Pharisees. They told Jesus that she had been caught in the very act of adultery and that in the Law of Moses it said that she should be stoned! They asked Jesus, 'What do you say?' Jesus calmly stooped down and wrote on the ground with His finger as though He had not heard them. When they continued to barrage Him with the same question, He eventually raised himself up and said to them, "He who is without sin among you, let him throw a stone at her first." (See John Chapter 8 for the full story). And then he just stooped back down and went back to his writing on the ground. One by one, from the oldest to the youngest, those people left them. (I can just imagine each man in his turn, his own conscience convicting him, letting the stone in his hand fall to the ground beside him with a thud; and I say stone, but they were pretty hefty in size considering that they were each hand chosen by those intent on putting that woman to death). Eventually, when they had all gone, Jesus and the woman were left alone. Jesus then raised Himself up and looking at the woman, He asked her, "Woman, where are those accusers of yours? Has no one condemned you?" She told him, "No one, Lord." At this point, our compassionate Jesus must have looked straight into her soul and spirit, with the most loving look this poor woman had ever received before, and spoken gently to her, "Neither do I condemn you; go and sin no more." To me, this is one of the greatest examples in the Bible of the heart of Jesus. We would all do well to keep this in mind every day throughout our lives.

Getting back to talking about the subject of the busyness of our lives, we can all rest easy in the freeing news of GOD's Word that we *don't* have to live with those nagging thoughts all the time. GOD never intended for anything to drag us down. In the Word, it is declared to us, "I am come that they might have life, and that they might have it more abundantly." (John 10:10 b ESV) "The Lord makes firm the steps of the one who delights in Him" (Psalm 37:23 NIV) and "The heart of man plans his way, but the LORD establishes his steps." (Proverb 16:9 ESV) That is our promise *that we do not need to carry the burden or the responsibility of planning our own lives.* Truly, GOD establishes our steps! We can simply trust in the Lord to take care of us and lead us day by day. The Lord confirms this in Matthew 6:25-26, "Therefore I tell you, do not worry about your life, what you will eat or drink; or about your body, what you will wear. Is not life more than food, and the body more than clothes? Look at the birds of the air; they do not sow or reap or store away in barns, and yet your heavenly Father feeds them. Are you not much more valuable than they?" (Matthew 6:25-26 NIV).

Some people may be questioning, "How can I know what GOD's plan is for my life?" Simple, by spending time with GOD in His Word and in prayer, you will learn to know His voice and His leading better and better. Wisdom tells us that the more we practice at something, the easier it will become for us. This is how excellence is attained. Well, the same principle applies with GOD. The more time we spend with Him, the more we will know Him. The more time we spend in the Word, the more our hearts will be filled up with the Truth, and the more time that we spend doing this is right in line with how much the Word will be working for us in our lives. A little Word, a little effect and evidence of change; a lot of Word, a lot of effect and evidence of change.

Just imagine Jesus standing at someone's door, gifts in hand for them, and they are saying, "Oh, thanks, but I'm too busy right now for that healing ministry You've bought (with Your blood) for me. Besides, I think it would be better suited to so and so at our church." Or "Gee,

Jesus, I really appreciate that you want to teach me how to pray today, but I am really busy right now. Maybe you could try coming back tonight after 10:00 or 11:00? Or maybe even tomorrow would be better for us both?" Perhaps these are not the exact words we have spoken or thought when we felt the Lord's Spirit drawing us to commune with Him, but if you are anything like me, then this is pretty accurate. The LORD sends His Spirit to draw us into communing with Him, and into communion with Him. He wants us to know and understand THE BLOOD COVENANT that we have with Him. He knows that if we do not know *or* understand this covenant, then we cannot operate in the blessings that He has for us in our lives. He purchased all of these things with his own blood. Would we really turn Jesus away if He came in the physical realm to our front door, bearing gifts for us? No, of course not! In our overflowing happiness and joy at seeing our beloved Savior, we would set everything else aside!

Revelation 3:20 (AMP):

"Behold, I stand at the door and knock; if anyone hears and listens to and heeds My voice and opens the door, I will come in to him and will eat with him, and he [will eat] with Me."

Let's try to imagine Jesus standing at our front door, a loving smile on His face, and His arms packed full of all of the good gifts He has bought for us. Now, the next time we feel the prompting of the Holy Spirit to spend some time with Him, in the Word and in prayer, we'll open the door. This is vitally important to our relationship with Him. Not only is this the easiest way to receive from Him His thoughts for our lives, but also what we have inside of those gifts He's given us and how to use them. How many times have we opened a box and read the words, "Read instructions before assembling."? A lot, right? Well, that is very applicable to us in our relationship with the LORD GOD. His Holy Spirit desires to teach us how to assemble our lives so that we can live the best and highest use of them. However, if we won't take the time to read His 'Instruction Book' and converse with Him in prayer, this will be not only difficult but impossible. GOD created each of us for a customized and specific calling. He placed within us specific gifts in order to fulfill those callings and only by our being used according to His plans can we ever live truly joyful and (completely) fulfilled lives. To accomplish that we must spend quality time alone with Him. To not listen to GOD will only cause us confusion, pain, and failure, as all of us can attest. How many times in the past have we messed up because we chose to do something without checking with the LORD first and later we ended up crying out, "Oh, GOD, help me!"? The Word of GOD says, "He knows the future!" Praise, GOD! By going to the One with foresight first, we can avoid a lot of trouble later! That is exactly what Jesus did at all times. There isn't one place in the Bible where we can read Jesus praying, "Oh, Father, if only I had prayed first. I would have known that the blind man didn't have the faith to be healed and he wouldn't have walked into that tree!" With that said, we shall get back to the first chapter of the Gospel of John.

Jesus also knew that there would be many others, us included, who would receive Him and all He had for them. So let's read about it in John 1, verses 12 and 13 to see what Jesus believes (knows to be true) about His Covenant with us. "But to as many as did receive and welcome Him, He gave the authority (power, privilege, right) to become the children of GOD, that is, to those who believe in (adhere to, trust in, and rely on) His name – [Isa. 56:5], who owe their birth neither to bloods nor to the will of the flesh [that of physical impulse], nor to the will of man [that of a natural father], but to GOD. [They are born of GOD!]" (John 1:12-13 AMP).

Here we see that Jesus promises that to all those who would believe in Him as the Saving Light of the World and come to Him as their Savior, He will give the authority to become the children of GOD. We will want to look back into the Old Testament to the book of Deuteronomy, the 28th chapter. This will help us to get a clearer insight into just exactly what we are entitled to as Children of the Most High GOD through Jesus Christ (the Anointed One) when we are walking in relationship and obedience to GOD.

WHAT JESUS BELIEVES

"IF YOU will listen diligently to the voice of the Lord your GOD, being watchful to do all His commandments which I command you this day, the Lord your GOD will set you high above all the nations of the Earth. And all these blessings shall come upon you and overtake you if you heed the voice of the Lord your GOD. Blessed shall you be in the city and blessed shall you be in the field. Blessed shall be the fruit of your body and the fruit of your ground and the fruit of your beasts, the increase of your cattle and the young of your flock. Blessed shall be your basket and your kneading trough. Blessed shall you be when you come in and blessed shall you be when you go out. The Lord shall cause your enemies who rise up against you to be defeated before your face; they shall come out against you one way and flee before you seven ways. The Lord shall command the blessing upon you in your storehouse and in all that you undertake. And He will bless you in the land which the Lord your GOD gives you. The Lord will establish you as a people holy to Himself, as He has sworn to you, if you keep the commandments of the Lord your GOD and walk in His ways. And all people of the earth shall see that you are called by the name [and in the presence] of the Lord, and they shall be afraid of you. And the Lord shall make you have a surplus of prosperity, through the fruit of your body, of your livestock, and of your ground, in the land which the Lord swore to your fathers to give you. The Lord shall open to you His good treasury, the heavens, to give the rain of your land in its season and to bless all the work of your hands; and you shall lend to many nations, but you shall not borrow. And the Lord shall make you the head, and not the tail; and you shall be above only, and you shall not be beneath, if you heed the commandments of the Lord your GOD which I command you this day and are watchful to do them. And you shall not turn aside from any of the words which I command you this day, to the right hand or to the left, to go after other gods to serve them" (Deuteronomy 28:1-14 AMP).

Jesus came to fulfill these promises for us. However, if we chose to open the door to sin and allow it a governing place in our lives, then satan will be quick to take his throne within our heart and rule from

WHAT JESUS BELIEVES

each and every place he can. Words and actions will always give evidence of what is in a man's heart. *Out of the abundance of a man's heart will he speak.* (see: Matthew 12:34, Luke 6:45 and James 3:10) We know what Jesus said about satan, the thief, in John 10:10 AMP "The thief comes only in order to steal and kill and destroy." That is exactly what he does if he can get access to it. If he can't he will still keep trying for it, so don't get discouraged when you feel things coming against you in life. <u>Jesus experienced this opposition too, but He was victorious in GOD. As we live and move and have our being in Him, we will be victorious too.</u> GOD is maturing us by growing us up in His perfect Love. In John 10:10 AMP Jesus also says, "I came that they may have and enjoy life, and have it in abundance (to the full, till it overflows)." Has anybody ever had a life that is so full of GOD's Love and GOD's Promise of Prosperity and GOD's Power and GOD's Victories that it overflows with joy and abundance because of His blessings? That life is His plan for you!

Wow! Is there anything that you could possibly want that is not promised to you in the first 13 verses of Deuteronomy 28? No? I couldn't find any either! At this point, I feel led to stop and tell you that the Lord specifically wants you to meditate on these verses, one verse each day, for the next month. A helpful tip would be to read one each morning while you are fresh, and your mind is clear and alert. In this way, you can meditate on your (special) verse all day, which will *greatly* increase your faith You may want to write it down on a piece of paper and take it with you wherever you go so that you can read it and re-read it, wholly meditating on it, again and again, until it becomes Rhema to you.

Logos is the Word of GOD, past, present and future. Rhema is what He is speaking to us through His Word. The Word of GOD says, "But when He, the Spirit of Truth (the Truth-giving Spirit) comes, He will guide you into all the Truth (the whole, full Truth). For He will not speak His own message [on His own authority]; but He will tell whatever He hears [from the Father; He will give the message that has been given to Him], and He will announce and declare to you the things that are to come [that will happen in the future]" (John 16:13 AMP). Isn't that exciting?! This is how you will receive Rhema, the revelation of what He [GOD through the Holy Spirit] is speaking to you, while you are reading the Logos! The Holy Spirit Himself WILL lead you into all (GOD's) Truth for your life! The whole full Truth of that Rhema (revelation) that GOD is speaking to you (through His Word) at that exact point in time! Anyone reading the Word with an open heart will always get both Logos and Rhema from GOD.

Jesus believes (knows [past present future]) He is the Son of the living GOD; therefore, Jesus operated in the authority of the Son of GOD (see Mt 7:29 and Mk 1:22), His miracles being His proof to us, the Church. Jesus believes that (through Him) we have become Children of GOD. He also believes that as heirs of GOD, we are entitled to all of the blessings *of* GOD. Jesus believes that we will do greater things than He has done as we operate in the gifts He has given us through the power of the precious Holy Spirit. He knows that He has blessed us with every good gift that we could possibly imagine as listed in the first 13 verses of the 28th chapter of Deuteronomy. By meditating on the Word of GOD each day, the Holy Spirit will give the Rhema of what GOD is speaking to us through that Word (the verse/s) for that day. In this way, we can all get a fresh Word from GOD every day!

Now that we have some specific Logos (what GOD has said) on what Jesus believes; and as we study it more by re-reading it, praying it over our lives (which includes speaking it aloud) and meditating on it in our hearts, we will acquire more and more of GOD's Rhema (GOD's revelation of what He is saying) regarding His Word. Now, that's exciting! Trust GOD to teach you as you do this and you will begin to operate in the ways of our LORD Jesus, because you, like Jesus, are believing GOD the Father!

"Jesus saw Nathanael coming toward Him and said concerning him, See! Here is an Israelite indeed [a true descendant of Jacob], in whom there is no guile nor deceit nor falsehood nor duplicity! Nathanael said to Jesus, How do You know me? [How is it that You know these things about me]? Jesus answered him, before [ever] Philip called you, when you were still under the fig tree, I saw you. Nathanael answered, Teacher, You are the Son of GOD! You are the King of Israel! Jesus replied, because I said to you, I saw you beneath the fig tree, do you believe in and rely on and trust in Me? You shall see greater things than this! Then He said to him, I assure you, most solemnly I tell you all, you shall see Heaven opened, and the angels of GOD ascending and descending upon the Son of Man!" [Gen. 28:12; Dan. 7:13] (John 1:47-51 AMP).

Jesus sees you too, right where you are in your life, and He wants you to see greater things than you have ever seen! You are going up to a higher place in the Spirit than you have ever been before! So get your basket out, and as you spend your time with GOD in the Word today, be ready and expectant for Him to fill up your basket to overflowing with His gifts!

"In My Presence is fullness of joy! Come away with Me! I have so much to tell you!"
Holy Spirit

2

"Everything That the Father HAS Is Mine"
John 16:15

Did you know that Jesus gave us that promise more than 2000 years ago? Now you may wonder, "Then why is the Church in such a bad state if that is true?" Well, if you had been given an inheritance of $7 million, you would think that was terrific, wouldn't you? I imagine that right away you would start thinking of all the different things you could do with your newly-acquired wealth, *but* what if you didn't know that you had inherited that $7 million? What if you hadn't read the Will that said you had been allotted that $7 million? Then you would simply live on in the same way that you always had, and that $7 million would just sit there, unspent, in a bank deposit waiting for you, wouldn't it? Well, that's exactly the way it can be with the Church (the Body of Christ). Most of the Church doesn't even know it has access to a Will, a perfect Will from GOD for each of our lives.

"I love you. I have wonderful things for you! Your treasure is hidden within My Word and within My heart. Come, I will help you find it. Soon you will know and believe!"
Living LOGOS

Some of you may be wondering, "What kind of an inheritance do I have in this Will? Also, how can I get my hands on it?" Those are both very valid and important questions, and they are both easily answered. We can each receive our due inheritance through Jesus Christ (the Anointed One) by His Anointing (the Holy Spirit), which is the very power of GOD. Therefore, each of us as Believers of Jesus Christ (the Anointed One) have a Spiritual Bank Account with GOD, a joint bank account really, with Jesus. We don't get a Visa Card type account that we need to pay for because that would be works, and works are under the Law. Besides, Jesus already paid for all of our debts, with his Blood and His Life, on the cross.

"For no person will be justified (made righteous, acquitted and judged acceptable) in His sight by observing the works prescribed by the Law. For [the real function of] the Law is to make men recognize and be conscious of sin [not mere perception, but an acquaintance with sin, which works toward repentance, faith and holy character]."

*"You cannot earn what has already been given to you.
Salvation and the gifts accompanying it are free."*
Holy Spirit

"But now, the righteousness of GOD has been revealed independently and altogether apart from the Law, although actually it is attested by the Law and the Prophets, Namely, the righteousness of GOD, which comes by believing with personal trust and confident reliance on Jesus Christ (the Messiah). [And it is meant] for all who believe. For there is no distinction, since all have sinned and are falling short of the honor and glory which GOD bestows and receives. **[All] are justified and made upright and in right standing with GOD, freely and gratuitously by His grace (His unmerited favor and mercy), through the redemption which is [provided] in Christ Jesus, Whom GOD put forward [before the eyes of all] as a mercy seat and propitiation by His blood [the cleansing and life-giving sacrifice of atonement and reconciliation, to be received] through faith.** This was to show GOD's righteousness, because in His divine forbearance, He had passed over and ignored former sins without punishment. It was to demonstrate and prove at the present time (in the now season) that He Himself is righteous and that He justifies and accepts as righteous him who has [true] faith in Jesus. Then what becomes of [our] pride and [our] boasting? It is excluded (banished, ruled out entirely). On what principle? [On the principle] of doing good deeds? No, but on the principle of faith. For we hold that a man is justified and made upright by faith independent of and distinctly apart from good deeds (works of the Law). [The observance of the Law has nothing to do with justification]. Or is GOD merely [the GOD] of Jews? Is He not the GOD of Gentiles also? Yes, of Gentiles also, since it is one and the same GOD Who will justify the circumcised by faith [which germinated from Abraham] and the uncircumcised through their [newly-acquired] faith. [For it is the same trusting faith in both cases, a firmly relying faith in Jesus Christ]. Do we then by [this] faith make the Law of no effect, overthrow it or make it a dead letter? Certainly not! On the contrary, we confirm and establish and uphold the Law" (Romans 3:20-31 AMP).

> *"It is not by your good works that you are saved.*
> *It is by your simple childlike faith in Me."*
> *Holy Spirit of Jesus the Christ*

"[BUT] IF so, what shall we say about Abraham, our forefather humanly speaking – [what did he find out? How does this affect his position, and what was gained by him]? For if Abraham was justified (established as just by acquittal from guilt) by good works [that he did, then] he has grounds for boasting. But not before GOD! For what does the Scripture say? Abraham believed in (trusted in) GOD, and it was credited to his account as righteousness (right living and right standing with GOD) [Gen. 15:6]. Now to a laborer, his wages are not counted as a favor or a gift, but as an obligation (something owed to him). **But to one who, not working [by the Law], trusts (believes fully) in Him Who justifies the ungodly, his faith is credited to him as righteousness (the standing acceptable to GOD).** Thus David congratulates the man and pronounces a blessing on him to whom GOD credits righteousness apart from the works he does: Blessed and happy and to be envied are those whose iniquities are forgiven and whose sins are covered up and completely buried. Blessed and happy and to be envied is the person of whose sin the Lord will take no account nor reckon it against him [Ps. 32:1, 2]. Is this blessing (happiness) then meant only for the circumcised, or also for the uncircumcised? We say that **faith was credited to Abraham as**

righteousness. How then was it credited [to him]? Was it before or after he had been circumcised? It was not after, but before he was circumcised. He received the mark of circumcision as a token or an evidence [and] seal of the righteousness which he had by faith while he was still uncircumcised – [faith] so that he was to be made the father of all who [truly] believe, though without circumcision, and who thus have righteousness (right standing with GOD) imputed to them and credited to their account, as well as [that he be made] the father of those circumcised persons who are not merely circumcised, but also walk in the way of that faith which our father Abraham had before he was circumcised. **For the promise to Abraham or his posterity, that he should inherit the world, did not come through [observing the commands of] the Law but through the righteousness of faith** [Gen. 17:4-6; 22:16-18]. If it is the adherents of the Law who are to be the heirs, then faith is made futile and empty of all meaning and the promise [of GOD] is made void (is annulled and has no power). For the Law results in [divine] wrath, but where there is no Law there is no transgression [of it either]. Therefore, [inheriting] the promise is the outcome of faith and depends [entirely] on faith, in order that it might be given as an act of grace (unmerited favor), to make it stable and valid and guaranteed to all his descendants – **not only to the devotees and adherents of the Law, but also to those who share the faith of Abraham, who is [thus] the father of us all. As it is written, I have made you the father of many nations.** [He was appointed our father] in the sight of GOD in Whom he believed, Who gives life to the dead and speaks of the nonexistent things that [He has foretold and promised] as if they [already] existed [Gen. 17:5]. [For Abraham, human reason for] hope being gone, hoped in faith that he should become the father of many nations, as he had been promised, so [numberless] shall your descendants be [Gen. 15:5]. He did not weaken in faith when he considered the [utter] impotence of his own body, which was as good as dead because he was about a hundred years old, or [when he considered] the barrenness of Sarah's [deadened] womb [Gen. 17:17; 18:11]. No unbelief or distrust made him waver (doubtingly question) concerning the promise of GOD, but **he grew strong and was empowered by faith as he gave praise and**

glory to GOD, fully satisfied and assured that GOD was able and mighty to keep His Word and to do what He had promised. That is why his faith was credited to him as righteousness (right standing with GOD). **But [the words], it was credited to him, were written not for his sake alone, but [they were written] for our sakes too. [Righteousness, standing acceptable to GOD] will be granted and credited to us also who believe in (trust in, adhere to, and rely on) GOD, Who raised Jesus our Lord from the dead**, Who was betrayed and put to death because of our misdeeds and was raised to secure our justification (our acquittal), [making our account balance and absolving us from all guilt before GOD]" (Romans 4:1-25 AMP).

GOD gives us proof of this Spiritual Bank Account when Jesus says, "But when He, the Spirit of Truth (the Truth-giving Spirit) comes, He will guide you into all the Truth (the whole, full Truth). For He will not speak His own message [on His own authority]; but He will tell whatever He hears [from the Father; He will give the message that has been given to Him], and He will announce and declare to you the things that are to come [that will happen in the future]. He will honor and glorify Me, because He will take of (receive, draw upon) what is Mine and will reveal (declare, disclose, transmit) it to you. Everything that the Father has is Mine. That is what I meant when I said that He [the Spirit] will take the things that are Mine and will reveal (declare, disclose, transmit) it to you" (John 16:13-15 AMP). GOD's will is to [fully] reveal to you 'His Will' for your life. As you get into the Word, GOD will reveal His Rhema (what GOD is speaking to *you* through the Bible). Rhema will come to you in the Presence of the Holy Spirit. If you desire to experience His Presence, spend time with Him. While speaking with His disciples, Jesus revealed to them that He was only able to hear GOD through the Holy Spirit. Just think about how much time Jesus spent communing with GOD through the Holy Spirit. The Holy Spirit acted as the wire or transmitter between the Father and the Son. We need to remember that when Jesus came to Earth in order to make this thing work, He (Jesus) had to live as a man dealing with all the temptations that are common to Mankind.

WHAT JESUS BELIEVES

"But the Helper, the Holy Spirit, whom the Father will send in My name, He will teach you all things, and bring to your remembrance all things that I said to you."
(John 14:26 NKJV)

Christ (Greek) / Messiah (from Hebrew) : anointing / anointed one. When the books of the Bible were translated into English in the original King James Version, for a reason untold to us, the translators left the Greek and Hebrew words 'Christ' and 'Messiah' untranslated. Sadly, most other translations have done the same thing. This resulted in a great loss to us of the knowledge and understanding of the Power that we have inherited from GOD through Jesus; Jesus, Who was and is the Anointed One. GOD's desire is for us to fully understand the Anointing that has been given to us through our relationship with GOD through Jesus His Son. When we understand this, there will be nothing that is impossible for us. It will be done on earth as it is in Heaven for GOD's will is being accomplished through His Power.]

"The greatest Power is Love."
Holy Spirit

All through both the Old and New Testaments, we find evidence of the Anointed One (the Messiah, the Christ). In Luke 4:17–21 AMP, it says this about Jesus, "And there was handed to Him [the roll of] the book of the prophet Isaiah. He opened (unrolled) the book and found the place where it was written [Isa. 61:1-2] **the Spirit of the Lord [is] upon Me, because He has anointed Me [the Anointed One, the Messiah] to preach the good news (the Gospel) to the poor; He has sent Me to announce release to the captives and recovery of sight to the blind, to send forth as delivered those who are oppressed [who are downtrodden, bruised, crushed, and broken down by calamity], To proclaim the accepted and acceptable year of the Lord [the day when salvation and the free favors of GOD profusely abound]** [Isa.

61:1-2]. Then He rolled up the book and gave it back to the attendant and sat down; and the eyes of all in the synagogue were gazing [attentively] at Him. And He began to speak to them: Today this Scripture has been fulfilled while you are present and hearing."

"To be Anointed is to be given Power. When you are in Me, you are Anointed in My Anointing. Therefore you carry My Power. Do you want to use it?"
Holy Spirit

Here, Jesus was telling the listeners, "I Am the Anointed One! I Am the One that GOD has promised to send to you, here in the book of Isaiah! I Am the One that was prophesied to remove your burdens and break your yolks of bondage/addiction: yolks of poverty, yolks of depression, yolks of lust, yolks of despair and oppression, any and all yolks that have been set upon mankind as a result of the evil one. You don't have to wait any longer to be set free. Here I Am. Come to Me and get your freedom!"

After all that, do you know what those people answered Him in verse 22? Let's read it together, "And all spoke well of Him and marveled at the words of grace that came forth from His mouth;" sounds good so far, doesn't it? But let's look at the rest of that verse: "and they said, is not this Joseph's Son?" (Luke 4:22 AMP). Well, they might have been alright if they hadn't looked at Jesus' roots in the natural. They were basically saying, "Your words *sound good* and all that, *but you're just Joseph the Carpenter's son.* We knew your daddy, and you can't possibly be the Anointed One!"

Anytime we look at our situation in the natural, we will start to sink in our faith levels. GOD has clearly stated in His Word that **"Faith is the act of believing that which you cannot see."** Here is the exact verse, "Now faith is the substance of things hoped for, the evidence of things not seen" (Hebrews 11:1 KJV). Second Corinthians 5:7 NKJV says, "For we walk by faith, not by sight." **Our minds will always get us into trouble when we try to figure something out on our own.**

WHAT JESUS BELIEVES

The Word says that GOD has given to us "the mind of Christ." We need to learn to utilize it.

"Word + Prayer + Meditation = Revelation"
Holy Spirit

"You are in The Revelation Zone"
Holy Spirit

"<u>**Let this same attitude and purpose and [humble] mind be in you which was in Christ Jesus: [Let Him be your example in humility]**</u><u> Who, although being essentially One with GOD and in the form of GOD [possessing the fullness of the attributes which make GOD GOD], did not think this equality with GOD was a thing to be eagerly grasped or retained, but stripped Himself [of all privileges and rightful dignity], so as to assume the guise of a servant (slave), in that He became like men and was born a human being</u>" (Philippians 2:5-7 AMP). (Try reading the above verse 3 times and really let each word soak in. It is one of the best revelations of the Bible. As you meditate say, "You did this for me." ♡).

"In My Presence, there is everything good."
Holy Spirit

"For who has known or understood the mind (the counsels and purposes) of the Lord so as to guide and instruct Him and give Him knowledge? But we have the mind of Christ (the Messiah) and do hold the thoughts (feelings and purposes) of His heart" [Isa. 40:13] (1 Corinthians 2:16 AMP).

"Do you lack Wisdom? Ask in Faith. Faith is the switch that activates the Power which IS the Anointing. Ask without doubting and you shall receive."
Holy Spirit

WHAT JESUS BELIEVES

He gave us the mind of the Anointed One and His Anointing (the Holy Spirit) so that we would not have to work out problems on our own. GOD never intended for man to create his own destiny. It wasn't GOD who said, "Kay sera sera, whatever will be will be." GOD has a wonderful plan and a wonderful destiny for us and as we follow it, He will give us the fulfillment that we have been longing to experience. As Jesus spoke to the people in his hometown, they couldn't see past the fact that He was the Carpenter's son. The eyes of their understanding were darkened because of the smallness of their faith in GOD. They did not believe that a great GOD would do things in such a humble manner, but the Bible says that Jesus humbled Himself and came to Earth as a man for us and in obedience to GOD. They never saw the whole beauty of the awesomeness of GOD in the way He sent His Son to Earth to deal with mankind's problem of sin. All this crowd ever saw was 'a Carpenter's son,' for they declared, "Is not this Joseph's son?"

At this, Jesus went on to say "...certainly ye will say to Me this simile, Physician, heal thyself; as great things as we heard done in Capernaum, do also here in thy country" (Luke 4:23 YLT98). At this point, He knew that they wanted Him (Jesus) to do some fantastic miracle for them to prove that He was the Anointed One sent by GOD. Some of you may be thinking, "Well, is that too much to ask?" It may not have been too much to ask if their hearts had been right, but I believe that Jesus looked into those stone-cold hearts, and saw that even if He did perform a miracle, they would still find reasons to believe that He was not the Anointed One.

"Pride blinds the mind to Truth. Only Revelation from GOD brings in the Light of Wisdom. I Am the One Who enlightens the eyes of your understanding."
Holy Spirit

Jesus was always in direct communication with GOD through the Holy Spirit, and it tells us in the Bible He knew then what was in the hearts of these men and women from His town of Nazareth [See John 6:14-

15] "and He said, `Verily I say to you -- No prophet is accepted in his own country; and of a truth I say to you, Many widows were in the days of Elijah, in Israel, when the Heaven was shut for three years and six months, when great famine came on all the land, and unto none of them was Elijah sent, but -- to Sarepta of Sidon, unto a woman, a widow; and many lepers were in the time of Elisha the prophet, in Israel, and none of them was cleansed, but -- Naaman the Syrian' " (Luke 4:24-27 YLT98). **What can Faith do for you?**

"Faith activated is Faith in motion. Let's GO!"
Holy Spirit

"Do not let Doubt toss you as a wave on a stormy sea. Doubt will certainly drive you if you allow it. Have Faith! Only Believe, little lamb, I will give you your (heart's) desire."
Holy Spirit

Now, you can imagine how big it went over with these people when Jesus was telling them, to their faces, "I'm not sent to a single one of you!" You may ask, but didn't Jesus die for the whole wide world? Sure, He did! He's a just and fair GOD, but it also tells us that GOD knew ahead of time who would be His and who wouldn't. In other words, GOD knew ahead of time which people would accept Jesus and believe in Him, and which wouldn't. GOD didn't believe in wasting time by casting His pearls before swine, and we shouldn't either. That is why it is so important that we stay in direct communication with GOD at all times. He will show us when to talk, what to say, and when to just walk away and leave. The answers to these questions will be deposited in you as you pray in the Spirit. <u>The Word declares that we *speak mysteries* when we pray in the Spirit. These mysteries are the answers to our every problem.</u>

"Come and let me pray through you and you will see my Power too!"
Holy Spirit

Praying in the Spirit gives us the answer from the inside out! Instead of our mind getting it first, and then completely misunderstanding the answer, GOD reveals it first to our spirit. In doing this, Holy Spirit is able to give us complete and perfect revelation. Through praying in the Spirit, *we first speak these mysteries* in prayer; and then when the need to speak out the answer (the wisdom that we have been praying into our spirit man) comes, we can because we have been spiritually filled up with His Wisdom; His Wisdom gained through our time praying (speaking) all of those mysteries in the Spirit! The wisdom that we have spoken in our spirit language comes flowing forth from our lips, as Rhema Word! (What GOD is saying!) *Many people do not pray in the Spirit much because they do not know what they are praying.* **If they knew that what they were praying about in the Spirit would eventually come out of their mouth as a victory for them, they would pray continually as we are told to do!** Who of us *doesn't* want victory over our situations? We all want it!

The enemy does not understand our (heavenly) spirit language and so he can't stop what GOD is doing in us through the praying in of these mysteries. The enemy can only halt us by distraction. Don't let him do it! He knows that we are empowered through praying in the Spirit and will do anything to stop it.

> *"Victory will always come if you won't give up. Keep praying in the Spirit and breathing (speaking) the Word. This will birth what you have been standing and believing for. I know the secret things. (Then) Be still and know that I am GOD and I love you."*
> **Holy Spirit**

King David declares, "I was cast upon You from my very birth; from my mother's womb You have been my GOD" (Psalm 22:10 AMP). The Living Bible puts it this way in verses 9-11, "You took me safely from my mother's womb and brought me through the years of infancy. I have depended upon you since birth; you have always been my GOD." GOD really does know ahead of time who will trust and rely on Him and who won't.

GOD has created a plan designed specifically for each of us. This is our heart's Perfect Desire, even though we may not know it yet. Though we all work together as the Body of Christ on this Earth, we each have individual tasks that we need to perform in order for the Body of Christ to function properly. You may say, "Oh, it really doesn't matter what I do. I'm not important enough to make any difference at all." That's simply a lie of the devil, and don't you buy it! You are very important to the Body of Christ! As a matter of fact, the rest of us cannot function properly without you. "That's just not possible," you say, "and where is that written in the Bible?" It's right here in 1 Corinthians 12: 5–31 (AMP): "And there are distinctive varieties of service and ministration, but it is the same Lord [Who is served]. And there are distinctive varieties of operation [of working to accomplish things], but it is the same GOD Who inspires and energizes them all in all. But to each one is given the manifestation of the [Holy] Spirit [the evidence, the spiritual illumination of the Spirit] for good and profit. To one is given in and through the [Holy] Spirit [the power to speak] a message of wisdom, and to another [the power to express] a word of knowledge and understanding according to the same [Holy] Spirit; to another [wonder-working] faith by the same [Holy] Spirit, to another the extraordinary powers of healing by the one Spirit; to another the working of miracles, to another prophetic insight (the gift of interpreting the divine will and purpose); to another the ability to discern and distinguish between [the utterances of true] spirits [and false ones], to another various kinds of [unknown] tongues, to another the ability to interpret [such] tongues. All these [gifts, achievements, abilities] are inspired and brought to pass by One and the same [Holy] Spirit, Who apportions to each person individually [exactly] as He chooses. For just as the body is a unity and yet has many parts, and all the parts, though many, form [only] one body, so it is with Christ (the Messiah, the Anointed One). For by [means of the personal agency of] One [Holy] Spirit we were all, whether Jews or Greeks, slaves or free, baptized [and by baptism united together] into one body, and all made to drink of one [Holy] Spirit. For the body does not consist of one limb or organ but of many. If the foot should say, because I am not the hand, I do not belong to the body, would it be therefore not [a part] of the body? If the ear should say, because I am not the eye, I do not belong to the body, would it be therefore not [a part] of the body? If the whole body were an eye, where [would be the sense of] hearing? If the whole body were an ear, where [would be the sense of] smell? But as it is, GOD has placed and arranged the limbs and organs in the body, each [particular one] of them, just as He wished and saw fit and with the best adaptation. But if [the whole] were all a single organ, where would the body be? And now there are [certainly] many limbs and organs, but a single body. And the eye is not able to say to the hand, I have no need of you, nor again the head to the feet, I have no need of you. But instead, there is [absolute] necessity for the parts of the body that are considered the more weak. And those [parts] of the body which we consider rather ignoble are [the very parts] which we invest with additional honor, and our unseemly parts and those unsuitable for exposure are treated with seemliness (modesty and decorum), which our more presentable parts do not require. But GOD has so adjusted (mingled, harmonized, and subtly proportioned the parts of) the whole body, giving the greater honor and richer endowment to the inferior parts which lack [apparent importance], so that there should be no division or discord or lack of adaptation [of the parts of the body to each other], but the members all alike should have a mutual interest in and care for one another. And if one member suffers, all the parts [share] the suffering; if one member is honored, all the members [share in] the enjoyment of it. Now you [collectively] are Christ's body and [individually] you are members of it, each part severally and distinct [each with his own place and function]. So GOD has appointed some in the Church [for His own use]: first apostles (special messengers); second prophets (inspired preachers and expounders); third teachers; then wonder-workers; then those with ability to heal the sick; helpers; administrators; [speakers in] different (unknown) tongues. Are all apostles (special messengers)? Are all prophets (inspired interpreters of the will and purposes of GOD)? Are all teachers? Do all have the power of performing miracles? Do all possess extraordinary powers of healing? **<u>Do all speak with tongues?</u>**" This is talking about the gift of tongues when someone has a message for the Body of Christ (the Church) and they give it in tongues (an unknown language), and they or someone else is given the interpretation of it from the Holy Spirit of GOD. (It is not to be confused with (personal) praying in the Spirit in an unknown language. That is freely accessible and necessary to all of us as the Lord Jesus promised to fill us with power from on High before He left to go back up into Heaven. That promise was fulfilled at Pentecost in the upper room with the first 120 when they were filled with the Spirit and given the evidence of tongues (praying and praising GOD in unknown languages). As said earlier, that promise is still in effect for us today. (Read Acts Chapter 2). Praying in tongues as stated in Acts 2 is not the same as 1 Corinthians 12:10, which is talking about speaking in tongues. Speaking in tongues is when one would give the Church Body in general a message from the LORD as the Lord gives the message to and through the speaker in another language, be it an Earthly or Heavenly language. In this kind of tongues (giving a message from GOD publicly), there will always be an interpretation or the person who has given it is told not to give them anymore.

"The fear of man brings a snare, but My perfect love will cast fear out every time. Fear has no right to hold you. Use the Name (Jesus) and the Blood! Hell trembles in fear when you do!"
Holy Spirit

Now, let's finish up 1 Corinthians 12 "Do all interpret? But earnestly desire and zealously cultivate the greatest and best gifts and graces (the higher gifts and the choicest graces). And yet I will show you a still more excellent way [one that is better by far and the highest of them all – love]" (1 Corinthians 12:5-31 AMP).

GOD already knows ahead of time each sin we are going to commit and He is committed to forgiving us of those sins when we ask Him to because of the precious blood of His Son, Jesus. For those of us who have been caught up in the lie of satan (I never capitalize his name) that says: the sins that we have committed are just *too many* or *too awful* to ever be forgiven by the LORD, Jesus' blood blows that lie right out of the water! We need to grasp the truth that GOD knew ahead of time just what He was committing to when He got called each one of us. **His fervent and forgiving Love covers a multitude of sins for the repentant heart that comes to Him.** "If we confess our sins, He is faithful and just to forgive us our sins and to cleanse us from all unrighteousness" (1 John 1:9 NKJV). "And above all things have fervent love for one another, for 'love will cover a multitude of sins' " (1 Peter 4:8 NKJV).

Anyone who takes Jesus as Lord is in Covenant with GOD, Blood Covenant! As you read and study the Bible more and more, you will gain revelation knowledge about just how seriously GOD takes His Covenants. Remember, when you entered into Covenant to make Jesus the Lord of your life, and Jehovah your Father and GOD, then He also entered into Covenant with you to make you His Heir and the Righteousness of Christ Jesus. You can rest in the assurance that no matter how badly you feel about the sin you've committed, you can't destroy the Righteousness of Christ (the Anointed One) Jesus, so you can't destroy your Righteousness either! "For He hath made Him to be sin for us, Who knew no sin; that we might be made the righteousness of GOD in Him" (2 Corinthians 5:21 KJV). *Each time you ask forgiveness from a repentant heart, GOD is faithful and just to cleanse you by covering your sin with the precious blood of Jesus. Take courage faithful heart!*

"There is a way that seems right unto a man, but the end of that way is death. I Am the Only Way, come to Me and live free! Only My Blood can cleanse you of all your sins. Come, find your peace in Me, you've been hurting for a long time."
Holy Spirit the Spirit of Jesus Christ

Romans 10:6-11 AMP says, "But the righteousness based on faith [imputed by GOD and bringing right relationship with Him] says, Do not say in your heart, Who will ascend into Heaven? that is, to bring Christ down; or who will descend into the abyss? that is, to bring

WHAT JESUS BELIEVES

Christ up from the dead [as if we could be saved by our own efforts] [Deut. 30:12-13]. But what does it say? The Word (GOD's message in Christ) is near you, on your lips and in your heart; that is, the Word (the message, the basis and object) of faith which we preach [Deut. 30:14], Because *if* you acknowledge and confess with your lips that Jesus is Lord and in your heart believe (adhere to, trust in, and rely on the truth) that GOD raised Him from the dead, **you will be saved**. For with the heart a person believes (adheres to, trusts in, and relies on Christ) and so is justified (declared righteous, acceptable to GOD), and with the mouth he confesses (declares openly and speaks out freely his faith) and confirms [his] salvation. The Scripture says, No man who believes in Him [who adheres to, relies on, and trusts in Him] will [ever] be put to shame or be disappointed" [Ps. 34:22; Isa. 28:16; 49:23; Jer. 17:7]. Romans 10:13 promises, "For everyone who calls upon the name of the Lord [invoking Him as Lord] will be saved" [Joel 2:32]. This is your assurance of your salvation if you have chosen Jesus as Lord. If you haven't, why don't you just take a moment to say this prayer, and you too can be assured of your own salvation?

> *"Dear Jesus, I need you in my life. I confess that I am a sinner. I confess that I need you to be Lord of my life. I ask you now to be my Savior and my Lord and to forgive me of all my sins. Now I receive what you gave to me 2000 years ago at the cross, my redemption from sin. I also receive my healing for which you were whipped with 39 lashes. I confess with my lips that Jesus is my Lord as commanded in Romans 10:10 (AMP), "For with the heart a person believes (adheres to, trusts in, and relies on Christ) and so is justified (declared righteous, acceptable to GOD), and with the mouth he confesses (declares openly and speaks out freely his faith) and confirms [his] salvation." And I believe and claim your Word in Romans 10:11 (AMP) where "The Scripture says, No man who believes in Him [who adheres to, relies on, and trusts in Him] will [ever] be put to shame or be*

disappointed" [Ps. 34:22; Isa. 28:16; 49:23; Jer. 17:7]. Now, I thank You, Lord Jesus, for doing all of this for me and dying in my place. I thank You, GOD, for sending your Son, Jesus, to die for me and to be made sin in my place, and I receive you now as my GOD and my Heavenly Father. I ask you also to breathe on me, as Jesus breathed on His disciples and said to them "Receive the Holy Spirit!" [John 20:22] Send now Your Precious Holy Spirit to me to live in me, to fill me with Your power from on High [Luke 24:49] to lead me into all truth [John 16:13] and to strengthen me, with evidence of tongues, as promised in Acts Chapter 2. I ask this all in the precious name of Jesus Christ, Amen."

If you have just said that prayer for the first time, or if you have just rededicated your life to Jesus, then make sure you tell somebody right away; and also be sure to get connected up with a good Holy Spirit filled group of Believers in your area right away. Most importantly, enjoy getting to know GOD by reading His Word, the Bible, on a daily basis and see what He has to say to you each day! Right now, up in Heaven, the angels are rejoicing over your salvation! Jesus (the Word) declares, "Likewise, I say unto you, there is joy in the presence of the angels of GOD over one sinner that repenteth" (Luke 15:10 KJV). So you can just imagine Saints and angels up in Heaven having a celebration over your salvation, right now! Praise GOD! And, "Welcome to the family of GOD! You are now a joint heir with Christ, beloved!"

Let's turn back to Luke 4, where Jesus had just finished telling the Nazarene crowd of their unbelief and they have turned into an angry, murderous mob. Let's start with verse 29, "And rising up, they pushed and drove Him out of the town, and [laying hold of Him] they led Him to the [projecting] upper part of the hill on which their town was built, that they might hurl Him headlong down [over the cliff]"(Luke 4:29 AMP).

Now, remember these are the same people that you may have been concerned over a few verses ago. You see, GOD really does know the heart of each person; and it's a good thing that He showed His Son, Jesus, what they were about to do to Him or He might have had to perform the miracle of walking on air! Let's see what Jesus does, "But passing through their midst, He went on His way" (Luke 4:30 AMP). Jesus didn't even waste his breath arguing with them. He just walked right through their midst and they didn't even notice Him leaving them and going the other way!

> *"Knowing hearts is what I do."*
> **Holy Spirit**

You see, the Lord knew before He came to Earth as a man that even though He would come ['that all men through Him might be saved' (see also Mark 16:16)], not all men *would* receive Him. We have also seen that GOD always made it clear to Jesus who would and who would not receive Him. By GOD showing His Son the hearts and minds of man, Jesus was able to immediately sort out the chaff from the wheat. In this way, we see that Jesus didn't go around wasting the allotted time He had been given on Earth to teach and to do GOD's will.

Now, *knowing* that we are brothers and sisters of Christ, as stated in Romans 8:29, "For those whom He foreknew [of whom He was aware and loved beforehand], He also destined from the beginning [foreordaining them] to be molded into the image of His Son [and share inwardly His likeness], that He might become the firstborn among many brethren" (Romans 8:29 AMP), we can also rest assured that as our time too on the Earth is allotted, GOD will indeed reveal to us the hearts and minds of those around us.

I realize that I am reiterating this point, but it is just that important for us to remember. GOD is all Wisdom and we need to remember that GOD is not going to entrust us with something unless we are indeed trustable. I have seen that He does in His grace allow us to make mistakes, but those kinds of mistakes must be limited by GOD in order to protect the hearts and lives of others. When GOD shows us something personal about the life of another person, we need to take it to Him in prayer and find out <u>exactly</u> what we are to do with this piece of information (knowledge). He may just want us to pray about it and not do or say anything else for that person at all. At other times, He may tell us a 'Word of Wisdom' to give to that person to help or encourage them in their life. One thing that we would never, never, never want to do would be to speak to anyone else about it. Unless we are specifically told by GOD to do so, we need to be very careful to protect the knowledge that GOD has entrusted to us. It helps us when we remember the command to "Do unto others as you would have them do unto you," for if we would not want someone passing on any information about us, then we need to give them the same respect. GOD will never reveal things to us to bring us glory, but only to bring glory to Himself; and to bring others to that glorious knowledge of His Son, Jesus.

If you had read on in Luke 4, you would have found that Jesus didn't go away licking His emotional wounds from the cruel acts of the crowd as they screamed at Him and tried to end His life by pushing him off of a cliff. Why? Because He didn't have any emotional wounds. To have emotional wounds, He would have had to have held the crowd as being in the right and GOD as being in the wrong. Since that simply wasn't true (as GOD is perfect), after He disappeared from their view, He headed on down to Capernaum, a town of Galilee; and there He continued on with His next assignment from the Father. Since Jesus wasn't found "boo-hooing" in his prayer closet over the events of the day, so you and I shouldn't be found doing that either. If we are about our Father's business and someone doesn't like what GOD speaks to us, we don't need to be offended. He (Jesus) continued on knowing the hearts of those He had left behind, so you and I can do it too! Remembering that, just like Jesus, we need do only what the Father tells us to do. Mankind has free will, and many will not accept the Words we have to say to them from the Father.

WHAT JESUS BELIEVES

That doesn't make GOD wrong when they don't receive His Words of Truth, so it doesn't make us wrong either. It simply means that we are following in the footsteps of Christ when we are persecuted by others (even those closest to us) because He (Jesus) was persecuted too.

> *Why don't you take some time right now to open your Bible and look up the verses that you have written down in your notebook or in your notes on these pages? First, may I suggest that you begin by asking GOD, in prayer, to open up His Word to you; and then thanking Him, in advance for doing so? Then will help you to come into a deeper knowledge of Him and His will for your life, as Holy Spirit (Himself) guides you into all Truth! Come into His presence expecting to hear from Him, just like Jesus did, trusting Him to show you what* **He wants you to know**!

"Anytime you call upon Me, I will answer you. My heart longs to share with you the deep things, the secret things of My heart, the Father's heart."
Holy Spirit

"A meek and quiet spirit is a good place to hear GOD."
Holy Spirit

3

The Anointing

Now let's talk about the Anointing, because the Anointing of GOD is how we too will discern (know) the thoughts and intents of the heart of man. The Anointing of GOD isn't simply something 'cosmos' that will float into our lives and hover around us with an almost perceptible 'aura' and magically put the knowledge of GOD into our heads...

The Anointing is the Holy Spirit. He is our constant connection with GOD. He is the One (yes, He is a real person, even though you don't see Him) that the Lord promised to send down to "lead us into all truth."

Now, notice our promise is to be led into **all** truth, and not partial truth! Grab your Bible now and open it to John 16:13 and we'll look at our promise on this. [I will be quoting out of the Amplified Bible again. I really like the depth of interpretation that it offers.]

"But when He, the Spirit of Truth (the Truth-giving Spirit) comes, He will guide you into all the Truth (the whole, full Truth). For He will not speak His own message [on His own authority]; but He will tell whatever He hears [from the Father; He will give the message that has been given to Him], and He will announce and declare to you the things that are to come [that will happen in the future]" (John 16:13 AMP).

Isn't this just exactly what happened to Jesus? He received the guidance of the Holy Spirit. The Holy Spirit spoke Words of Knowledge

WHAT JESUS BELIEVES

to Jesus. GOD was speaking to the people, through the Holy Spirit, through His Son, Jesus. Did His disciples even realize that it was actually GOD speaking to them? "Yes." And "No."

"Yes," they realized that the Holy Spirit spoke the Words and Knowledge of GOD to Jesus. Even Peter said, "You are the Christ!" (The Anointed One of which the Scripture foretold). [Remember, Jesus was living here in an Earth suit of dirt just like you and I; and He needed guidance, just like you and I]. The reason He never sinned was due to the fact that He walked inerrant (without error) by laying down His fleshly will (sinful human nature) and walking in complete obedience to GOD, His Heavenly Father, even to the laying down of His life for us at the cross.

"No," they did not recognize that Jesus and GOD the Father were really and truly One. We can read this in the Bible when we look at John 14; Let's read starting from verse 1 so we can understand fully what Jesus was dealing with regarding unbelief, even in His own disciples.

Let's set the scene in our minds. Jesus was reclining at the table with eleven of His twelve disciples. Judas had already left the meal (after satan had entered into him) to go and betray Jesus (for the 30 pieces of silver). This is that significant, historical meal that is referred to as "The Last Supper." It was so named because this was the last meal that Jesus shared with His Disciples before His crucifixion. This was the first time that wine and bread were served to Believers, being representative of His blood that would be shed for them and the entire human race; and of His body which would be broken (hung on a cross until dead) for them and also for the entire human race. This event is also known as the first Communion. (See Luke 22 for this story).

The Disciples had been with Him and had heard Him speaking and teaching the Words of GOD for three years now. They have seen Him perform every conceivable miracle, even to the raising up of the dead back to life again! He has taught them by example, by parables (short stories that illustrate moral lessons) with deep spiritual insights, and by His perfect example in every way.

Jesus knows that tonight He is going to be arrested and on the 'morrow, He will be put to death on a cross. His final hours are spent with the other eleven disciples, doing what He has constantly done since first starting out with them. He is teaching them of the things to come, teaching them to stand in prayer, and He is imparting to them His great faith and His great hope by the words He speaks and the Faith He exhibits (all evidence of the Holy Spirit being with Him, but they still don't fully understand all of this yet). He knows that when He is arrested, great fear will come upon His little flock of men, and as any good Shepherd, He is trying to bring them comfort and safety by assuring them that the wolf (satan) won't win and everything will turn out right! He wants them to know that He is to be leaving them shortly to go and make Heavenly homes for each of them. Thus assuring them that He will come back to get them and that they will live forever with He Himself and the Father.

"DO NOT let your hearts be troubled (distressed, agitated). You believe in and adhere to and trust in and rely on GOD; believe in and adhere to and trust in and rely also on Me. In My Father's house there are many dwelling places (homes). If it were not so, I would have told you; for I am going away to prepare a place for you. And when (if) I go and make ready a place for you, I will come back again and will take you to Myself, that where I am you may be also. And [to the place] where I am going, you know the way. Thomas said to Him, Lord, we do not know where You are going, so how can we know the way?" (John 14:1-5 AMP).

Right here, we can see that after all Jesus had taught to them and promised to them, they still were not comprehending who Jesus was; or from Whom He had come and to Whom He would be shortly returning.

WHAT JESUS BELIEVES

"Jesus said to him, I am the Way and the Truth and the Life; no one comes to the Father except by (through) Me. If you had known Me [had learned to recognize Me], you would also have known My Father. From now on, you know Him and have seen Him. Philip said to Him, Lord, show us the Father [cause us to see the Father – that is all we ask]; then we shall be satisfied" (John 14:6-8 AMP).

Get ready, here it comes! "Jesus replied, Have I been with all of you for so long a time, and do you not recognize and know Me yet, Philip? Anyone who has seen Me has seen the Father. How can you say then, Show us the Father? Do you not believe that I am in the Father, and that the Father is in Me? What I am telling you I do not say on My own authority and of My own accord; but the Father Who lives continually in Me does the (His) works (His own miracles, deeds of power). Believe Me that I Am in the Father and the Father in Me; or else believe Me for the sake of the [very] works themselves. [If you cannot trust Me, at least let these works that I do in My Father's name convince you]" (John 14:9-11 AMP).

At this point, you would think they would all understand the Spiritual Oneness of the Father and the Son, and fall prostrate on the floor before Him, but it is not until after the resurrection that this happens.

Let's quickly turn to John 20 and start with verse 1. "NOW ON the first day of the week, Mary Magdalene came to the tomb early, while it was still dark, and saw that the stone had been removed from (lifted out of the groove across the entrance of) the tomb. So she ran and went to Simon Peter and the other disciple, whom Jesus [tenderly] loved, and said to them, they have taken away the Lord out of the tomb, and we do not know where they have laid Him! Upon this, Peter and the other disciple came out and they went toward the tomb" (John 20:1-3 AMP).

See any life-changing faith so far? Neither do I, so let's keep reading. "And they came running together, but the other disciple outran Peter and arrived at the tomb first. And stooping down, he saw the linen cloths lying there, but he did not enter. Then Simon Peter came up, following him, and went into the tomb and saw the linen cloths lying there; but the burial napkin (kerchief) which had been around Jesus' head, was not lying with the other linen cloths, but was [still] rolled up (wrapped round and round) in a place by itself. Then the other disciple, who had reached the tomb first, went in too; and he saw and was convinced and believed" (John 20:4-8 AMP).

Yep, they are both thinking together, "He's been stolen!"

"For as yet they did not know (understand) the statement of Scripture that He must rise again from the dead. [Ps. 16:10.] Then the disciples went back again to their homes (lodging places). But Mary remained standing outside the tomb sobbing. As she wept, she stooped down [and looked] into the tomb. And she saw two angels in white sitting there, one at the head and one at the feet, where the body of Jesus had lain. And they said to her, Woman, why are you sobbing? She told them, because they have taken away my Lord, and I do not know where they have laid Him. On saying this, she turned around and saw Jesus standing [there], but she did not know (recognize) that it was Jesus. Jesus said to her, Woman, why are you crying [so]? For Whom are you looking? Supposing that it was the gardener, she replied, Sir, if you carried Him away from here, tell me where you have put Him and I will take Him away" (John 20:9-15 AMP).

Even though we don't see Mary understanding the Truth about "her Lord," we do see her 'love for her Lord.' How sad and how happy this must have made Jesus feel. "Jesus said to her, Mary! Turning around she said to Him in Hebrew, Rabboni! – which means Teacher or Master" (John 20:16 AMP). Now she knows!

"Jesus said to her, Do not cling to Me [do not hold Me], for I have not yet ascended to the Father. But go to My brethren and tell them, I am ascending to My Father and your Father, and to My GOD and your GOD. Away came Mary Magdalene, bringing the disciples news (word) that she had seen the Lord and that He had said these things to her. Then on that same first day of the week, when it was evening, though the disciples were behind closed doors for fear of the Jews, Jesus came and stood among them and said, Peace to you! So saying, He showed them His hands and His side. And when the disciples saw the Lord, they were filled with joy (delight, exultation, ecstasy, rapture)" (John 20:17-20 AMP).

Now, would be the point where they would fall at His feet in understanding and great joy with the true understanding and knowledge of Who He is! What a glorious ecstasy it must have been to have the One they loved the most in the world back with them! Can you imagine the tears of joy they must have cried? And the shouts of glorious love they must have made? Can you imagine your own joy and relief in seeing Jesus if you had been there? So can I!

Verses 21, 22, and 23 are also very important teachings for us and so we will include them now and look back to them for more insight at a later point in this chapter. "Then Jesus said to them again, Peace to you! [Just] as the Father has sent Me forth, so I am sending you. And having said this, He breathed on them and said to them, Receive the Holy Spirit! [Now having received the Holy Spirit, and being led and directed by Him] if you forgive the sins of anyone, they are forgiven; if you retain the sins of anyone, they are retained" (John 20:21-23 AMP).

Jesus spoke to them in Faith of the Holy Spirit indwelling them. At this point, they were prepared to receive Him by Jesus breathing on them, but He would actually manifest Himself (the Holy Spirit) on that Day of Pentecost when He came as "a rushing, mighty wind, and appearing as tongues of fire on each of them!" [See Acts 1:4–9 and all of Acts Chapter 2].

Now as we read verse 24, we can see and understand why people of the Church today often referred to the disciple Thomas as "doubting Thomas." "But Thomas, one of the Twelve, called the Twin, was not with them when Jesus came. So the other disciples kept telling him, we have seen the Lord! But he said to them, unless I see in His hands the marks made by the nails and put my finger into the nail prints, and put my hand into His side, I will never believe [it]. Eight days later, His disciples were again in the house, and Thomas was with them. Jesus came, though they were behind closed doors, and stood among them and said, Peace to you! Then He said to Thomas, Reach out your finger here, and see My hands; and put out your hand and place [it] in My side. Do not be faithless and incredulous, but [stop your unbelief and] believe! Thomas answered Him, My Lord and my GOD! Jesus said to him, because you have seen Me, Thomas, do you now believe (trust, have faith)? Blessed and happy and to be envied are those who have never seen Me and yet have believed and adhered to and trusted and relied on Me" (John 20:24-29 AMP).

John 21:14 records witness of the third time Jesus appeared to His disciples after being resurrected from the dead. We can gather from this that Jesus was still going and doing the will of His Father by appearing and teaching the lambs of His flock, as directed by GOD. Now, we will go back to before His crucifixion and learn more about how He operated under the Anointing (Holy Spirit), while here on the Earth.

As Jesus heard the Word and Knowledge of GOD, He only acted on it in the way the Holy Spirit of GOD directed Him to. You may ask, "You mean Jesus had to ask GOD [the Father] what to say, and where to go, and what to do?" Yes! He told us this in John 5:30 when He said, "I am able to do nothing from Myself [independently, of My own accord — but **only** as I am taught by GOD and as I get His orders]. Even as I hear, I judge [I decide as I am bidden to decide. As the voice comes to Me, so I give a decision], and My judgment is right (just, righteous), because I do not seek or consult My own will [I have no desire to do what is pleasing to Myself, My own aim, My own purpose] but **only** the will and pleasure of the Father Who sent Me" (John 5:30 AMP).

WHAT JESUS BELIEVES

First, we saw that Jesus came to Earth as the Anointed One, Who was prophesied about in the Old Testament Scriptures long ago. Next, we saw that it was the Holy Spirit in Him that let Him know just what the Father was speaking to Him. In this case, we can see that the Holy Spirit is like the telephone line between Jesus and the Father while Jesus walked this Earth as a man.

In the next paragraph, we will go back to the lineage of Jesus and read about His ancestors. We will see how long before His birth on this planet, the Holy Spirit, that precious Anointing of GOD, was already at work on the hearts of mankind in preparation for their Messiah, and the healing of the rift between GOD and man. Jesus was able to perform all of the incredible miracles He performed while on the Earth through that Anointing. In this way, the Holy Spirit was like the power line between the Father and the Son. Looking back through history, we will see the Holy Spirit in many capacities, not the least of which is the Father's love.

"When the lights in the heavens came on, I was there! We did all of this because of our love for you! Nothing was too much to give for you. Nothing. Jesus agrees 100%."
Holy Spirit

When a child, you may have heard the saying, "one, two, skip a few, ninety-nine, one hundred!" Well, that is a little bit like what we are going to do now. The first man was Adam and his wife's name was Eve. They are recorded in Genesis 1 as the first man and the first woman. All life on this Earth today started originally with the two of them. Skipping on down some (if you really want to know the relatives in between you can start reading about them in Genesis 5), we come to their great (x 8) grandson, Noah. [In Biblical numerology 8 represents *new beginning*.] The Word tells us that Noah was a righteous man in GOD's sight and so when GOD destroyed the Earth by flood, Noah and his wife and their three sons Shem, Ham, and Japheth, were all saved with the animals in the Ark (Genesis 6–9). This speaks for itself that all mankind also came forth from the loins of Noah and his descendants.

For those of you who like to study genealogies, you would enjoy doing one on Noah's three sons, for out of them came the races of our day. Although they have split into many factions that we term 'Nationalities,' they all had one beginning, Noah, and before him, Adam. Hence, we really are just one big family, "red and yellow, black and white, we are precious in his sight!" Whether or not the world likes it, we are truly brothers of one blood!

Now, let's jump on down to Abraham and Sarah; formerly Abram and Sarai (Genesis17). (Again for those genealogy lovers, see Genesis 10 and 11!). They begat (or had) Isaac, who had Jacob, whom GOD renamed Israel. (You can read the full stories of these three families and what they did in Genesis 14-49). Israel (Jacob) had 12 sons. From oldest to youngest, these were their names: Reuben, Simeon, Levi, Judah, Dan, Naphtali, Gad, Asher, Issachar, Zebulun, (daughter named Dinah), Joseph, and Benjamin. (For genealogy buffs, Chapters 29 and 30 are a must!).

The twelve sons of Jacob, whom GOD renamed Israel, are the roots from which the twelve tribes of Israel sprang.

King David. Just his name inspires images of great battle conquests, if you know even a little about Bible history! King David, as told in the Bible, comes from the "shoot (branch) of Judah." (Again, all genealogy buffs can read about David's lineage in the First Book of the Chronicles, Chapter 2. All of the barest genealogy, to David's time, without their whole stories can also be found in Chapters 1 and 2). King David, the same David who killed the giant, Goliath (1 Samuel 17 and 18), was declared in the Word as "a man after GOD's own heart."

First Samuel 13:14 (AMP) says, "...the Lord has sought out [David] a man after His own heart, and the Lord has commanded him to be prince and ruler over His people..." Psalm 89:20 AMP says, "I have found David My servant; with My holy oil have I anointed him." [Acts 13:22]. GOD's holy oil as stated here in Psalm 89:20 is representative of the Anointing of the Holy Spirit on King David's life. David needed this Anointing in order to lead his people rightly before GOD.

If you have read somewhat about David, you can see mistakes that he made during his lifetime, but when <u>he was obedient to the leading of the Holy Spirit, that Anointing on his life, he was able to lead the people correctly in the sight of GOD</u>. It is encouraging to know that a man like David could make mistakes and always come back to the GOD he loved, knowing that forgiveness was waiting to be given to him, just as soon he was obedient and repented before GOD.

Acts 13:22-23 (AMP) tells us, "And when He had deposed him (Saul), He raised up David to be their king; of him He bore witness and said, I have found David son of Jesse <u>a man after My own heart</u>, **who will do all My will and carry out My program fully**. [1 Sam. 13:14; Ps. 89:20; Isa. 44:28]. Of this man's descendants, GOD has brought to Israel a Savior [in the person of Jesus], according to His promise" (Acts 13:22-23 AMP).

If you have done some reading of the Psalms, then you have read how blessed David was by GOD, but you have also seen how human David was in his cries for help to GOD. That is not to his detriment, for he knew where his Source of strength and safety was and that was in the Lord. The Psalms themselves that he wrote in the Bible were all done under the power of the Anointing. [Just reading Psalms 103 and 104 will put you in awe of our GOD]!

Since the day that David was first called, we see evidence of the Anointing of the Holy Spirit upon his life. Samuel, the judge (and prophet) of Israel during David's youth, came to the home of Jesse, David's father, and asked to see his sons. The Lord, by His Holy Spirit (the Anointing), had spoken to Samuel and told him that one of the sons of Jesse was chosen by Him (GOD) to be the new king of Israel.

The old king had sinned against GOD and GOD was going to remove him from leading His people Israel.

Samuel had Jesse bring to stand before him each of his seven sons, "When they had come, he looked on Eliab [the eldest son] and said, surely the Lord's anointed is before Him. But the Lord said to Samuel, Look not on his appearance or at the height of his stature, for I have rejected him. For the Lord sees not as man sees; for man looks on the outward appearance, but the Lord looks on the heart. Then Jesse called Abinadab and made him pass before Samuel. But Samuel said, neither has the Lord chosen this one. Then Jesse made Shammah pass by. Samuel said, nor has the Lord chosen him. Jesse made seven of his sons pass before Samuel. And Samuel said to Jesse, The Lord has not chosen any of these. Then [he] said to Jesse, Are all your sons here? [Jesse] said, There is yet the youngest; he is tending the sheep. Samuel said to Jesse, Send for him; for we will not sit down to eat until he is here" (1 Samuel 16:6-11 AMP).

Right here is a good analogy between David and Jesus. They were both keepers of their fathers' sheep. David kept a flock of real sheep for his earthly father before he was ever given the responsibility of GOD's flock, the Israelites. Jesus shepherded a group of people destined to be the beginning of the greatest flock the world has ever known, the flock that still continues to this day and goes by the title of Christian!

> *"David was a man after My own heart!"*
> **Spirit of the Father (Holy Spirit)**

Also, David and Jesus were both kings. David was an earthly king and he eventually reigned over all of Israel. Jesus was King of Kings and He reigns forever! "And He has on His robe and on His thigh a name written: KING OF KINGS AND LORD OF LORDS" (Revelation 19:16 NKJV). "... Jesus Christ, the faithful witness, the firstborn from the dead, and the ruler over the kings of the Earth. To Him Who loved us and washed us from our sins in His own blood, and has made us kings and priests to His GOD and Father, to Him be glory and dominion forever and ever. Amen" (Revelation 1:5-6 NKJV).

When he did arrive, "Then Samuel took the horn of oil and anointed David in the midst of his brothers; and the Spirit of the Lord came mightily upon David from that day forward. And Samuel arose and went to Ramah" (1 Samuel 16:13). (Remember that horn of oil is again symbolic in the physical of what happened to David in the spiritual. GOD's Holy Spirit, the Anointing of (Jehovah) GOD, was upon David from that day forward. Again, that is how he was able to write [prophetic] psalms (songs). It is also how he was able to guide and direct GOD's people, GOD's way).

"Psalm 103
Meditate upon My Words to you. Will you sing this Psalm aloud in Worship to Me? I love to hear you sing."
Holy Spirit of GOD

Going back to Jesus' very beginning here on Earth as a human will help us to better understand GOD's awesome Holy Spirit Anointing. "Now the birth of Jesus Christ took place under these circumstances: When His mother Mary had been promised in marriage to Joseph, before they came together, she was found to be pregnant [through the power] of the Holy Spirit" (Matthew 1:18 AMP).

Flipping over to Luke 1, let's read about Mary, the mother of Jesus, and her cousin Elizabeth. "In the days when Herod was king of Judea there was a certain priest whose name was Zachariah, of the daily service (the division) of Abia; and his wife was also a descendant of Aaron, and her name was Elizabeth. And they both were righteous in the sight of GOD, walking blamelessly in all the commandments and requirements of the Lord. But they had no child, for Elizabeth was barren; and both were far advanced in years. Now while on duty, serving as priest before GOD in the order of his division, as was the custom of the priesthood, it fell to him by lot to enter [the sanctuary of] the temple of the Lord and burn incense [Exod. 30:7]. And all the throng of people were praying outside [in the court] at the hour of incense [burning]. And there appeared to him an angel of the Lord, standing at the right side of the altar of incense. And when Zachariah saw him, he was troubled, and fear took possession of him. But the angel said to him, Do not be afraid, Zachariah, because your petition was heard, and your wife Elizabeth will bear you a son, and you must call his name John [GOD is favorable]. And you shall have joy and exultant delight, and many will rejoice over his birth, for he will be great and distinguished in the sight of the Lord. And he must drink no wine nor strong drink, and he will be filled with and controlled by the Holy Spirit even in and from his mother's womb [Num. 6:3]. And he will turn back and cause to return many of the sons of Israel to the Lord their GOD, and he will [himself] go before Him in the spirit and power of Elijah" [the power of Elijah = the Anointing] "to turn back the hearts of the fathers to the children, and the disobedient and incredulous and unpersuadable to the wisdom of the upright [which is the knowledge and holy love of the will of GOD] – in order to make ready for the Lord a people [perfectly] prepared [in spirit, adjusted and disposed and placed in the right moral state]" [Isa. 40:3; Mal. 4:5-6] (Luke 1:5-17 AMP).

Moving on down to verse 26, we read, "Now in the sixth month [after that], the angel Gabriel was sent from GOD to a town of Galilee named Nazareth, to a girl never having been married and a virgin engaged to be married to a man whose name was Joseph, a descendant of the house of David; and the virgin's name was Mary. And he came to her and said, Hail, O favored one [endued with grace]! The Lord is with you! Blessed (favored of GOD) are you before all other women! But when she saw him, she was greatly troubled and disturbed and confused at what he said and kept revolving in her mind what such a greeting might mean. And the angel said to her, Do not be afraid, Mary, for you have found grace (free, spontaneous, absolute favor and loving-kindness) with GOD. And listen! You will become pregnant and will give birth to a Son, and you shall call His name Jesus. He will be great (eminent) and will be called the Son of the Most High; and the Lord GOD will give to Him the throne of His forefather David, and He will reign over the house of Jacob throughout the ages; and of His reign there will be no end [Isa. 9:6-7; Dan. 2:44], and Mary said to the angel, How can this be, since I have no [intimacy with any man as a] husband? Then the angel said to her, The Holy Spirit will come upon you, and the power of the Most High will overshadow you [like a shining cloud]; and so the holy (pure, sinless) Thing (Offspring) which shall be born of you will be called the Son of GOD. [Exod. 40:34; Isa. 7:14]. And listen! Your relative Elizabeth in her old age has also conceived a son, and this is now the sixth month with her who was called barren. For with GOD nothing is ever impossible and no word from GOD shall be without power or impossible of fulfillment" (Luke 1:26-37 AMP).

This is a "good Word" from GOD and would be a good one to jot down in your notebook, "For with GOD **nothing** is ever impossible and no word from GOD shall be without power or impossible of fulfillment" (Luke 1:37 AMP).

"Then Mary said, Behold, I am the handmaiden of the Lord; let it be done to me according to what you have said. And the angel left her" (Luke 1:38 AMP).

Food for thought: 'If we would just place our complete trust in GOD, what things could He do in our own lives?'

"And at that time Mary arose and went with haste into the hill country to a town of Judah, and she went to the house of Zachariah and, entering it, saluted Elizabeth. And it occurred that when Elizabeth heard Mary's greeting, the baby leaped in her womb, and Elizabeth was filled with and controlled by the Holy Spirit. And she cried out with a loud cry, and then exclaimed, Blessed (favored of GOD) above all other women are you! And blessed (favored of GOD) is the Fruit of your womb! And how [have I deserved that this honor should] be granted to me, that the mother of my Lord should come to me? For behold, the instant the sound of your salutation reached my ears, the baby in my womb leaped for joy" (Luke 1:39-44 AMP).

That kind of Anointing sounds like the kind of Anointing [with power] we would love to have on our lives and operate in, doesn't it? And that kind of joy and knowledge is the kind we too would love to have operating in our lives, isn't it? The good news is that this Anointing is exactly the same today as [it was] then! It is the same precious Holy Spirit, the same marvelous, awesome [power of] GOD that is waiting for us to yield to Him; to be fully utilized [operated in] by each of us as believers and followers of Christ Jesus!

"And blessed (happy, to be envied) is she who believed that there would be a fulfillment of the things that were spoken to her from the Lord. And Mary said, my soul magnifies and extols the Lord, and my spirit rejoices in GOD my Savior, for He has looked upon the low station and humiliation of His handmaiden. For behold, from now on all generations [of all ages] will call me blessed and declare me happy and to be envied! For He Who is almighty has done great things for me – and holy is His name [to be venerated in His purity, majesty and glory]! And His mercy (His compassion and kindness toward the miserable and afflicted) is on those who fear Him with godly reverence, from generation to generation and age to age [Ps. 103:17]. He has shown strength and made might with His arm; He has scattered the proud and haughty in and by the imagination and purpose and designs of their hearts. He has put down the mighty from their thrones and exalted those of low degree. He has filled and satisfied the hungry with good things, and the rich He has sent away empty-handed [without a gift]. He has laid hold on His servant Israel [to help him, to espouse his cause], in remembrance of His mercy, Even as He promised to our forefathers, to Abraham and to his descendants forever" [Gen. 17:7; 18:18; 22:17; 1 Sam. 2:1-10; Mic. 7:20] (Luke 1:45-55 AMP).

Overcome by the Holy Spirit, both Elizabeth and Mary had prophesied; and Elizabeth's baby, who would grow up to be John the Baptist, was filled with the Holy Spirit (the Anointing) and 'leaped in her womb for joy!' the instant Mary's salutation reached Elizabeth's ears! (Luke 1:41 AMP).

Now let's read about Jesus' birth and the events that surrounded it. "IN THOSE days it occurred that a decree went out from Caesar Augustus that the whole Roman Empire should be registered. This was the first enrollment, and it was made when Quirinius was governor of Syria. And all the people were going to be registered, each to his own city or town. And Joseph also went up from Galilee from the town of Nazareth to Judea, to the town of David, which is called Bethlehem, because he was of the house and family of David, to be enrolled with Mary, his espoused (married) wife, who was about to become a mother [Matt. 1:18-25]. And while they were there, the time came for her delivery, and she gave birth to her Son, her Firstborn; and she wrapped Him in swaddling clothes and laid Him in a manger, because there was no room or place for them in the inn. And in that vicinity there were shepherds living [out under the open sky] in the field, watching [in shifts] over their flock by night. And behold, an angel of the Lord stood by them, and the glory of the Lord flashed and shone all about them, and they were terribly frightened. But the angel said to them, Do not be afraid; for behold, I bring you good news of a great joy which will come to all the people. For to you is born this day in the town of David a Savior, Who is Christ (the Messiah) the Lord! [Mic. 5:2]. And this will be a sign for you [by which you will recognize Him]: you will find [after searching] a Baby wrapped in swaddling clothes and lying in a manger [1 Sam. 2:34; 2 Kings 19:29; Isa. 7:14]. Then suddenly there appeared with the angel an army of the troops of Heaven (a Heavenly Knighthood), praising GOD and saying, Glory to GOD in the highest [Heaven], and on Earth peace among men with whom He is well pleased [men of goodwill, of His favor]. When the angels went away from them into Heaven, the shepherds said one to another, Let us go over to Bethlehem and see this thing (saying) that has come to pass, which the Lord has made known to us. So they went with haste and [by searching] found Mary and Joseph, and the Baby lying in a manger. And when they saw it, they made known what had been told them concerning this Child, and all who heard it were astounded and marveled at what the shepherds told them. But Mary was keeping within herself all these things (sayings), weighing and pondering them in her heart. And the shepherds returned, glorifying and praising GOD for all the things they had heard and seen, just as it had been told them" (Luke 2:1-20 AMP).

Upon entering the place where the newborn Jesus lay, we can just imagine how they must have peered in at that little face and being overcome themselves by the Holy Spirit, they too fell down at His feet to worship Him! Oh, what a wonderful sight that must have been. And all the while Mary storing all of these things up in her heart. What joy she must have felt at giving birth to the Savior of the World, the long-awaited Messiah! She must have experienced that beautiful Anointing of GOD's Spirit every day that her Son, Jesus, was with her! Oh, to have experienced that too....

In Matthew 2, you can read about the wise men who saw the star and came from the East to worship Him and bring Him gifts. The same Anointing brought them to Jesus' side. History tells us that it probably took about <u>two years</u> for the men to make their Journey to Bethlehem. Now that's the kind of faith that perseveres until the journey is accomplished.

The Anointing on Jesus is what kept Him safe and alive until **He chose** to lay down His life for us at the cross. satan tried to kill Jesus through King Herod's decree by killing all of the baby boys in Bethlehem <u>two years</u> old and under, but GOD warned Joseph by an angel in a dream, "Now after Jesus was born in Bethlehem of Judea in the days of Herod the king, behold, wise men from the East came to Jerusalem, saying, "Where is He who has been born King of the Jews? For we have seen His star in the East and have come to worship Him." When Herod the king heard this, he was troubled, and all Jerusalem with him. And when he had gathered all the chief priests and scribes of the people together, he inquired of them where the Christ was to be born. So they said to him, "In Bethlehem of Judea, for thus it is written by the prophet: 'But you, Bethlehem, in the land of Judah, Are not the least among the rulers of Judah; For out of you shall come a Ruler Who will shepherd My people Israel.' " Then Herod, when he had secretly called the wise men, determined from them what time the star appeared. And he sent them to Bethlehem and said, "Go and search carefully for the young Child, and when you have found Him, bring back word to me, that I may come and worship Him also." When they heard the king, they departed; and behold, the star which they had seen in the East went before them, till it came and stood over where the young Child was. When they saw the star, they rejoiced with exceedingly great joy. And when they had come into the house, they saw the young Child with Mary His mother, and fell down and worshiped Him. And when they had opened their treasures, they presented gifts to Him: gold, frankincense, and myrrh. Then, being divinely warned in a dream that they should not return to Herod, they departed for their own country another way. Now when they had departed, behold, an angel of the Lord appeared to Joseph in a dream, saying, "Arise, take the young Child and His mother, flee to Egypt, and stay there until I bring you word; for Herod will seek the young Child to destroy Him." When he arose, he took the young Child and His mother by night and departed for Egypt, and was there until the death of Herod, that it might be fulfilled which was spoken by the Lord through the prophet, saying, "Out of Egypt I called My Son." Then Herod, when he saw that he was deceived by the wise men, was exceedingly angry; and he sent forth and put to death all the male children who were in Bethlehem and in all its districts, from two years old and under, according to the time which he had determined from the wise men. Then was fulfilled what was spoken by Jeremiah the prophet, saying: "A voice was heard in Ramah, Lamentation, weeping, and great mourning, Rachel weeping for her children, Refusing to be comforted, Because they are no more" (Matthew 2:1-18 NKJV).

Kept by the Holy Spirit, they lived in Egypt until Herod's death. "Now when Herod was dead, behold, an angel of the Lord appeared in a dream to Joseph in Egypt, saying, 'Arise, take the young Child and His mother, and go to the land of Israel, for those who sought the young

Child's life are dead.' Then he arose, took the young Child and His mother, and came into the land of Israel. But when he heard that Archelaus was reigning over Judea instead of his father Herod, he was afraid to go there. And being warned by GOD in a dream, he turned aside into the region of Galilee. And he came and dwelt in a city called Nazareth, that it might be fulfilled which was spoken by the prophets, "He shall be called a Nazarene" (Matthew 2:19-23 NKJV).

The Anointing of the Holy Spirit will watch over us day and night. Whether He speaks to us in or through our dreams, or whether He speaks to our heart, whether He assigns an angel to come and speak to us while we are awake or asleep, all of these are also solid ways that (the Anointing) Holy Spirit speaks to us. Our job is to *give ear* and obey. (**"give ear": take heed**)

> *Jesus definition of taking heed to His Father:*
> *"Prompt Obedience. Perfect Obedience."*
> *Holy Spirit*

"Now His parents went to Jerusalem every year to the Passover Feast [Deut.16:1-8; Exod. 23:15]. And when He was twelve years [old], they went up, as was their custom. And when the Feast was ended, as they were returning, the boy Jesus remained behind in Jerusalem. Now His parents did not know this, but, supposing Him to be in the caravan, they traveled on a day's journey; and [then] they sought Him [diligently, looking up and down for Him] among their kinsfolk and acquaintances. And when they failed to find Him, they went back to Jerusalem, looking for Him [up and down] all the way. After three days they found Him [came upon Him] in the [court of the] temple, sitting among the teachers, listening to them and asking them questions. And all who heard Him were astonished and overwhelmed with bewildered wonder at His intelligence and understanding and His replies" (Luke 2:41-47 AMP). Notice especially verse 47, "**And all who heard Him were astonished and overwhelmed with bewildered wonder at His intelligence and understanding and His replies**" (Luke 2:47 AMP). Jesus was 12 years old.

We know that the Holy Spirit descended and alighted upon Him like a dove when He was 30 years old, but this is prior to that event (when He is still a child). Even so, we see (this) Wisdom [of GOD (Anointing) (upon Him, operating through Him)] (is) from above: Stephen speaks by unction of (the Holy Spirit) Wisdom (from GOD), "But they were not able to resist the intelligence and the wisdom and [the inspiration of] the Spirit with which and by Whom he spoke" (Acts 6:10 AMP).

Paul writes about this wisdom in his letter to the Colossians, "My purpose is that their hearts, joined together in love, may be encouraged. May they have all the riches of the full assurance of understanding, leading to a true knowledge of the mystery of GOD — that is, Messiah. In Him all the treasures of wisdom and knowledge are hidden" (Paul's Letter to the Colossians 2:2-3 TLV).

"Run to Me, My Child."
Holy Spirit

James writes to the twelve tribes (of GOD) scattered abroad about this same wisdom (that Jesus walked in and lived the example of perfectly), "JAMES, a servant of GOD and of the Lord Jesus Christ, to the twelve tribes scattered abroad [among the Gentiles in the dispersion]: Greetings (rejoice)!" (James 1:1 AMP), "But the wisdom from above is first of all pure (undefiled); then it is peace-loving, courteous (considerate, gentle). [It is willing to] yield to reason, full of compassion and good fruits; it is wholehearted and straightforward, impartial and unfeigned (free from doubts, wavering, and insincerity) (James 3:17 AMP).

The questions Jesus posed, His understanding and the replies He answered to the teachers in the Temple all exhibited the Wisdom of GOD to such an extent that it says, "<u>all who heard Him were astonished and overwhelmed with bewildered wonder</u> at <u>His intelligence</u> and <u>understanding</u> and <u>His replies</u>" (Luke 2:47 AMP).

Do you suppose (during Jesus' time with them) He asked them Who Isaiah 6 is speaking of? "AND THERE shall come forth a Shoot out of the stock of Jesse [David's father], and a Branch out of his roots shall grow and bear fruit [Isa. 4:2; Matt. 2:23; Rev. 5:5; 22:16]. And the Spirit of the Lord shall rest upon Him – the Spirit of wisdom and understanding, the Spirit of counsel and might, the Spirit of knowledge and of the reverential and obedient fear of the Lord – and shall make Him of quick understanding, and His delight shall be in the reverential and obedient fear of the Lord. And He shall not judge by the sight of His eyes, neither decide by the hearing of His ears; But with righteousness and justice shall He judge the poor and decide with fairness for the meek, the poor, and the downtrodden of the earth; and He shall smite the earth and the oppressor with the rod of His mouth, and with the breath of His lips He shall slay the wicked. And righteousness shall be the girdle of His waist and faithfulness the girdle of His loins" (Isaiah 11:1-5 AMP).

How interesting that a little child shall *also* lead them... "And the wolf shall dwell with the lamb, and the leopard shall lie down with the kid, and the calf and the young lion and the fatted domestic animal together; and a little child shall lead them" (Isaiah 11:6 AMP).

If only they had known that the little child (of 12 years of age) before them was LORD GOD ALMIGHTY, KING of Kings and LORD of Lords, the One Who would lead Heavens' Armies forth! "I am the Alpha and the Omega, the Beginning and the End, says the Lord GOD, He Who is and Who was and Who is to come, the Almighty (the Ruler of all)" [Isa. 9:6] (Revelation 1:8 AMP). "He had seven stars in His right hand; a sharp double-edged sword came from His mouth, and His face was shining like the sun at midday. When I saw Him, I fell at His feet like a dead man. He laid His right hand on me and said, "Don't be afraid! I am the First and the Last, and the Living One. I **was** dead, but look — I am alive forever and ever, and I hold the keys of death and Hades" (Revelation 1:16-18 HCSB). "And I saw Heaven opened, and behold a white horse; and He that sat upon him was called Faithful and True, and in righteousness He doth judge and make war. His eyes were as a flame of fire, and on His head were many crowns; and He had a name written, that no man knew, but He Himself. And He was clothed with a vesture dipped in blood: and his name is called The Word of GOD. And the armies which were in Heaven followed him upon white horses, clothed in fine linen, white and clean. And out of His mouth goeth a sharp sword, that with it He should smite the nations: and He shall rule them with a rod of iron: and He treadeth the winepress of the fierceness and wrath of Almighty GOD. And He hath on His vesture and on His thigh a name written, KING OF KINGS, AND LORD OF LORDS" (Revelation 19:11-16 KJV).

If only they knew that the One spoken of in Isaiah 53 (the entire chapter speaks of Him), "Who would have believed what we just heard? When was the Lords' Power revealed through Him? He sprouted up like a twig before GOD, like a root out of parched soil; He had no stately form or majesty that might catch our attention, no special appearance that we should want to follow Him" (Isaiah 53:1-2 NET). If they only knew when they read Psalm 22, "I was cast upon You from birth. From My mother's womb You have been My GOD" (Psalms 22:10 NKJV). If only they knew...

To all of that, I say, "The beginning of Wisdom is: get Wisdom (skillful and godly Wisdom)! [For skillful and godly Wisdom is the principal thing]. And with all you have gotten, get understanding (discernment, comprehension, and interpretation)" [James 1:5] (Proverbs 4:7 AMP).

And when His parents found Him? "And when they saw Him, they were amazed: and His mother said unto Him, Son, why hast Thou thus dealt with us? Behold, Thy father and I have sought Thee sorrowing. And He said unto them, how is it that ye sought Me? Wist ye not that I must be about My Father's business? And they understood not the saying which He spake unto them. And He went down with them, and came to Nazareth, and was subject unto them: but His mother kept all these sayings in her heart. And Jesus increased in wisdom and stature, and in favour with GOD and man" (Luke 2:48-52 KJV).

WHAT JESUS BELIEVES

Jesus lived at home and helped His family until the time that He was thirty. When Jesus did start His three years of preaching the good news to the poor, healing of the brokenhearted, proclamation of liberty to the captives, recovery of sight to the blind, and setting at liberty those who were oppressed, He did so under the direction of the Holy Spirit, which as we have already discussed is the Anointing. GOD first sent John the Baptist out ahead of Him (Jesus) to declare His coming and prepare the hearts of the people.

"IN THOSE days there appeared John the Baptist, preaching in the Wilderness (Desert) of Judea and saying, Repent (think differently; change your mind, regretting your sins and changing your conduct), for the Kingdom of Heaven is at hand. This is he who was mentioned by the prophet Isaiah when he said, the voice of one crying in the wilderness (shouting in the desert), Prepare the road for the Lord, make His highways straight (level, direct) [Isa. 40:3]. This same John's garments were made of camel's hair, and he wore a leather girdle about his waist; and his food was locusts and wild honey [Lev. 11:22; 2 Kings 1:8; Zech. 13:4]. Then Jerusalem and all Judea and all the country round about the Jordan went out to him; and they were baptized in the Jordan by him, confessing their sins. But when he saw many of the Pharisees and Sadducees coming for baptism, he said to them, you brood of vipers!" [John the Baptist could not have known the hearts of men, except by the Holy Spirit (we know he was filled with the Holy Spirit from his mother's womb)]. "Who warned you to flee and escape from the wrath and indignation [of GOD against disobedience] that is coming? <u>Bring forth fruit that is consistent with repentance</u> [let your lives prove your change of heart]; and do not presume to say to yourselves, we have Abraham for our forefather; for I tell you, GOD is able to raise up descendants for Abraham from these stones! And already the ax is lying at the root of the trees; every tree therefore that does not bear good fruit is cut down and thrown into the fire. I indeed baptize you in (with) water because of repentance [that is, because of your changing your minds for the better, heartily amending your ways, with abhorrence of your past sins]. But He Who is coming after me is mightier than I, Whose sandals I am not worthy or fit to take off or carry; He will baptize you with the Holy Spirit and with fire. His winnowing fan (shovel, fork) is in His hand, and He will thoroughly clear out and clean His threshing floor and gather and store His wheat in His barn, but the chaff He will burn up with fire that cannot be put out" (Matthew 3:1-12 AMP).

Jesus also went out to John and was baptized (Luke 3:21-22; John 1:29–34) in the Jordan River. "Then Jesus came from Galilee to the Jordan to John to be baptized by him. But John protested strenuously, having in mind to prevent Him, saying, it is I who have need to be baptized by You, and do You come to me?" [Another example of the Holy Spirit showing John the Baptist the heart]. "But Jesus replied to him, Permit it just now; for this is the fitting way for [both of] us to fulfill all righteousness [that is, to perform completely whatever is right]. Then he permitted Him. And when Jesus was baptized, He went up at once out of the water; and behold, the Heavens were opened, and he [John] saw the Spirit of GOD descending like a dove and alighting on Him. And behold, a voice from Heaven said, This is My Son, My Beloved, in Whom I delight!" [Ps. 2:7; Isa. 42:1] (Matthew 3:13-17 AMP).

As we read about the life of Jesus, you may wonder how all of this is going to connect to you, and how all of this applies to your walk with the Lord today. Pretty simple really, Jesus was the perfect example of walking in the Anointing (the [perfect] direction and will) of GOD at all times, right? Right! When we read about Jesus' life, and we see the timing and order in which GOD executed (His will) in Jesus' life [as in Executively led from the One with the Highest Position], we can start to see the timing and direction of GOD in our own lives.

It also gives us great hope, knowing that GOD knew in advance all of the mistakes we would make and He decided to give us the Anointing anyway. Now, that's grace! Not to be confused with a license to sin, but grace, unmerited favor directed at us from GOD! *It is the goodness of GOD that leads us to repentance (See: Romans 2).* A repentant heart can always receive cleansing from sin. (See

WHAT JESUS BELIEVES

Revelation 3:19) Thank GOD for the blood of Jesus which can wash away each stain!

"Come to the fountain as oft as you like
There's cleansing of sin both by day and by night.
There's power in the Blood which cannot be turned off
From the Victory gained when I died on the cross!"
Spirit of Jesus the Messiah

When we read about the complete and unquestioning obedience of Jesus to His Father, GOD, and then we read about the outcome to all that He did and how it all came out *perfectly*, we are able to gain more strength from GOD by operating in His faith through His all-knowing direction. Thank GOD that He does know our story's ending and thank GOD that if we will obey Him and trust Him, that ending will be victorious!

As we continue to study the Word about Jesus' walk and His Anointing, we can see how He applied the Anointing to the various situations He encountered; and we, in turn, can use them as food, spiritual food, to feed on. That way, when we encounter a similar opportunity to one of those that Jesus encountered, and **we are led to do something in the Supernatural [by the Power of GOD thru the Holy Spirit], by faith we can and we will**! All because we have been feeding off of and meditating on all of these wonderful and faith-filled miraculous stories that we have read about Jesus!

The next situation the Word tells us about Jesus (in Matthew) is that He was directed by the Holy Spirit to go out into the wilderness, "THEN JESUS was led (guided) by the [Holy] Spirit into the wilderness (desert) to be tempted (tested and tried) by the devil (satan). And He went without food for forty days and forty nights, and later He was hungry [Exod. 34:28; 1 Kings 19:8]. And the tempter came and said to Him, If You are GOD's Son, command these stones to be made [loaves of] bread. But He replied, it has been written, Man shall not live and be upheld and sustained by bread alone, but by every Word that comes forth from the mouth of GOD [Deut. 8:3]. Then the devil took Him into the holy city and placed Him on a turret (pinnacle, gable) of the temple sanctuary. [Neh. 11:1; Dan. 9:24]. And he said to Him, If You are the Son of GOD, throw Yourself down; for it is written, He will give His angels charge over you, and they will bear you up on their hands, lest you strike your foot against a stone [Ps. 91:11-12]. Jesus said to him, On the other hand, it is written also, you shall not tempt, test thoroughly, or try exceedingly the Lord your GOD [Deut. 6:16]. Again, the devil took Him up on a very high mountain and showed Him all the kingdoms of the world and the glory (the splendor, magnificence, preeminence, and excellence) of them. And he said to Him, these things, all taken together, I will give You, if You will prostrate Yourself before me and do homage and worship me. Then Jesus said to him, Begone, satan! For it has been written, you shall worship the Lord your GOD, and Him alone shall you serve" [Deut. 6:13] (Matthew 4:1-10 AMP).

Through all of the temptations, Jesus stayed strong and resolute to the Truth, not bending to the will of satan in any way. He did not wish to acquire earthly wealth nor earthly glory for Himself. His (Jesus') only desire was to serve the Father and bring Him glory. When Jesus said, "Begone, satan! For it has been written, you shall worship the Lord your GOD, and Him alone shall you serve," Jesus was showing us that in *not being covetous*, He was able to freely receive all that GOD had for Him.

In the world's system of doing things, 'more is better.' If it costs more, it must be better. If we own more of it, we must be better. If we have a higher position in a company and earn more money, our life must be better. All of these things are simply items that come with the Earth. They are all temporary things, even our jobs. We are not taking any of it to Heaven with us when we go! GOD wants us to receive all that He has for us, but *what we do with what we have is what will count*.

Jesus teaches us to be a servant one to another and to esteem others as higher than ourselves. "And Jesus called them to Him and said, you know that the rulers of the Gentiles lord it over them, and their great men hold them in subjection [tyrannizing over them]. Not so shall it be among you; but whoever wishes to be great among you must be your servant, and whoever desires to be first among you must be your slave – Just as the Son of Man came not to be waited on but to serve, and to give His life as a ransom for many [the price paid to set them free]" (Matthew 20:25-28 AMP). Jesus washed the disciples' feet as an example of this, "[NOW] BEFORE the Passover Feast began, Jesus knew (was fully aware) that the time had come for Him to leave this world and return to the Father. And as He had loved those who were His own in the world, He loved them to the last and to the highest degree. So [it was] during supper, satan having already put the thought of betraying Jesus in the heart of Judas Iscariot, Simon's son, [That] Jesus, knowing (fully aware) that the Father had put everything into His hands, and that He had come from GOD and was [now] returning to GOD, got up from supper, took off His garments, and taking a [servant's] towel, He fastened it around His waist. Then He poured water into the washbasin and began to wash the disciples' feet and to wipe them with the [servant's] towel with which He was girded. When He came to Simon Peter, [Peter] said to Him, Lord, are my feet to be washed by You? [Is it for You to wash my feet?] Jesus said to him, You do not understand now what I am doing, but you will understand later on. Peter said to Him, You shall never wash my feet! Jesus answered him, unless I wash you, you have no part with (in) Me [you have no share in companionship with Me]. Simon Peter said to Him, Lord, [wash] not only my feet, but my hands and my head too! Jesus said to him, anyone who has bathed needs only to wash his feet, but is clean all over. And you [My disciples] are clean, but not all of you. For He knew who was going to betray Him; that was the reason He said, not all of you are clean." [Take note here that Jesus is serving the sinner as well as the saint; hence He died for all mankind when He went to the cross. Not just for those whom He knew would be His, but baring also the sin of **all** mankind. Whether or not His free gift is received, it was/is the choice of each person. In this, He didn't leave anyone out. All mankind has or will have the choice to receive Jesus as Lord. And that means that all mankind has the choice as to whether or not they have their sins forgiven]. "So when He had finished washing their feet and had put on His garments and had sat down again, He said to them, do you understand what I have done to you? You call Me the Teacher (Master) and the Lord, and you are right in doing so, for that is what I am. If I then, your Lord and Teacher (Master), have washed your feet, you ought [it is your duty, you are under obligation, you owe it] to wash one another's feet. For I have given you this as an example, so that you should do [in your turn] what I have done to you. I assure you, most solemnly I tell you, a servant is not greater than his master, and no one who is sent is superior to the one who sent him. If you know these things, blessed and happy and to be envied are you if you practice them [if you act accordingly and really do them]" (John 13:1-17 AMP).

Jesus set that example so that we would *not* lift ourselves up into pride, thus causing ourselves a great fall. "Pride goes before destruction, and a haughty spirit before a fall" (Proverbs 16:18 NKJV). Jesus knows this to be true and He never once took on a Spirit of Pride. He watched many a man fall upon the Earth, from His seat in Heaven, before He came down as our Savior. He watched satan fall from Heaven when he was cast out because he had lifted himself up in pride. satan is so evil that he even convinced one third of the angels to follow him instead of GOD. Now those fallen angels are all cast out of Heaven too!

Pride is completely destructive! Don't let yourself entertain any prideful thoughts even for a minute! They **can** and **will** destroy you and your life! <u>There is safety in following the footsteps of Jesus</u>.

Now, let's look at two other Scriptures which give us good evidence that Jesus didn't struggle with pride. Even though satan must have tried to tempt Him with it, again and again, He <u>never</u> fell into it. In

John 5:41 and 8:50, we are shown proof that Jesus never had to seek His own glory.

First John 5:41 AMP, "I receive not glory from men [I crave no human honor, I look for no mortal fame]."

Next, John 8:50 AMP, "However, I am not in search of honor for Myself. [I do not seek and am not aiming for My own glory]. There is One Who [looks after that; He] seeks [My glory], and He is the Judge."

The following verse in John 8:51 promises us eternal life. Sadly, those who were living in 'the world' and following their fleshly (sinful) nature, didn't understand what Jesus was teaching them at all.

Let's read verses 51 through 59 together, "I assure you, most solemnly I tell you, if anyone observes My teaching [lives in accordance with My message, keeps My Word], he will by no means ever see and experience death. The Jews said to Him, now we know that You are under the power of a demon (insane). Abraham died, and also the prophets, yet You say, if a man keeps My Word, he will never taste of death into all eternity. Are You greater than our father Abraham? He died, and all the prophets died! Who do You make Yourself out to be? Jesus answered, If I were to glorify Myself (magnify, praise, and honor Myself), I would have no real glory, for My glory would be nothing and worthless. [My honor must come to Me from My Father]. It is My Father Who glorifies Me [Who extols Me, magnifies, and praises Me], of Whom you say that He is your GOD. Yet you do not know Him or recognize Him and are not acquainted with Him, but I know Him. If I should say that I do not know Him, I would be a liar like you. But I know Him and keep His Word [obey His teachings, am faithful to His message]. Your forefather Abraham was extremely happy at the hope and prospect of seeing My day (My incarnation); and he did see it and was delighted [Heb. 11:13]. Then the Jews said to Him, You are not yet fifty years old, and have You seen Abraham? Jesus replied, I assure you, most solemnly I tell you, before Abraham was born, I AM" [Exod.

3:14] (John 8:51-58 AMP). "Then they took up stones to throw at Him; but Jesus hid Himself and went out of the temple, going through the midst of them, and so passed by" (John 8:59 NKJV). Once again, through the power of the Anointing, Jesus was able to walk right through a crowd and those old hypocrites couldn't even see Him!

Jesus operated in service to GOD. He was the best example of a servant that this world has ever known. He was the perfect example of a servant. It is what He did on the Earth. He never followed after any spirit, but the Spirit of GOD. He never went along with the crowd and did whatever they were doing so that He could fit in. And He never did anything without being led of GOD. This was how He stayed in the Anointing 24/7! If Jesus did it and He said that we would be operating under the guidance of the same Spirit of GOD that He operated under, we can live our lives walking in the Anointing too!

Jesus said, "He who believes [who adheres to and trusts in and relies on the Gospel and Him Whom it sets forth] and is baptized will be saved [from the penalty of eternal death]; but he who does not believe [who does not adhere to and trust in and rely on the Gospel and Him Whom it sets forth] will be condemned. **And these attesting signs will accompany those who believe: in My name they will drive out demons; they will speak in new languages; they will pick up serpents;"** [Remember when the deadly Viper bit the Apostle Paul and he shook it off and was unharmed? (Acts 28)] **"and [even] if they drink anything deadly, it will not hurt them; they will lay their hands on the sick, and they will get well**" (Mark 16:16-18 AMP).

"So then the Lord Jesus, after He had spoken to them, was taken up into Heaven and He sat down at the right hand of GOD [Ps. 110:1]. And they went out and preached everywhere, while the Lord kept working with them and confirming the message by the attesting signs and miracles that closely accompanied [it]. Amen (so be it)" (Mark 16:19-20 AMP). These are the last recorded instructions that Jesus spoke to His little flock before He was taken up into Heaven. How important do you think they are to Jesus that His followers obey them? Knowing that Jesus only did what He saw the Father doing and (He) only spoke what He heard the Father speaking, How important is it to the Father for Jesus' last words to be obeyed?

Combine that promise with the command given to the disciples (and to us) in Matthew 28:19-20, and **we can clearly see that we have rightful and GOD given authority to do all these things.** "Go then and make disciples of all the nations, baptizing them into the name of the Father and of the Son and of the Holy Spirit, Teaching them to observe everything that I have commanded you, and behold, I am with you all the days (perpetually, uniformly, and on every occasion), to the [very] close and consummation of the age. Amen (so let it be)" (Matthew 28:19-20 AMP).

Isn't it exciting to know that Jesus, the same yesterday, today, and forever, has given us the same commandment as He gave to His first disciples? Why don't you take a minute to pray and ask the Father what His plans are for you today? Maybe there is someone close by who needs a touch from GOD today...

Do you dare to go out and do, what Jesus believes?

"Ask Me to show you how much I love you."
Holy Spirit of GOD

"There is a place of rest inside My Spirit
Where man cannot dwell, but by My Spirit.
Therein you will find All Peace, therein you will know My Love."
Holy Spirit

WHAT JESUS BELIEVES

PART TWO

Walking in the Glory

4

The Disciples

"GOD is ever ready to pour out a blessing. We, in turn, need to know how to receive."
(Insight from Holy Spirit – my mentor and friend)

James lifted the net, again, nothing...It had been the same all night **long**, only now it was early morning and the lightening water surrounding his small boat was taking on the crimson colors of a clear dawn. He looked at his brother, John; his face seemed to mirror the frustration that he himself was feeling. Nathaniel sat in the boat peering over the edge into the water. Was he looking for fish or was he somewhere else altogether? Thomas stood quietly at the stern of the boat with his hands folded behind his back. His face looked Heavenwards, but his eyes were closed. Praying? Maybe...It seemed they had all done a lot of that lately. Simon Peter was staring at the empty net they had pulled into the boat only minutes before. What was he thinking about? Was he remembering the few fish that Jesus had multiplied into thousands on two different occasions? Was he remembering that last supper they had all shared together before Jesus' crucifixion? Or possibly, he was just wondering what they all were: "Where was Jesus now?"

James remembered the first time he had seen Jesus, "Follow me, and I will make you fishers of men." He had called out first to Simon (now called Peter) and Andrew his brother. Both Simon Peter and Andrew had immediately left their nets and followed Jesus.

"Going on from there, He saw two other brothers, James (himself), the son of Zebedee, and John his brother, in the boat with Zebedee their father, mending their nets. "He (Jesus) called them, and immediately they left the boat and their father, and followed Him" (Matthew 4:21, 22 NKJV).

First, they had gone all over Galilee with Him. Everywhere Jesus went, He would teach in their synagogues, preach the Gospel of the Kingdom, and heal all kinds of sickness and all kinds of disease among the people.

"Then His fame went throughout all Syria; and they brought to Him all sick people who were afflicted with various diseases and torments, and those who were demon-possessed, epileptics, and paralytics; and He healed them. Great multitudes followed Him — from Galilee, and from Decapolis, Jerusalem, Judea, and beyond the Jordan" (Matthew 4:24-25 NKJV).

"And seeing the multitudes, He went up on a mountain, and when He was seated His disciples came to Him" (Matthew 5:1 NKJV). They always came to Him, James thought; somehow they were drawn to Him wherever He was. The love that Jesus had for them was truly unlike any they had ever known. Somehow they could sense that no matter what they had done, He loved them. And no matter what they would do, He always would. Unconditional love; that was the kind it was, unconditional. He (James) could feel it even now...

"Then He opened His mouth and taught them, saying: Blessed are the poor in spirit, for theirs is the Kingdom of Heaven. Blessed are those who mourn, for they shall be comforted. Blessed are the meek, for they shall inherit the earth. Blessed are those who hunger and thirst for righteousness, for they shall be filled. Blessed are the merciful, for they shall obtain mercy. Blessed are the pure in heart, for they shall see GOD. Blessed are the peacemakers, for they shall be called sons of GOD. Blessed are those who are persecuted for righteousness' sake, for theirs is the Kingdom of Heaven. Blessed are you when they revile and persecute you, and say all kinds of evil against you falsely for My sake. Rejoice and be exceedingly glad, for great is your reward in Heaven, for so they persecuted the prophets who were before you. You are the salt of the earth; but if the salt loses its flavor, how shall it be seasoned? It is then good for nothing but to be thrown out and trampled underfoot by men. You are the light of the world. A city that is set on a hill cannot be hidden. Nor do they light a lamp and put it under a basket, but on a lampstand, and it gives light to all who are in the house. Let your light so shine before men, that they may see your good works and glorify your Father in Heaven. Do not think that I came to destroy the Law or the Prophets. I did not come to destroy but to fulfill. For assuredly, I say to you, till Heaven and Earth pass away, one jot or one tittle will by no means pass from the Law till all is fulfilled. Whoever therefore breaks one of the least of these commandments, and teaches men so, shall be called least in the Kingdom of Heaven; but whoever does and teaches them, he shall be called great in the Kingdom of Heaven. For I say to you, that unless your righteousness exceeds the righteousness of the scribes and Pharisees, you will by no means enter the Kingdom of Heaven. You have heard that it was said to those of old, 'You shall not murder, and whoever murders will be in danger of the judgment.' But I say to you that whoever is angry with his brother without a cause shall be in danger of the judgment. And whoever says to his brother, 'Raca!' shall be in danger of the council. But whoever says, 'You fool!' shall be in danger of hell fire. Therefore if you bring your gift to the altar, and there remember that your brother has something against you, leave your gift there before the altar, and go your way. First be reconciled to your brother, and then come and offer your gift. Agree with your adversary quickly, while you are on the way with him, lest your adversary deliver you to the judge, the judge hand you over to the officer, and you be thrown into prison. Assuredly, I say to you, you will by no means get out of there till you have paid the last penny. You have heard that it was said to those of old, 'You shall not commit adultery.' But I say to you that whoever looks at a woman to lust for her has already committed adultery with her in his heart. If your right eye causes you to sin, pluck it out and cast it from you; for it is more profitable for you that one of your members perish, than for your whole body to be cast into hell. And if your right hand causes you to sin, cut it off and cast it from you; for it is more profitable for you that one of your members perish, than for your whole body to be cast into hell. Furthermore, it has been said, 'Whoever divorces his wife, let him give her a certificate of divorce.' But I say to you that whoever divorces his wife for any reason except sexual immorality causes her to commit adultery; and whoever marries a woman who is divorced commits adultery" (Matthew 5:2-32 NKJV). James could remember hearing Jesus speak these words to them as if they had been spoken yesterday. It was about three years now since he had first heard these words taught.

Many times, they did not fully comprehend what Jesus spoke to them; well, most times really. But often after Jesus would tell them a parable, He would explain it to the twelve of them. "And He said to them, To you it has been given to know the mystery of the Kingdom of GOD; but to those who are outside, all things come in parables, so that 'Seeing they may see and not perceive, and hearing they may hear and not understand; Lest they should turn, and their sins be forgiven them' " (Mark 4:11-12 NKJV). Jesus had spoken this to them right after He had talked to a great multitude gathered to Him by the sea. There had been so many people there that Jesus had put Himself into a boat and He had taught them from the sea while the multitude stayed on the shore. Jesus had been teaching them many things by parables and He had said to them in His teaching, "Listen! Behold, a sower went out to sow. And it happened, as he sowed, that some seed fell by the wayside; and the birds of the air came and devoured it. Some fell on stony ground, where it did not have much earth; and immediately it sprang up because it had no depth of earth. But when the sun was up it was scorched, and because it had no root it withered away. And some seed fell among thorns; and the thorns grew up and choked it, and it yielded no crop. But other seed fell on good ground and yielded a crop that sprang up, increased and produced: some thirtyfold, some sixty, and some a hundred." And He said to them, "He who has ears to hear, let him hear!" (Mark 4:3-9

NKJV). It was when He was alone and those around Him with the twelve asked Him about the parable that He had said, 'they were given to know the mystery of the Kingdom.' Then Jesus had explained the parable to them. "And He said to them, do you not understand this parable? How then will you understand all the parables? The sower sows the Word. And these are the ones by the wayside where the Word is sown. When they hear, satan comes immediately and takes away the Word that was sown in their hearts. These likewise are the ones sown on stony ground who, when they hear the Word, immediately receive it with gladness; and they have no root in themselves, and so endure only for a time. Afterward, when tribulation or persecution arises for the Word's sake, immediately they stumble. Now these are the ones sown among thorns; they are the ones who hear the Word, and the cares of this world, the deceitfulness of riches, and the desires for other things entering in choke the Word, and it becomes unfruitful. But these are the ones sown on good ground, those who hear the Word, accept it, and bear fruit: some thirtyfold, some sixty, and some a hundred" (Mark 4:13-20 NKJV). James felt honored when He'd spoken those words.

He also knew that when Jesus had spoken of cutting off your hand if it causes you to sin meant that one was to get whatever was causing him to sin out of his life! He wasn't really saying, "If you keep pointing your finger at people and coveting what they own you should cut off that pointer finger and gouge out your eyes." He was saying, "Don't covet what isn't yours. Don't be envious." Now he knew a lot more about right and wrong.

James remembered another time, a morning when Jesus had been hungry and had seen a fig tree in the distance..."Now in the morning, as He returned to the city, He was hungry. And seeing a fig tree by the road, He came to it and found nothing on it but leaves, and said to it, "Let no fruit grow on you ever again." Immediately the fig tree withered away. And when the disciples saw it, they marveled, saying, how did the fig tree wither away so soon?" So Jesus answered and said to them, "Assuredly, I say to you, if you have faith and do not

WHAT JESUS BELIEVES

doubt, you will not only do what was done to the fig tree, but also if you say to this mountain, 'Be removed and be cast into the sea,' it will be done. And whatever things you ask in prayer, believing, you will receive" (Matthew 21:18-22 NKJV). Jesus had taught them many Scriptures on faith. Chuckling to Himself, He thought of Thomas and the words He had spoken. The other 10 of them had seen Jesus the day He had arisen from the dead. He had appeared to them "...when the doors were shut where the disciples were assembled, for fear of the Jews, Jesus came and stood in the midst, and said to them, 'Peace be with you.' When He had said this, He showed them His hands and His side. Then the disciples were glad when they saw the Lord. So Jesus said to them again, 'Peace to you!' As the Father has sent Me, I also send you. And when He had said this, He breathed on them, and said to them, 'Receive the Holy Spirit.' If you forgive the sins of any, they are forgiven them; if you retain the sins of any, they are retained" (John 20:19-23 NKJV).

"Now Thomas, called the Twin, one of the twelve, was not with them when Jesus came. The other disciples therefore said to him, we have seen the Lord. So he said to them, unless I see in His hands the print of the nails, and put my finger into the print of the nails, and put my hand into His side, I will not believe." Still smiling, James mused on in his memory, "And after eight days His disciples were again inside, and Thomas with them. Jesus came, the doors being shut, and stood in the midst, and said, 'Peace to you!' " (John 20:24-26 NKJV).

James could still see the look of amazement on Thomas' face and, if possible, a look of even more incredulous amazement covered his face when Jesus spoke these words to him, "Then He said to Thomas, reach your finger here, and look at My hands; and reach your hand here, and put it into My side. Do not be unbelieving, but believing" (John 20:27-28 NKJV).

At this, Thomas had hit his knees and cried out, "...My Lord and my GOD!" Jesus said to him, "Thomas, because you have seen Me, you have believed. *Blessed are those who have not seen and yet have believed*" (John 20:29 NKJV). Poor Thomas! What a story to have to tell one's grandchildren! Truly they had all learned from Thomas' experience. Deep inside, they knew it could have happened to any one of them.

James thought back to the 70 others that He had appointed. Jesus had "...sent them two by two before His face into every city and place where He Himself was about to go. Then He (Jesus) said to them, the harvest truly is great, but the laborers are few; **therefore pray the Lord of the harvest to send out laborers into His harvest**. Go your way; behold, I send you out as lambs among wolves. Carry neither money bag, knapsack, nor sandals; and greet no one along the road. But whatever house you enter, first say, 'Peace to this house.' And if a son of peace is there, your peace will rest on it; if not, it will return to you. And remain in the same house, eating and drinking such things as they give, for the laborer is worthy of his wages. Do not go from house to house. Whatever city you enter, and they receive you, eat such things as are set before you. And <u>heal the sick there, and say to them, 'The Kingdom of GOD has come near to you</u>" (Luke 10:1-9 NKJV).

Jesus also told the 70, "But whatever city you enter, and they do not receive you, go out into its streets and say, 'The very dust of your city which clings to us we wipe off against you. Nevertheless know this, that the Kingdom of GOD has come near you.' But I say to you that it will be more tolerable in that Day for Sodom than for that city. Woe to you, Chorazin! Woe to you, Bethsaida! For if the mighty works which were done in you had been done in Tyre and Sidon, they would have repented long ago, sitting in sackcloth and ashes. But it will be more tolerable for Tyre and Sidon at the Judgment than for you. And you, Capernaum, who are exalted to Heaven, will be brought down to Hades. <u>He who hears you hears Me, he who rejects you rejects Me, and he who rejects Me rejects Him who sent Me</u>" (Luke 10:10-16 NKJV).

"Then the seventy returned with joy, saying, Lord, even the demons are subject to us in Your name" (Luke 10:17 NKJV).

"And He said to them, I saw satan fall like lightning from Heaven. Behold, I give you the authority to trample on serpents and scorpions, and over all the power of the enemy, and nothing shall by any means hurt you" (Luke 10:18-19 NKJV).

Then he remembered Jesus telling them, "Nevertheless do not rejoice in this, that the spirits are subject to you, but rather rejoice because your names are written in Heaven" (Luke 10:20 NKJV).

> *"I knew your end from your beginning...*
> *Every faltering step and every victory*
> *And I loved you."*
> **Holy Spirit of Father GOD**

He praised GOD that his name was written in Heaven with the other disciples; well, all except one and he was dead now. Jesus had said that it would have been better for Judas if he had not been born. He had told him this about the one who would betray Him, and Judas had gone anyway! James just couldn't imagine doing that! How could anyone *not* love Jesus, and yet he saw many, many who didn't. They had crucified him. He did not understand how a man so full of love and goodness could not be loved by all. Apparently, pride was a strong evil thing, for it had kept many men from inheriting the Kingdom of Heaven! How sorry he felt for those who were so blinded by pride. To imagine eternity without his Jesus in it was to him worse than the thought of being in hell! Oh, how he loved his Master! Everywhere He went, He did good things for others. Healing, healing, always healing...whether it was healing of the body or healing of the mind (by forgiving them of their sins and sometimes even casting devils out of them). Peter stirred from his reverie and James looked in his direction. Seeing the expression on each other's face, they smiled at one another. Yes, they had both been thinking about Jesus.

WHAT JESUS BELIEVES

"What were you remembering about him?" Peter asked in his deep yet gentle voice.

"I was remembering the way He healed all who came to Him. I was thinking of His great love for all of us." After a short pause, James continued, "I was remembering the shocked expression on Thomas' face when Jesus appeared and said, '...Reach your finger here, and look at My hands; and reach your hand here, and put it into My side. Do not be unbelieving, but believing' " (John 20:27 NKJV).

Now, it was Peter's turn to chuckle. "I remember that too. You know, it could have been any of us that had doubted."

"I know. I was thinking about that too. All the same, we all learned from Thomas' experience."

"Too true. Too true," Peter replied. Gazing out towards the horizon on the opposite shore, Simon Peter spoke clearly the words his Lord had spoken to them all, "Whoever receives this little child in My name receives Me; and whoever receives Me receives Him who sent Me. <u>For he who is least among you all will be great...but whoever wishes to be great among you must be your servant, and whoever desires to be first among you must be your slave – just as the Son of Man came not to be waited on but to serve, and to give His life as a ransom for many</u>" (See Luke 9:48 NKJV and Matthew 20:26-28 AMP).

"He certainly did teach us to serve," Peter went on. "Remember the night that Jesus washed all of our feet? I told Him, 'You shall never wash my feet!' Jesus answered me, 'Unless I wash you, you have no part with Me.' Then I said to Him, "Lord, not only my feet, but my hands and my head too!" When Jesus replied, "Anyone who has bathed needs only to wash his feet, but is clean all over. And you [My disciples] are clean, but not all of you. For He knew who was going to betray Him; that was the reason He said, not all of you are clean." Jesus was not only showing us how to serve one another and others too, but He was also showing us that when our walk with Him is right and clean, then our whole self, including our heart, is also pure. He knew that Judas was unclean in his heart toward Himself and us. How could we *not* have known that Judas Iscariot was so bad? Then again, I denied knowing Him three times!" Grunting in disgust at himself, Peter sat down on the still wet (fishing) net. James waited for him to notice the dampness, but when he gave no sign of it, he turned away. Peter was definitely strong-willed, but very, very zealous for the Lord. This made for an interesting combination. James' mind drifted off to the time on the mountain when Jesus had been transfigured before Peter, John and himself.

Not turning around, he spoke again to Peter, "Have you ever been more afraid than when Jesus took you and John and myself up on that high mountain and when we awoke to find Jesus face was shining like the sun, his clothing was dazzling and white, brighter than anyone could bleach it **and** He was speaking with Moses and Elijah!?(See John 13:8-11 AMP).

Peter laughed softly, "I still cannot believe that I offered *to build* three shelters for them!"

"At least *you* had the courage to talk!" At this, they both burst into laughter!

"I still haven't told anyone about that. Have you?"

"No, I haven't. He is risen now, so I guess I could have told someone if I had wanted to, but I haven't." James went on, "Another thing that I remember being half scared out my wits at was standing by that man possessed with the legion of demons! When Jesus had commanded, "Come out of the man, you unclean spirit! And He asked him, what is your name?" When a voice inside the man said, "My name is Legion, for we are many. And he kept begging Him urgently not to send them [himself and the other demons] away out of that region." When he said, 'we are many,' I thought, 'We are not! Let's go!' But Jesus just told them to "Go." And that was the end of it. (See Matthew 8:28-34)

WHAT JESUS BELIEVES

After seeing Jesus exercise that kind of Power over demons, I haven't been afraid of them since! It's great not to have any fear where they're concerned.

"Yes, it is. Do you know what scared me the most?"

"Was it when Jesus came walking out to us all on the water during that terrible storm?"

"Yes, how did you know?" James replied.

"Simple, we all had one of the worst scares of our lives that night! Remember the storm...the waves..."

"But the boat was by this time out on the sea, many furlongs [a furlong is one-eighth of a mile] distant from the land, beaten and tossed by the waves, for the wind was against them. And in the fourth watch [between 3:00–6:00 a.m.] of the night, Jesus came to them, walking on the sea. And when the disciples saw Him walking on the sea, they were terrified and said, it is a ghost! And they screamed out with fright. But instantly He spoke to them, saying, Take courage! I AM! Stop being afraid!" [Exod. 3:14] (Matthew 14:24-27 AMP).

"Yeah, and I with my 'great faith' shouted, 'Lord, if it is You, command me to come to You on the water. He said, 'Come! So I got out of the boat and walked on the water, and I came toward Jesus.' But then I looked down and that was it! Sink City!" (See Matthew 14:28, 29 AMP).

James interjected, "I thought that you would drown out there the second you stepped out of the boat. When you walked on that water, I think the eyes of all of us still in the boat almost popped out of our heads in amazement!"

"It really was amazing to walk on that water, but at the time, sinking never really occurred to me. All I could see and think about was my

WHAT JESUS BELIEVES

Jesus! And then I started to notice things, the howling of the wind, *its strength, and not Jesus*, the waves *all around me*...Did you notice that while I had my eyes on Jesus and was walking in faith, the waves never went over me?"

"Yes," replied James, with a chuckle. "You didn't start sucking in water until you were in the process of drowning and screaming for your life!"

"I'm getting to that part, I'm getting to it," said Peter, his eyes sparkling with laughter. Then getting sober he continued, "When I looked down, it was like the solid foundation under my feet just melted away and I started to sink. It was a terrifying feeling; I can tell you! Then I finally got part of my wits about me, at least enough to cry out to the Lord for help. When I cried out, 'Lord, save me!" 'instantly Jesus reached out His hand and *caught and held me*, saying to me, O you of little faith, why did you doubt?' "I have never felt safer than I did at that moment!" (See Matthew 14:30-31 AMP).

"I think we all felt safe, really safe, for the first time in our lives! Somehow, *we all knew* that He was the Son of GOD. Nothing has ever felt like that, *knowing* that you were in the presence of the Son of the Almighty GOD! That was the first time where I really experienced worship that strongly!"

"I know what you mean," replied Peter.

"So do I," choroused the others one at a time. Looking at each other, they all felt the bond. Remembering the things that Jesus had done had brought the past painfully into the present.

"When do you think we will see Him again?"

"How long do you think He'll stay with us this time?"

"I miss Him!"

"So do I!"

"So do I!"

"So do I!!"

"So do I!"

"I was wondering how long He would remain on Earth before He returns to His Father in Heaven," Nathanael stated.

"I've been wondering the same thing, but not wanting to hear the answer," said John. "It seems like already He is helping us get used to Him not being around."

"That never occurred to me," commented Thomas. "But now that you mention it, for some reason, it doesn't feel like it is going to be very long."

"I felt that too,"...murmured assents...

"We can't even catch fish without Him." They all chuckled at this and then looked down in discouragement at the still empty net. They were all concerned about surviving, now that Jesus wasn't with them all the time anymore.

Looking onto the morning shoreline, the disciples noticed a man standing alone on the beach, "...Children, have you any food?" They answered Him, "No." And He said to them, "Cast the net on the right side of the boat, and you will find some." So they cast, and now they were not able to draw it in because of the multitude of fish. Therefore, that disciple whom Jesus loved said to Peter, 'It is the Lord!' Now, when Simon Peter heard that it was the Lord, he put on *his* outer garment (for he had removed it), and plunged into the sea. But the other disciples came in the little boat (for they were not far from land, but about two hundred cubits), dragging the net with fish. Then, as soon as they had come to land, they saw a fire of coals there, and fish laid on it, and bread. Jesus said to them, "Bring some of the fish which you have just caught." Simon Peter went up and dragged the net to land, full of large fish, one hundred and fifty-three. And although there were so many, the net was not broken. Jesus said to them, "Come and eat breakfast." Yet none of the disciples dared ask Him, "Who are You?" — knowing that it was the Lord. Jesus then came and took the bread and gave it to them, and likewise the fish. This is now the third time Jesus showed Himself to His disciples after He was raised from the dead. So when they had eaten breakfast, Jesus said to Simon Peter, "Simon, son of Jonah, do you love Me more than these?" He said to Him, "Yes, Lord; You know that I love You." He said to him, "Feed My lambs." He said to him again a second time, "Simon, son of Jonah, do you love Me?" He said to Him, "Yes, Lord; You know that I love You." He said to him, "Tend My sheep." He said to him the third time, "Simon, son of Jonah, do you love Me?" Peter was grieved because He said to him the third time, "Do you love Me?" And he said to Him, "Lord, You know all things; You know that I love You." Jesus said to him, "Feed My sheep. Most assuredly, I say to you, when you were younger, you girded yourself and walked where you wished; but when you are old, you will stretch out your hands, and another will gird you and carry you where you do not wish. This He spoke, signifying by what death he would glorify GOD. And when He had spoken this, He said to him, 'Follow Me.' " Then Peter, turning around, saw the disciple whom Jesus loved following, who also had leaned on His breast at the supper, and said, "Lord, who is the one who betrays You?" Peter, seeing him, said to Jesus, "But Lord, what about this man?" Jesus said to him, "If I will that he remain till I come, *what is that to you*? You follow Me. Then this saying went out among the brethren that this disciple would not die. Yet Jesus did not say to him that he would not die, but, 'If I will that he remain till I come, what is that to you?' This is the disciple who testifies of these things, and wrote these things; and we know that his testimony is true. And there are also many other things that Jesus did, which if they were written one by one, I suppose that <u>even the whole world itself could</u>

WHAT JESUS BELIEVES

<u>not contain the books that would be written. Amen</u>" (See John 21:5-25 NKJV). We end this part here in the book of John the 21st chapter.

Obviously, if you have read the Bible, you know that these conversations between the men on the boat were not in it. They were simply written here to help emphasize the reality of the men and their lives. They were real men, flesh and bones; and they had real problems occur in their lives, but the difference between these men and ourselves is that they walked with Jesus while He was on this Earth. You and I still walk with Him, only it's via the precious Holy Spirit. We are entitled to the same Power. We are entitled to the same miracles. We are entitled to the same promises. Not only are we entitled to work on Jesus' behalf, we are commanded to do so!

Here comes Jesus delegating His power to them. "Jesus approached and, breaking the silence, said to them (and us!), All authority (all power of rule) in Heaven and on Earth has been given to Me. Go then and make disciples of all the nations, baptizing them into the name of the Father and of the Son and of the Holy Spirit, Teaching them" (*us again*!) "to observe **everything** that I have **commanded** you, and behold, **I am with you <u>all the days</u> (perpetually, uniformly, and on every occasion), to the [very] close and consummation of the age.** Amen (so let it be)" (Matthew 28:18-20 AMP).

Mark 16:15-19 (AMP) shows us some more of what GOD expects to do *through us* by the Power of his Anointing. "And He said to them, Go into all the world and preach and publish openly the good news (the Gospel) to every creature [of the whole human race]. He who believes [who adheres to and trusts in and relies on the Gospel and Him Whom it sets forth] and is baptized will be saved [from the penalty of eternal death]; but he who does not believe [who does not adhere to and trust in and rely on the Gospel and Him Whom it sets forth] will be condemned. **And these attesting signs will accompany those who believe: in My name they will drive out demons; they will speak in new languages.**" Right there; that blows the 'lie' of satan that praying in tongues is not for every Christian Believer right out of the water! <u>Read Acts Chapter 2, if you haven't already, to see the power of the Holy Ghost that you are entitled to.</u> Also, looking up the Holy Spirit or Holy Ghost in a good Bible Concordance and studying the Scriptures will give you a good understanding on the Holy Spirit. Looking under the word "tongues" will help you to grow in your understanding of your Heavenly spirit language. "They will pick up serpents; and [even] if they drink anything deadly, it will not hurt them." The Bible says in Psalm 91:11-12, "For He will order His angels to protect you wherever you go. They will hold you up with their hands so you won't even hurt your foot on a stone" (Psalms 91:11-12 NLT), but I won't test GOD by jumping off of the Empire State Building! When Jesus was led by the Spirit into the wilderness to be tempted, He fasted for forty days and then satan came to test Him. In one of the temptations, satan tried to tempt Jesus by using Psalm 91 to try to get Jesus to sin. "Then the devil took Him up into the holy city, set Him on the pinnacle of the temple, and said to Him, 'If You are the Son of GOD, throw Yourself down. For it is written: He shall give His angels charge over you, and, in their hands they shall bear you up, lest you dash your foot against a stone.' " Jesus said to him, "It is written again, 'You shall not tempt the Lord your GOD' " (Matthew 4:5-7 NKJV). Now we'll get back to Mark 16:18 **"THEY (BELIEVERS) WILL LAY THEIR HANDS ON THE SICK, AND THEY WILL GET WELL."** Can anybody out there possibly misinterpret this Scripture? I cannot see how, but sadly there is still wrong teaching on this even today. "So then the Lord Jesus, after He had spoken to them, was taken up into Heaven and He sat down at the right hand of GOD" [Ps. 110:1]. This verse makes it clear to us that this <u>is</u> the very last statement that Jesus made before returning to Heaven to reign beside the Father. It bears saying again that it must have been important to Jesus that we remember this or He would not have saved it till the very last. It was the thing He wanted them to meditate on. *In meditating on any Scripture, the Holy Spirit will always give us a bigger understanding of it. It somehow becomes 'more real' to us than our situation and that is how miracles occur.*

WHAT JESUS BELIEVES

If you need an answer to prayer on something that you may have been struggling with, why don't you go to the Word right now and find a Scripture that relates to it? By meditating on it, you are allowing the Holy Spirit to open up the truth of that Scripture to you. You may even want to invite Him to help you understand the Word better. He likes that. Remember, He is a part of the Trinity and He is your friend too. GOD and Jesus and the Holy Spirit are the best friends you'll ever have. They will **never** be too busy for you.

"...but there is a friend who sticks closer than a brother" (Proverbs 18:24 AMP). That's Him!

"Greater love has no one than this, than to lay down one's life for his friends. You are My friends if you do whatever I command you."
Jesus - (John 15:13-14 NKJV)

WHAT JESUS BELIEVES

Do you dare to believe what Jesus believes? If you do, then you are also His friend!

5

Follow by Example

"For those whom He foreknew [of whom He was aware and loved beforehand], He also destined from the beginning [foreordaining them] to be molded into the image of His Son [and share inwardly His likeness], that He might become the firstborn among many brethren" (Romans 8:29 AMP).

Jesus. Just the name brings images to our minds. Jesus, healing the sick. Jesus, teaching on a hillside. Jesus, walking on water. Jesus, casting out demons. Jesus, forgiving. Jesus, multiplying the fish. Jesus, sleeping during a storm. We could go on and on! When we see all the images of Jesus, we see Jesus as He was 2000 years ago. We don't see Jesus, as He really is today, our big brother. Yes, our big brother! Read that verse above again, it says, "That He might become the firstborn among many brethren." "...many brethren." That's us! Praise GOD, Jesus is our big brother! And our Father, GOD, sent Him to us to be the example for you and me, and every other sibling that would follow in His footsteps.

As defined, earlier in the book, "<u>we</u> have the mind of Christ" [Christ: the Anointed One and His Anointing (Holy Spirit)]. We also know that 'the Anointing' is the person of the Holy Spirit. This being true, He indwells in us as promised. Jesus said, "Abide in Me, and I in you. As the branch cannot bear fruit of itself, unless it abides in the vine, neither can you, unless you abide in Me" (John 15:4 NKJV), and "Or do you not know that your body is the temple of the Holy Spirit who is in you, whom you have from GOD, and you are not your own?" (1 Corinthians 6:19 NKJV). [First Corinthians is a letter to the Church in Corinth from the Apostle Paul, under the unction of the Holy Spirit, after Holy Spirit was sent to abide with us].

The Bible promised that Jesus' body would not see corruption. satan thought that he, himself, had won that battle at the cross. In reality, after the price had been paid for our sins (by the Son laying down His life in accordance to the will of the Father for the sins of all mankind), JESUS WAS GIVEN IMMEDIATE AUTHORITY to take the keys of Death and Hell, and that is just what He did! Plus, remember the thief on the cross, the one that had begged Jesus to remember him when He came into His Kingdom? "And Jesus said to him, Assuredly, I say to you, **today you will be with Me in Paradise**" (Luke 23:43 NKJV). Jesus spoke clearly of His body being the temple of the Holy Spirit. "Jesus answered and said to them, Destroy this temple, and in three days I will raise it up" (John 2:19 NKJV). Today, there remains a vagueness in the Church Body as to *how GOD raised up His Son from death*. GOD used His Powerful Holy Spirit which had *indwelt* Jesus' body while on this Earth! "Whoosh!" Amazing Holy Spirit; He is Zoe and He is Dunamis! By Who's power do you think Lazarus was raised from the dead, and also Jairus' daughter and all the other people that were raised from the dead in Jesus' ministry?

> **Zoe**: phonetic spelling: dzo-ay' - *of the absolute fullness of life, both essential and ethical, which belongs to GOD* - Strong's Concordance: 2222.

> **Dunamis**: phonetic spelling: doo'-nam-is: *strength, power, ability, inherent power, power residing in a thing by virtue of its nature, or which a person or thing exerts and puts forth power for performing miracles* - Strong's: 1411.

When you read about the veil in the Temple being torn in two, that was the Holy Spirit's doing too! The tearing of the veil, which had previously separated the people from the Holy of Holies, was now removed because Jesus had paid the price and we, as Christians, could now stand clean (pure and forgiven) in the sight of GOD! We could now come right to the throne of GOD because of Jesus' shed blood! "Oh, what can wash away our sin? Nothing, but the blood of Jesus!" Where is the Holy of Holies on the Earth now? Father GOD would no longer have the Holy of Holies in a man-made temple; we would be His temples and we would commune directly with Him!

When the Pharisees and Sadducees had listened to Jesus speaking of Himself as the temple of the Holy Spirit, they were thinking that He was referring to a temple made by man's hands. When in fact, Jesus was referring to the temple in which the Holy Spirit (the Anointing of GOD) was residing, He Himself! "Now the Passover of the Jews was approaching, so Jesus went up to Jerusalem. There He found in the temple [enclosure] those who were selling oxen and sheep and doves, and the money changers sitting there [also at their stands]. <u>And having made a lash (a whip) of cords, He drove them all out of the temple [enclosure] – both the sheep and the oxen – spilling and scattering the brokers' money and upsetting and tossing around their trays (their stands). Then to those who sold the doves He said, take these things away (out of here)! Make not My Father's house a house of merchandise (a marketplace, a sales shop)! [Ps. 93:5]. And His disciples remembered that it is written [in the Holy Scriptures], Zeal (the fervor of love) for Your house will eat Me up. [I will be consumed with jealousy for the honor of Your house.]</u>" [Ps. 69:9]. Do we see how zealously honoring Jesus is!? "Then the Jews retorted, what sign can You show us, seeing You do these things? [What sign, miracle, token, indication can You give us as evidence that You have authority and are commissioned to act in this way?]" How was it that the Jews retorting were indignant and angry at Jesus' actions, towards the defilement of the temple, instead of standing side by side with Him and assisting to drive out the money changers? Religious spirits not only lie, but they can blind their host (or oppressed one) to the truth. "**Jesus answered them, Destroy (undo) this temple, and in three days I will raise it up again.** Then the Jews replied, it took forty-six years to build this temple (sanctuary), and will You raise it up in three days? But He had spoken of the temple which was His body" (John 2:13-21 AMP). The GOD of the Universe, incarnate in man, is down on the Earth speaking to them (the Jews, those *waiting* for Messiah), and they don't even recognize Him [and, in fact, came against Jesus]! When you read *and in three days I will raise it up again*, don't forget that *Jesus was given all authority* AND that *the Father, Son, and Holy Spirit are One.*

The Holy of Holies *was* the holiest place on Earth. Understanding that we are now a temple of GOD's Holy Spirit, let's read 1 Corinthians 3:16-17. "Do you not know that you are the temple of GOD and that the Spirit of GOD dwells in you?" (1 Corinthians 3:16 NKJV). "If anyone does hurt to GOD's temple or corrupts it [with false doctrines] or destroys it, GOD will do hurt to him and bring him to the corruption of death and destroy him. For the temple of GOD is holy (sacred to Him) and that [temple] you [the believing Church and its individual believers] are" (1 Corinthians 3:17 AMP). These verses are really worth meditating on. They strengthen your inner man which affects all of you.

We are told in Philippians to, "Let this mind be in you..." What mind? The mind of Christ. "Let this mind be in you which was also in Christ Jesus" (Philippians 2:5 NKJV). We aren't trying to be equal with GOD, but we *do* want to allow His Powerful Holy Spirit to flow through us. *We carry that same Spiritual Power* (Anointing) *within us* and *the Word teaches us to carry on in Jesus' footsteps.* We are told to "be imitators of Christ." If we are imitators of the Anointed One, then we will have the Anointing of GOD flowing through us because we are following in His footsteps and allowing the Holy Spirit, the powerful Anointing of GOD, to flow through us (See Philippians 2:5-15, 1 Corinthians 2:16 & Ephesians 5:1, 2).

Will SOME of us be persecuted for following in Jesus' footsteps? No, ALL of us who follow in Jesus' footsteps will be persecuted. Let's read about it in 1 Peter 2:19–25 "For one is regarded favorably (is approved, acceptable, and thankworthy) if, as in the sight of GOD, he endures the pain of unjust suffering. [After all] what kind of glory [is there in it] if, when you do wrong and are punished for it, you take it patiently? **But if you bear patiently with suffering [which results]**

when you do right and that is undeserved, it is acceptable and pleasing to GOD. For even to this were you called [it is inseparable from your vocation]. For Christ also suffered for you, leaving you [His personal] example, so that you should follow in His footsteps. He was guilty of no sin, neither was deceit (guile) ever found on His lips [Isa. 53:9]. When He was reviled and insulted, He did not revile or offer insult in return; [when] He was abused and suffered, He made no threats [of vengeance]; but he trusted [Himself and everything] to Him Who judges fairly. He personally bore our sins in His [own] body on the tree [as on an altar and offered Himself on it], that we might die (cease to exist) to sin and live to righteousness. **By His wounds, you have been healed. For you were going astray like [so many] sheep, but now you have come back to the Shepherd and Guardian (the Bishop) of your souls**" [Isa. 53:5, 6] (1 Peter 2:19-25 AMP). Did you notice the part that said, '*by His wounds (stripes) you were healed?*' That is one of the most important Scriptures in the Bible regarding your promise of health and healing. Jesus was lashed 39 times for us before they hung Him on the cross for our sins. *Did you know that all major diseases root from 39 original diseases*? That's right! "But He was wounded for our transgressions, He was bruised for our iniquities; the chastisement for our peace was upon Him, and by His stripes we are healed" (Isaiah 53:5 NKJV).

Now, let's get back to that part about us following in His footsteps regarding suffering unjustly. Did you catch the part where the Amplified Bible clarifies saying, '*it is inseparable from our vocation?*' So, yes, the suffering unjustly is there and we are told to bear it patiently. We are told in verse 23 that Jesus did not revile or offer insult back when He was reviled and insulted. It also says that He made no threats, not even when He suffered abuse. He trusted in GOD completely, even then.

Our meditating on the Word needs to come into action: *loving our enemies, praying for those who persecute us and returning good to those who render us evil*. When we react in love and forgiveness, we are being as sons should to our Father Who is in Heaven. He will judge the evil doers, but He will also reward us for obeying Him. *Just like Jesus, we need to offer the other cheek and not speak back tongue in cheek!*

"But I say to you, love your enemies, bless those who curse you, do good to those who hate you, and pray for those who spitefully use you and persecute you (Matthew 5:44 NKJV), not returning evil for evil or reviling for reviling, but on the contrary blessing, knowing that you were called to this, that you may inherit a blessing" (1 Peter 3:9 NKJV). "A good man out of the good treasure of his heart brings forth good; and an evil man out of the evil treasure of his heart brings forth evil. For out of the abundance of the heart his mouth speaks" (Luke 6:45 NKJV). "You have heard that it was said, an eye for an eye and a tooth for a tooth. But I tell you not to resist an evil person. But whoever slaps you on your right cheek, turn the other to him also" (Matthew 5:38-39 NKJV). "<u>But I say to you who are listening now to Me</u>: [in order to heed, make it a practice to] love your enemies, treat well (do good to, act nobly toward) those who detest you and pursue you with hatred, invoke blessings upon and pray for the happiness of those who curse you, implore GOD's blessing (favor) upon those who abuse you [who revile, reproach, disparage, and high-handedly misuse you]. To the one who strikes you on the jaw or cheek, offer the other jaw or cheek also; and from him who takes away your outer garment, do not withhold your undergarment as well. Give away to everyone who begs of you [who is in want of necessities], and of him who takes away from you your goods, do not demand or require them back again. And as you would like and desire that men would do to you, do exactly so to them. If you [merely] love those who love you, what quality of credit and thanks is that to you? For even the [very] sinners love their lovers (those who love them)" (Luke 6:27-32 AMP). Praise GOD that the more we practice walking in unconditional love, the more natural an action it will become for us as *out of the abundance (overflow) of the heart our mouth speaks* and our actions are in agreement! Love! **Love is the key!** (Reference Matthew 12:34 AMP).

Let's stop for a minute and get a mental picture of the Church today. How is Her health? No, the question is not: "How much did the offering bring in?" or "How much does my Pastor get paid each year?" It isn't even, "How many deacons do we have on our board?" If you are in a small church (congregation) you may be thinking, well, we have a nice choir and our Pastor preaches great Bible stories, but either way the question has still been left unanswered. The Church today must be looked at Worldwide. She may have body parts, i.e., individual Church bodies that are doing well in certain areas of ministry, 'operating in the gifts and/or prayer' and so they are healthy in those areas, but what GOD is coming back for is a whole (entire) 'Church without spot or wrinkle.' Let's go back and read about that starting in Ephesians 5:26.

"So that He might sanctify her, having cleansed her by the washing of water with the Word" (Ephesians 5:26 AMP). Many people do not go any deeper with this verse than, 'My sins are forgiven,' but that is not all that it means to us. When we are 'washed by the water with the Word,' *it is the Living Water that washes us and the Anointing (Holy Spirit) that teaches us, which brings us healing not only to our body but to our mind as well!* When that Word of GOD has so washed our minds, meaning we have read it and spoken it so many times that our minds have become *saturated* with the Word of GOD, it is at this point that the Word becomes more real to us than our situation. It is then we are able to receive from GOD due to *the washing of the water* (Living Water [*Power*-filled *Life*-changing *Water*]) *with the Word*. That Water is Dunamis (and it is) Zoe! It isn't the water that was dirty, but it is by the washing of the water, the Living Word of GOD, that you and I are made clean. It might have been easier understood if the translators had put it like this: 'So that He might sanctify Her (the Church / us), having cleansed Her by washing Her with the cleansing water of the Word.' When we read the Word, it always cleanses our mind.

The Truth will always separate the light from the darkness. Sin cannot stay hidden to us as Christians when we continually read the Word of

WHAT JESUS BELIEVES

GOD. Jesus' Word is truly a light in the darkness and this Light will always shine down and expose to us the *unrepented sin* within our heart. Understanding verse 26, we can go on to better understand verse 27. "That He might present the Church to Himself in glorious splendor, without spot or wrinkle or any such things [that she might be holy and faultless]" (Ephesians 5:27 AMP). Remember, a revelation is receiving Rhema. Rhema is GOD's knowledge imparted to us. We need to have Rhema regarding this.

Now at this point, I ask that you ask GOD to show you the fullness of the Truth in the statement I am about to make. <u>GOD is not coming back for a sick Church</u>. It is unscriptural to say that He is coming back for a sickly Church. I know that many of you have been taught that, but there is not anywhere in Scripture that Jesus told us to allow sickness any place in our lives. He never allowed it into His life and since we are told to do as He did, neither should you or I. Yes, there are sermons preached on Paul's 'thorn in the flesh,' but that was a messenger sent to buffet him by satan. It was not a disease (Ref. 2 Corinthians 12:7). Also, you may question Paul's eyesight because somebody told you that 'because Paul asked, "See how big I am writing to you with my own hand?" it meant that he had poor eyesight.' Nowhere in the New Testament is there even a hint that Paul had bad eyesight and needed help. He went around as *a testimony to the Power (and active Life) [Dunamis Zoe] of GOD*, not as a testimony to the weakness of GOD. It says of him that the scales fell off of his eyes and he could see clearly (Ref. Acts 9:18). Imagine how hard it would be for anyone to take him seriously as a called servant and healer of GOD, if he were to go around with bad eyesight. Can you see the expressions on the faces of the crowd as Paul asks, "Now who would like me to lay hands on them for their healing? Just come up *really* close to me where I can see you and we will pray." Pray what? The prayer of faith, as it says in James 5:14-15? How could he pray the prayer of faith over anybody if he himself lacked the faith to be healed and was himself sick in body with an eye disease? *You need to have a revelation about healing to walk in the Anointing of healing.*

"So then faith comes by hearing, and hearing by the Word of GOD" (Romans 10:17 NKJV).

It has been preached many times that in 2 Corinthians 12:9 where Paul uses the Word *infirmities*, he is referring to sickness or disease when in fact *Paul's use of **infirmities** is referring to his natural man's native weakness and frailty aside from the Power of GOD.* That being said, we can continue on learning about the Scripture so misinterpreted from 2 Corinthians 12. Where Paul declares, "Three times I called upon the Lord and besought [Him] about this and begged that it might depart from me; but He said to me...for My strength and power are made perfect (fulfilled and completed) and show themselves most effective in [your] weakness. Therefore, I will all the more gladly glory in my weaknesses and infirmities, that the strength and power of Christ (the Messiah) may rest (yes, may pitch a tent over and dwell) upon me!" (2 Corinthians 12:8, 9 AMP). We can see that *Paul is saying he is glad that the power of GOD is shown strong in himself; and this being obvious because he is human with human limitations, like any other man, aside from GOD. He knows that people seeing his human limitations and then hearing the **(irrefutable) wisdom** that GOD speaks through him and seeing the **(irrefutable) miracles** that GOD performs through him, cannot help but know that there is a greater One at work, in and through himself, than merely the man, Paul.*

When the World sees miracles being performed in impossible situations in our lives, then they too will know that One greater than ourselves is at work in our lives. Let's you and I become that walking testimony! *If the word is out that the World is due some kind of crisis, let's be the ones led by the Spirit of GOD.* **Let's all be a walking testimony of faith and miracles in action thus bringing much glory to our GOD**; **"For we walk by faith, not by sight"** (2 Corinthians 5:7 NKJV), **trusting in GOD completely, just like Jesus!** *These actions are real faith builders for those observing our reactions to these situations, be it spiritual, physical, mental or other.*

WHAT JESUS BELIEVES

We need to remember that we are always a visible testimony to somebody else. Jesus said to the woman healed of the issue of blood, that *her faith had made her well.* That same law applies to you and I. *According to our faith, it will be done unto us. Jesus gave us every example to live by, by first living by them Himself!*

"And suddenly, a woman who had a flow of blood for twelve years came from behind and touched the hem of His garment. For she said to herself, 'If only I may touch His garment, I shall be made well.' But Jesus turned around, and when He saw her He said, 'Be of good cheer, daughter; your faith has made you well.' And the woman was made well from that hour. And when He had come into the house, the blind men came to Him. And Jesus said to them, 'Do you believe that I am able to do this?' They said to Him, Yes, Lord. Then He touched their eyes, saying, 'According to your faith let it be to you.' And their eyes were opened..." (Matthew 9:20-22, 28-30 NKJV). (See also Mark Chapter 5 and Luke Chapter 8).

Jesus knew the Word of GOD because He had the Living Word of the Holy Spirit of GOD residing in Him and giving Him perfect revelation! We have the Holy Spirit of GOD residing in us and we can know the Word of GOD too. By reading it daily and making it more important to us than our physical meals, we cannot help but grow in the Wisdom and Knowledge of the Lord. It is a vital aspect of our lives. *Does it really need to be that important to us?* <u>Yes, it definitely does</u>! GOD's Word is Wisdom and GOD promises that giving attention to His Word (His Wisdom) is healthy for us in every way!

Let's read what the Bible says about *His Words* in Proverbs 4:20-22 (NKJV). "My son, give attention to my words; incline your ear to my sayings. **Do not let them depart from your eyes; Keep them in the midst of your heart; for they are life to those who find them, and health to all their flesh.**" *This involves studying the Word and it takes effort and self-discipline on our part,* which always goes against our fleshly desires. Our *flesh* desires to *veg out* on the couch and *watch television.* If we follow our fleshly desires, we are sure to remain weak within our spiritual man. Then when satan buffets us with his weapons of lies, we are almost always sure to fall because we did not arm ourselves with the Word of GOD and have on the Armor that Father provided for us (See Ephesians Chapter 6). When a time of trouble does come, it is always worth the time we will take to get inside GOD's Word and learn what our promises are (now)! When we learn what His promises to us are, we can know GOD's perfect Will. Each Promise is a Gem for Life!

By the way, **the Hebrew word for health in Proverb 4:22 is medicine. Therefore, it is medicine to all our flesh (body and mind).** Now, you would never think of going to the doctors for a prescription and not having that prescription filled, would you? You would know that just having that slip of paper with your prescription written on it would not make you better. You would have to go down to the drug store and get it filled by the pharmacist, and then you would need to follow the directions from your doctor that the pharmacist has had typed out for you on the label. That would probably mean taking it several times a day for several days, wouldn't it? The Word of GOD is far more valuable than any pharmaceutical prescription. *The Word is more to be desired than gold or silver for His Words of Wisdom are life and medicine to our spirit, soul, and body* (Ref. Proverbs Chapters 4 and 8). The answer for every provisional need is found in the Word of GOD. Wisdom will always get you there... [*Where? To your answer.*]

> *"I AM the Key to all Wisdom.*
> *I AM the Revelator."*
> **Holy Spirit**

Proverbs 8:1-3 (NKJV): "Does not Wisdom cry out, and understanding lift up her voice? She takes her stand on the top of the high hill, beside the way, where the paths meet. She cries out by the gates, at the entry of the city, at the entrance of the doors: To you, O men, I call, and my voice is to the sons of men. O you simple ones, understand prudence, and you fools, be of an understanding heart. Listen, for I will speak of excellent things, and from the opening of My lips will come right things; for My mouth will speak truth; wickedness is an abomination to My lips. All the words of My mouth are with righteousness; nothing crooked or perverse is in them. They are all plain to him who understands, and right to those who find knowledge. Receive My instruction, and not silver, and knowledge rather than choice gold; for Wisdom is better than rubies, and all the things one may desire cannot be compared with her. I, Wisdom, dwell with prudence, and find out knowledge and discretion. The fear of the Lord is to hate evil; pride and arrogance and the evil way and the perverse mouth I hate. Counsel is Mine, and sound Wisdom; I am understanding, I have strength. By Me kings reign, and rulers decree justice. By Me princes rule, and nobles, all the judges of the earth. I love those who love Me, and those who seek Me diligently will find Me. Riches and honor are with Me, enduring riches and righteousness. My fruit is better than gold, yes, than fine gold, and My revenue than choice silver. I traverse the way of righteousness, in the midst of the paths of justice, that I may cause those who love Me to inherit wealth, that I may fill their treasuries. The Lord possessed Me at the beginning of His way, Before His works of old. I have been established from everlasting, from the beginning, before there was ever an earth. When there were no depths I was brought forth, when there were no fountains abounding with water. Before the mountains were settled, before the hills, I was brought forth; while as yet He had not made the Earth or the fields, or the primal dust of the world. When He prepared the Heavens, I was there, when He drew a circle on the face of the deep, when He established the clouds above, when He strengthened the fountains of the deep, when He assigned to the sea its limit, so that the waters would not transgress His command, when He marked out the foundations of the earth, then I was beside Him as a master craftsman; and I was daily His delight, Rejoicing always before Him, Rejoicing in His inhabited world, and My delight was with the sons of men. Now therefore, listen to Me, My children, for blessed are those who keep My ways. Hear instruction and be wise, and do not disdain it. Blessed is the man who listens to Me, watching daily at My gates, waiting at the posts of My doors. For whoever finds Me finds life, and obtains favor from the Lord; but he who sins against Me wrongs his own soul; all those who hate Me love death."

Proverb 9:11 declares, "For by Me [Wisdom from GOD] your days shall be multiplied, and the years of your life shall be increased" (AMP). *Wisdom and knowledge are a part of GOD. As Wisdom is made known to us (revealed, taught) by the Holy Spirit, we are acquiring the ability to use more of GOD's Power (Zoe's Dunamis [Life's Power]) as we are filled up with more and more of GOD's Anointing. As we allow the Holy Spirit more room to move in our lives, we will start to see the miracles, like those that Jesus performed, being performed through us!* Why don't we all *take Wisdom* for the next seven days just like we would *take a prescription*? We can each look up a Scripture or Scriptures on Wisdom and write them down on a piece of paper and read them three times each day. Maybe we could meditate on them during our meals. I'm sure that we can all find a way to fit them into our busy schedules, just like we would fit taking a prescription from our doctors into our schedules. If the prescription read, *"Take with food,"* we would take the time to eat something before swallowing a pill. Let's apply it and see what the *"medicine of GOD"* accomplishes in our lives when we have been faithful to take it as we should! GOD loves us so much that He's serious about us. If He knows (created) *"the directions"* for a healthy life, shouldn't we be listening? The words to an old public service announcement for education just popped into my head, "Reading is fundamental!" Isn't that the truth?!

*"I will lead you into all Truth.
I will lead you into Peace."*
Holy Spirit

*"There is a place in My Spirit
Where Creativity begins.
There is a place in My Spirit
Where dreams are born.
There is a place in My Spirit
Where dreams are nurtured.
There is a place in My Spirit
Where dreams are fulfilled.
It all happens within the
Revelation Zone."*
Holy Spirit

6

Worship: Getting Intimate with GOD

"The Lord appeared from of old to me [Israel], saying, Yes, I have loved you with an everlasting love; therefore with loving-kindness have I drawn you and continued My faithfulness to you" [Deut. 7:8] (Jeremiah 31:3 AMP).

"Draw me! We will run after you!"
(Song of Solomon 1:4 AMP)
The Song of Songs!

As the Truth of the Word is revealed more and more to our hearts, we will walk more and more by the Spirit of GOD. This is what it means to be *led by the Spirit.* <u>We learn that worshiping GOD is our spirit communing with GOD's Spirit. It is Rhema (Revelation Knowledge) that reveals to us our need to worship GOD. It is that revelation in our spirit man that says, "Hey, this is what I was created to do!"</u> We will also find that without the help of the precious Holy Spirit, it would be impossible for us to truly worship GOD. *Worship is not something our soul (mind, will and emotions) does, it is a purely spiritual communing.* It is GOD helping man to worship GOD. You may wonder, "Why on earth would GOD work it this way?" He didn't. Originally, man was pure. He was sinless before the fall of Adam and Eve in the Garden of Eden (Genesis 1). Man had no sin whatsoever and so he was in no way separated from GOD. His heart was pure and the relationship with GOD that mankind had was one completely untouched by sin. It was a relationship consisting of man communing directly with GOD. "GOD said, Let Us [Father, Son, and Holy Spirit] make mankind in Our image, after Our likeness, and let them have complete authority over the fish of the sea, the birds of the air, the [tame] beasts, and over all of the earth, and over everything that creeps upon the earth [Ps. 104:30; Heb. 1:2; 11:3]. So GOD created man in His own image, in the image and likeness of GOD He created him; male and female He created them [Col. 3:9-10; James 3:8-9]. And GOD blessed them and said to them, Be fruitful, multiply, and fill the earth, and subdue it [using all its vast resources in the service of GOD and man]; and have dominion over the fish of the sea, the birds of the air, and over every living creature that moves upon the earth. And GOD said, See, I have given you every plant yielding seed that is on the face of all the land and every tree with seed in its fruit; you shall have them for food. And to all the animals on the earth and to every bird of the air and to everything that creeps on the ground–to everything in which there is the breath of life – I have given every green plant for food." [Even lions were vegetarians at this point.] "And it was so. And GOD saw everything that He had made, and behold, it was very good (suitable, pleasant) and He approved it completely. And there was evening and there was morning, a sixth day (Genesis 1:26-31 AMP).

"Now a river went out of Eden to water the garden; and from there it divided and became four [river] heads. The first is named Pishon; it is the one flowing around the whole land of Havilah, where there is gold. The gold of that land is of high quality; bdellium (pearl?) and onyx stone are there. The second river is named Gihon; it is the one flowing around the whole land of Cush. The third river is named Hiddekel [the Tigris]; it is the one flowing east of Assyria. And the fourth river is the Euphrates. And the Lord GOD took the man and put him in the Garden of Eden to tend and guard and keep it. And the Lord GOD commanded the man, saying, you may freely eat of every tree of the garden; but of the tree of the knowledge of good and evil and blessing and calamity you shall not eat, for in the day that you eat of it you shall surely die. Now the Lord GOD said, It is not good (sufficient, satisfactory) that the man should be alone; I will make him a helper meet (suitable, adapted, complementary) for him. And out of the ground the Lord GOD formed every [wild] beast and living creature of the field and every bird of the air and brought them to Adam to see what he would call them; and whatever Adam called every living creature, that was its name. And Adam gave names to all the livestock and to the birds of the air and to every [wild] beast of the field; but for Adam there was not found a helper meet (suitable, adapted, complementary) for him. And the Lord GOD caused a deep sleep to fall upon Adam; and while he slept, He took one of his ribs or a part of his side and closed up the [place with] flesh. And the rib or part of his side which the Lord GOD had taken from the man He built up and made into a woman, and He brought her to the man. Then Adam said, this [creature] is now bone of my bones and flesh of my flesh; she shall be called Woman, because she was taken out of a man. Therefore a man shall leave his father and his mother and shall become united and cleave to his wife, and they shall become one flesh [Matt. 19:5; 1 Cor. 6:16; Eph. 5:31-33]. And the man and his wife were both naked and were not embarrassed or ashamed in each other's presence" (Genesis 2:10-25 AMP).

So you can see, when GOD created Eden, it was the perfect garden! Incredible animals of every variety inhabited Eden. From the smallest to the largest, all the creatures in this garden got along! Adam was given the honor of naming every creation which lived and breathed within the garden, including his personal favorite, Woman! GOD lavished love on Adam; and Adam in return loved and worshiped his Creator. Adam and Eve never doubted the love of GOD. He was their adoring Father and they were His devoted children. Life was sweet...and *then* came the *temptation.* (Isn't that the way it always is? We are going along just fine with our life and *here comes satan*!)

Well, as you probably know, that old serpent of old, slyly sidled up to Eve and spoke to her of *things to be desired*. Yes, that old forked tongue, that was in evidence in the Garden of Eden is still in great evidence to this day! satan is very crafty, but the Word of GOD gives us warning that "the thief cometh not, but for to steal, and to kill, and to destroy..." (John 10:10 KJV), and that is exactly what he did with Adam and his wife, Eve. Stepping into his snare of temptation caused

WHAT JESUS BELIEVES

them not only the loss of the gorgeous Garden of Eden with its perfect lifestyle, but it also separated them in their walk with GOD and caused them to give over their dominion (control/authority over) of the World to satan. They were made to go out into this harsh cruel World of which satan had deceitfully gained dominion. Adam and Eve had unwittingly given their dominion (control) over to him when they accepted his lie and ate of the fruit of the tree (of knowledge of good and evil), which they had been commanded by GOD *not* to eat.

After eating the fruit, the Word of GOD tells us *that their eyes were opened and they knew they were naked and were ashamed.* What possible reason could they have to be *ashamed*, unless their minds were open to *unholy thoughts?* Now the *knowledge* that they had so *coveted* had been given to them. Sadly, satan had been given access to their minds as well. Once innocent minds were now bombarded with the depraved thoughts of a completely evil creature (satan). Hence, the beginning of the fall of mankind (disobedience to GOD, listening to satan, and coveting). If there were a graph of "thuds," meaning the falls of mankind throughout history, I think this would be the second to largest "thud" on the graph. The largest "thud" would have to be the one made by our wonderful Jesus when He took "the fall" for all of Mankind's sins (our sins) by (Him) dying for us on the cross.

Praise GOD, for this would have also been recorded as the greatest "triumph" in history, if there were a graph made of "triumphs!" Thank you, Jesus! **You are indeed, our Triumph!**

The Word of GOD tells us that "[GOD] disarmed the principalities and powers that were ranged against us and made a bold display and public example of them, in triumphing over them in Him and in it [the cross]" (Colossians 2:15 AMP). Colossians 2:13-14 AMP gives us a clear definition of what GOD did for us in regards to satan's control over mankind. "And you who were dead in trespasses and in the uncircumcision of your flesh (your sensuality, your sinful carnal nature), [GOD] brought to life together with [Christ], having [freely] forgiven us **all** our transgressions, having cancelled and blotted out and wiped away the handwriting of the note (bond) with its legal decrees and demands which was in force and stood against us (hostile to us). This [note with its regulations, decrees, and demands] He set aside and cleared completely out of our way by nailing it to [His] cross." **Yes, history heard a resounding "thud," but in that "thud" was that largest "Triumphant ring" this World has ever known! Praise GOD!** That resounding "thud" when Jesus gave His life for ours at the cross was satan's death knell! In **one** *fell* swoop, *GOD took it ALL back*! HalleluYah! Yes, all of it! He took back our right to have eternal life and communion with Him. He took back our right to perfect health. He took back our right to prosper in all things. He took back our right to a sound right mind. In all things, He took back our right to reign over this Earth and to *have dominion* over it, for He gave us His Name! Just think about what that entitles us to! If we were to sum it all up in one legal-sounding sentence, it might read something like this, "I, GOD, give My Children Power of Attorney to use My name, Jesus (Yeshua: Salvation, He Saves). Henceforth, whatever they ask of Me, in that given Name, shall be given unto them because I love them. Also, whatsoever they, My Children, bind on this Earth shall also be bound in Heaven, and whatsoever they, My Children, shall loose on this Earth shall also be loosed in Heaven. Whatever command they give to satan must promptly be obeyed by him. This legal and binding document will be backed completely by Myself and all the power attached to Me including My Angelic Host. Signed in "The Blood" by GOD the Father."

The Word says that His Name, Jesus, is "Far above all rule and authority and power and dominion and every name that is named [above every title that can be conferred], not only in this age and in this world, but also in the age and the world which are to come. And He has put all things under His feet and has appointed Him the universal and supreme Head of the Church [a headship exercised throughout the Church] [Ps. 8:6], which is His body, the fullness of Him Who fills all in all [for in that body lives the full measure of Him

WHAT JESUS BELIEVES

Who makes everything complete, and Who fills everything everywhere with Himself]" (Ephesians 1:21-23 AMP).

Now, the Word in John says (Jesus speaking), "And I will do [I Myself will grant] whatever you ask in My Name [as presenting all that I AM], so that the Father may be glorified and extolled in (through) the Son" [Exod. 3:14] (John 14:13 AMP). "You have not chosen Me, but I have chosen you and I have appointed you [I have planted you], that you might go and bear fruit and keep on bearing, and that your fruit may be lasting [that it may remain, abide], so that whatever you ask the Father in My Name [as presenting all that I AM], He may give it to you" (John 15:16 AMP.) "And when that time comes, you will ask nothing of Me [you will need to ask Me no questions]. I assure you, most solemnly I tell you, that My Father will grant you whatever you ask in My Name [as presenting all that I AM]. [Exod. 3:14]. Up to this time you have not asked a [single] thing in My Name [as presenting all that I AM]; <u>but now ask and keep on asking and you will receive, **so that your joy (gladness, delight) may be full and complete.**</u> I have told you these things in parables (veiled language, allegories, dark sayings); the hour is now coming when I shall no longer speak to you in figures of speech, but I shall tell you about the Father in plain words and openly (without reserve). At that time you will ask (pray) in My Name; and <u>I am not saying that I will ask the Father on your behalf [for it will be unnecessary]. For the Father Himself [tenderly] loves you because you have loved Me and have **believed** that I came out from the Father</u>" (John 16:23-27 AMP).

That is the power that you and I have in GOD. We have the name of Jesus. We have the Word of GOD, which is Jesus. (The Word of GOD tells us that Jesus is the Living Word. If you have never grasped the meaning of this try looking up John 1:1–4 and putting the name of "Jesus" in place of "the Word." It is a real eye-opening experience!) And we have the Holy Spirit, the Power of GOD at our fingertips. I do not say this lightly, but it is true, for the Word declares that "For GOD did not give us a spirit of timidity (of cowardice, of craven and cringing and fawning fear), but [He has given us a spirit] of Power and of Love and of calm and well-balanced mind and discipline and self-control" (2 Timothy 1:7 AMP). GOD gave us all of these things! They are all definitely great reasons to worship Him all by themselves, but amazingly when we get into deep worship, although all that He has done for us is still there, *all that He is* takes 'top billing!' I find myself saying again and again to him, "GOD you are......so GOD!" And He is!

We know that there has never been a time since the beginning of creation that GOD has forced mankind to worship Him. He never has and never will desire that kind of worship. What he wants and has always wanted is to be willfully worshiped. *He wants each of us to feel so loved (John 3:16) that it is our hearts' desire to have a deep spiritual relationship with Him, one in which we desire to pour out our love to Him freely and without reservation. One in which we choose to spend time with Him, doing nothing but worshiping Him, our spirit to His Spirit.*

Worshiping GOD is vital to a healthy relationship with Him. Without worship, we could never really know the intimate side of GOD. This side of His love is an *all-consuming fire*! (Ref. Deuteronomy 4:24 and Hebrews 12:29). New Christians often exhibit a beautiful love for the Lord. It is often visible to everyone in the Church. These young Christians have *a yearning in their spirit to know GOD*. They have a desire to become closer to Him. They have a need to become intimate with Him. Sadly, most have not often been encouraged along in their new love for the LORD. Instead, they have come under the cold comments of the flesh; <u>comments by Christians who have now grown cold and hard in their faith</u>. Or they may have come under fire of the enemy and received one of his fiery darts. Either type of attack may have come in the form of comments like: "I remember when I was a baby Christian. I *behaved* just like you do." Or "New Christians always *feel* this way! Enjoy it while it lasts!" Or "Don't worry about the way you are *acting*, you will act like the rest of us as you get more *mature* in the Lord." These comments often act as a large bucket of ice water on a hot fire. As if GOD would *ever take His Love away from us!* The kind of *uninhibited love* that these new Christians are showing *is the perfect example of loving the Lord!* It isn't the kind of love that wonders what people are doing with their hands raised in worship before the Lord. It is the kind of love that wonders *why everybody doesn't have their hands raised in worship before the LORD.* This kind of uninhibited Worship has often prompted an ignorant and envious thought or comment, such as "They are still so young that they don't know any better than to act that way in church!" *We all should be so blessed as to not know any better and Worship Him that way!*

As a young child, my mother taught me to sing songs to Jesus. *She taught me by example.* When she did her housework, she would sing a song about Jesus. When she would feel upset or hurt about something one of us had done, she would sing a song about Jesus. When we traveled in the car, she would help to while away the time by having us sing songs about Jesus. And when she would rock me to sleep at night, she would sing me songs about Jesus along with my other lullabies. As I grew, I followed in her footsteps and found myself singing songs about Jesus on almost any occasion. I could often be found singing, "Yes, Jesus loves me!" when someone had hurt my feelings and I felt *less than adequate.* Singing these songs during times of hardship and trial was a vital part of how I worked through those difficult times. I didn't know that singing songs about Jesus always draws the presence of the Holy Spirit to us in a *tangible* way. I only knew that when I sang to the LORD, an immense peace swept over my soul and healing began in my heart. It was the way that GOD poured new love for the one who had hurt me into my heart. It was a gateway to the promises of GOD, but I didn't know that at that time either. I only knew that it made me feel better to sing songs to GOD and to spend time with Him. One thing I have been assured of time and time again over the years, as I would come out of these sessions with the Lord, *I knew Father GOD and The Lord Jesus loved me!*

Emotionally painful times come to all of us in life. **Singing songs of praise and worship to the Lord at these difficult times will not only ease your pain but will also lift the burdens that have caused them to weigh so heavily on your mind.** While under the fullness of the

Anointing of Worship, the problems which had once seemed so big, seem suddenly to have lost their great importance. Is that because GOD doesn't care about our *little everyday problems*? No. It is because *GOD knows the answer to our little everyday problems and to every great big problem too.* **It's Him!** He knows that if we will let Him take us to that place of worship where we let all of our problems fall away, it is there that He can show us the much-needed answers to our problems.

In times of crisis: shut the doors, turn off the television, unplug the phone, and PRAISE, PRAISE, PRAISE with the Word of GOD being your guide until you are brought into the Healing Worship by the Holy Spirit! Oh, don't forget to have a pen handy to mark the answers He has shown you in your Bible, and to write down detailed notes about your answer including your Bible Scriptures! You will want to write down all the information you receive from the LORD GOD at this time for future reference. Worship is where you will get some of your most powerful teachings from the Holy Spirit. This happens because your mind is not tangled up with the things of this world while in deep worship to GOD. And since your mind <u>is not</u> tangled up with the affairs of this world, you will be able to hear from GOD <u>very clearly</u>! (For encouragement regarding hearing from GOD, look up John 10:27, and underline it or highlight it in your Bible for future reference and encouragement)!

There is a beautiful Anointing that falls on us when we worship GOD. Sometimes we laugh, sometimes we cry, sometimes we get very quiet in our spirit and just bask in His Presence, and sometimes it is a combination of them all. As said before, it is right at the moment when our <u>crisis seems to be the worst</u> that we need to <u>worship GOD the most</u>! It is during our worship of GOD, this spirit to spirit relationship / communing, that we will find our inner healing. GOD is the fullness of Life and Love; therefore, it is impossible to spend time in His presence without receiving healing. The more you need healing, the more time you need to set aside to worship and spend time with GOD! And this applies to *<u>any type of healing you need,</u>* ***<u>body or mind</u>!***

There is a *beautiful love letter* in the Bible; it is entitled *The Song of Songs*. Although many Bibles referred to it as *The Song of Solomon*, we will use its original title *The Song of Songs,* which means *The Best of Songs*. This is the literal translation of the Hebrew Shir hash-shirim and the Greek asma asmaton. The addition of *asher li-Shelomoth,* translated "w*hich is to Solomon,*" is the basis for the title commonly used in English, *The Song of Solomon (Ref. Zondervan AMP Bible 2010). This love letter was penned to us from the very heart of GOD!*

The Song of Songs is the beautiful and pure outcry of a Bride's love for her Groom and the Groom's love for His Bride. Representative of our (the Church's) love for GOD and GOD's love for His people, Israel. [Having been adopted in, we too are a part of GOD's family, a part of the family of His beloved Israel]! Let's immerse us a bit in *The Song of Songs*, so that we can get a taste of GOD's fathomless Love for us.

"Let him kiss me with the kisses of his mouth! [she cries. Then, realizing that Solomon has arrived and has heard her speech, she turns to him and adds]: For your love is better than wine!" (Song of Solomon 1:2 AMP). Here we can see that the only desire that this bride has is to lavish her love upon her beloved. She longs to be the one to receive his kisses, his love. She longs for an intimate relationship with him. That is GOD's desire for the Church today. He wants them to want Him above anything and anyone else. He wants us to desire His love and devotion. He wants us to love Him with a pure love from a sincere heart; a heart that yearns for His love...*a heart yearning to be intimate with Him*. In the book of Revelation, the Church is referred to as *the Bride of Christ*. Therefore, Jesus is the Bridegroom of the Church. The Word says that *He is coming back for a Church (Bride) without spot or wrinkle*. Matthew 25 refers to us as <u>wise virgins</u>. Let's read verses 1-13 together:

"THEN THE Kingdom of Heaven shall be likened to ten virgins who took their lamps and went to meet the Bridegroom. Five of them were foolish (thoughtless, without forethought) and five were wise (sensible, intelligent, and prudent). For when the foolish took their lamps, they did not take any [extra] oil with them; But the wise took flasks of oil along with them [also] with their lamps. While the Bridegroom lingered and was slow in coming, they all began nodding their heads, and they fell asleep. But at midnight there was a shout, Behold, the Bridegroom! Go out to meet him! Then all those virgins got up and put their own lamps in order. And the foolish said to the wise, give us some of your oil, for our lamps are going out. But the wise replied, there will not be enough for us and for you; go instead to the dealers and buy for yourselves. But while they were going away to buy, the Bridegroom came, and those who were prepared went in with Him to the marriage feast; and *the door was shut*. Later the other virgins also came and said, Lord, Lord, open [the door] to us! But He replied, I solemnly declare to you, I do not know you [I am not acquainted with you]. Watch therefore [give strict attention and be cautious and active], for you know neither the day nor the hour *when the Son of Man will come*" (Matthew 25:1-13 AMP). This is a warning and a command that we are to keep our lives filled up with GOD in order to be ready for Him when He comes. This is the only way for us to be that ready Bride that He is returning for *without spot or wrinkle*. The only way we can keep our hearts pure (virginal) is to spend time with GOD, worshiping Him. It is also during our worship of Him that He pours out His Anointing [oil] upon us, which is the reason we leave our sessions of Worship of Him <u>*feeling so 'filled up*</u>*!'* If His Anointing is Power, then we will be filled up with His Power. If His Anointing is Light, then we will be filled up with His Light. And since it is both, we will be filled up with His Revelation Knowledge! Now that's **powerful** oil!

Revelation 19:7-8 (AMP) Bible says, "Let us rejoice and shout for joy [exulting and triumphant]! Let us celebrate and ascribe to Him glory and honor, for the marriage of the Lamb [at last] has come, and His bride has prepared herself. [Ps. 118:24]. She has been permitted to dress in fine (radiant) linen, dazzling and white – for the fine linen is (signifies, represents) the righteousness (the upright, just, and godly living, deeds, and conduct, and right standing with GOD) of the saints (GOD's holy people)" (Revelation 19:7-8 AMP).

GOD is looking for those who will *worship Him*. Since "GOD is a Spirit (a spiritual Being) and those who worship Him must worship Him in spirit and in truth (reality)" (John 4:24 AMP) sometimes we have to pray in the desire to worship Him <u>because there is so much of 'us' in the way</u>. I have often started out a time of worshiping the Lord by just singing praise songs as they came to my mind. GOD has always honored my diligence in this, and before long a beautiful Anointing has fallen on me and I was then able to truly worship Him, my spirit to His Spirit. For those of you who have never really experienced worship, let me explain how it *can* happen. I say *can* because you are never really able to peg GOD. Just when you think that you have Him figured out, He'll surprise you!

During one of the hardest times of my life, GOD taught me how to worship Him and why I needed to worship Him. First, He spoke into my spirit in the midst of my pain. He led me to just walk around and sing songs *about* Him and to sing songs *to* Him. Before long, I would find myself singing songs *only* <u>to</u> Him. It was at this point that I could sense my inner self, my soul, crying out to GOD in the midst of my pain. It was also at this point that I could feel something within me connect with GOD. I received an inner knowing that He really cared about me and all that I was going through. An inner knowing that He was at that moment seeing to my needs. I did not know at first that this was my spirit man connecting to GOD's Spirit. My spirit was itself reaching out for the Source of its healing. It was reaching out for its Creator. His Word says that when we pray in the Spirit (in our spirit language) that it edifies our inner (spirit) man (1 Corinthians 14:4). Somehow, when we are praising GOD with our spirit, we are communing with Him, spirit to Spirit; and our spirit knows and understands things that our mind (soul) does not yet know and understand. **When praying in the spirit of GOD, our spirit is receiving the mysteries (answers) of GOD that our mind is not yet aware of**. (See 1 Corinthians 14:2-4). When this happens, I find that I have gone over into worship. There is a beautiful pervading sense of <u>*peace*</u> and <u>*joy*</u> and <u>*love*</u> when this happens. This is the *manifestation of the Holy Spirit* upon us and the sense of awed wonder that accompanies it, for the Lord is beyond adequate description.

> *"Grace held onto your hand.*
> *And Grace won't let go."*
> **Holy Spirit of Grace**

> *"When you feel Me, I Am here.*
> *When you do not, I Am still here.*
> *I will never leave you nor forsake you."*
> **Holy Spirit**

In the Old Testament, when the Spirit of GOD came down and filled the Temple during the daytime, a cloud of glory could be seen over the Temple. According to the Bible, [Moses recorded that] this **glory cloud** also filled the Holy of Holies, the innermost part of the Temple. This cloud radiated brightly with the Glory of GOD. When Moses would go into the Holy of Holies, before the Lord, it is written that he came out with the Glory of the LORD shining brightly upon his face. So brightly, in fact, that he had the need to wear a dark cloth over his head to shield the Israelites from the intense brightness! The Bible also tells us that it was this same (glory) cloud that led the Israelites by day across the desert. At night, it appeared to the Israelites as a pillar of fire. When it moved forward, the Israelites would pick up camp and move forward. When it stopped, they would stop and set up camp. There have been times during worship of the LORD that I have seen what I believe to be this same cloud of glory. I have seen this glory cloud descended in the spirit both in church and at home during worship of the LORD. At other times, it has been so tangible that even though I could not see it, I could feel it, for I could feel the presence of GOD all around me! Those are the times we fall to our knees before the LORD and cry out, "Abba! Father! GOD!"

"Ask me to give you an unquenchable hunger for worship!
Let Me show you what sheer joy feels like!"
Holy Spirit

"Slain in the Spirit" Or "Falling under the Power of GOD"

For those who have never experienced being *slain in the Spirit* or *falling under the power [anointing] of GOD,"* which are both the same thing, or to those who perhaps have never even heard of being *slain in the Spirit*, let's define it. *To be slain* can be simply defined as *to be killed* or *to be disposed of;* yet when we are *slain in the Spirit* or *go under in the Spirit of GOD*, we are still very much alive! In fact, it is one of the most Heavenly experiences we can have while we are still residing in our bodies on this Earth! I believe that it earned these definitions because, during this time of our *communing with GOD*, our flesh is so completely _not_ in control, one could temporarily term it as *slain* or *dead* to us. You will never feel *more alive* than you will when you have *gone under* in the Holy Ghost.

While slain in the Spirit, there will be times that people may see you laying prostrate on the floor with nothing apparent going on at all! While at other times, you may be praying or singing in your spirit language (tongues). You may be laughing and/or weeping. There may be a conversation going on between you and GOD, and should you speak out loud, one-half of the conversation may be heard by those around you!

There are many different experiences to be had while slain in the spirit, but _they will all involve getting closer to GOD_ and _they are all to be desired!_ Just one experience is guaranteed to change your perspective of GOD and life. Just one experience will help you to worship Him with more understanding of Who He is. If you have never experienced this, I suggest you pray that GOD will start blessing you with experiences of being slain in the Spirit. If you desire prayer regarding this, look for someone with the tangible Anointing of GOD on their life and ask them to come into agreement in prayer with you for it!

Transference of the Anointing

When you desire to operate in certain gifts of the Spirit, you look for someone who is already operating fluently in those Spiritual gifts. Then, when you find them and are <u>sure that their gift is proven (for real), you request them to pray over you for that same Anointing</u>. You are asking GOD to bless you with that gift by the *laying on of hands*. That is Scriptural as we can read in 1 Timothy 5:22, where we are commanded to not hastily lay hands on anyone. It doesn't mean that we are not to pray for one another's needs, it simply means that we are not to commission someone to a ministerial duty without the leading of the LORD to do so. This is why it is so important to find someone with the Anointing of GOD on their life, for the gift you desire, to pray over you. Let's read Acts 6:1–10 to get better insight (understanding) on this. "NOW ABOUT this time, when the number of the disciples was greatly increasing, complaint was made by the Hellenists (the Greek-speaking Jews) against the [native] Hebrews because their widows were being overlooked and neglected in the daily ministration (distribution of relief). So the Twelve [Apostles] convened the multitude of the disciples and said, It is not seemly or desirable or right that we should have to give up or neglect [preaching] the Word of GOD in order to attend to serving at tables and superintending the distribution of food. Therefore, select out from among yourselves, brethren, seven men of good and attested character and repute, full of the [Holy] Spirit and wisdom, whom we may assign to look after this business and duty. But we will continue to devote ourselves steadfastly to prayer and the ministry of the Word. And the suggestion pleased the whole assembly, and they selected Stephen, a man full of faith (a strong and welcome belief that Jesus is the Messiah) and full of and controlled by the Holy Spirit, and Philip, and Prochorus, and Nicanor, and Timon, and Parmenas, and Nicolaus, a proselyte (convert) from Antioch. These they presented to the apostles, who after prayer laid their hands on them." The Twelve (Apostles) convened the multitude of the ever increasing number of disciples and asked them to select out men of GOD who could attend to serving tables and superintending the distribution of food. This they did through prayer and the Anointing of GOD. Then, once they knew those that were chosen by the LORD GOD, they laid hands on them and prayed that they would have the gifts necessary to do their jobs. In essence, they prayed for GOD to give (transfer) the anointing that they (the twelve) had onto those chosen to take their place at those tasks. Hence, the *transference of the Anointing*. We'll finish reading verses 7–10 in order to find out what happens when an Anointing has been transferred over to someone [and just because someone has transferred their anointing (from the LORD) onto you, it does not mean that they have any less of it themselves. It works like love, the more you give away, the more you get to flow in]! "And the message of GOD kept on spreading, and the number of disciples multiplied greatly in Jerusalem; and [besides] a large number of the priests were obedient to the faith [in Jesus as the Messiah, through Whom is obtained eternal salvation in the Kingdom of GOD]. Now Stephen, full of grace (divine blessing and favor) and power (strength and ability) worked great wonders and signs (miracles) among the people. However, some of those who belonged to the synagogue of the Freedmen (freed Jewish slaves), as it was called, and [of the synagogues] of the Cyrenians and of the Alexandrians and of those from Cilicia and [the province of] Asia, arose [and undertook] to debate and dispute with Stephen. But they were not able to resist the intelligence and the wisdom and [the inspiration of] the Spirit with which and by Whom he spoke" (Acts 6:1-10 AMP).

When the Holy Ghost anoints us to do something, people may argue against it, but <u>it will be obvious to all that what we have done has been accomplished by none other than the power of Almighty GOD!</u> His power is His Glory. His Glory is His Anointing manifested.

(Remember, the power of GOD is the Anointing, a free and necessary gift as a follower of Jesus Christ and a child of GOD). Today, as yesterday, there will be those who are jealous of our abilities in the Lord, and they will try to disprove them, to thereby discredit us. (Acts 17:5; Mark 3:1–6; Matthew 9:28–34; Matthew 21:23–27; Matthew 26:3–5; Luke 6:6–11; Luke 11:15–54; Luke 13:10-17; Luke 20:1–19). The Pharisees and Sadducees were jealous of Jesus. They had Him killed because of the jealousy within them. They were *antichrist*. The Bible warns us that there will be those who are *antichrist*, which is <u>not</u> to be mixed up with <u>*the Antichrist*,</u> who is spoken of as associated with *the Beast*. <u>Those who are *antichrist* [little a] are those who are against the teachings of Christ (the Anointed One and His Anointing, which is inclusive of His Anointed (teaching) Word)</u>. In verse 10, it is clearly stated that these antichrist men were not able to resist the intelligence and the wisdom and the Spirit of GOD, with which and by Whom Stephen spoke. That same Holy Spirit that enabled Stephen to speak with power as he did was to the one *Words of Life*, and to the other (those antichrist) *words of death*. For to some, his words (from GOD via the Holy Spirit through Stephen) would lead to <u>their</u> repentance and eternal life, but to others the words he spoke would lead to their eternal destruction and separation from GOD on Judgment Day. This, because <u>they refused to turn from their sins, even when those sins had been pointed out to them by the Holy Ghost</u> through Stephen.

Just as Stephen was prayed over by those with the *gifts (Anointing) of GOD* that he needed to be equipped with, so should you and I be prayed over by those with the gifts that we need to be equipped with. When we go to a true man of GOD [one who operates in discernment and follows the leading of the Holy Spirit on a continual basis], that man of GOD will know by the Spirit [when he (or she) prays over us] the will of GOD. If the gift (Anointing) we are requesting is one GOD desires us to (continually) operate in (as a ministry/ministerial gifting), the man of GOD will pray for that anointing to come upon our life. If not, then the man of GOD will pray for us as he is directed to pray by the Holy Spirit. In other words, we may not be called to the

Office of a Prophet, but we may still get a prophetic Word from the LORD about something or someone from time to time. We may not be called to be a worship leader; hence, we would not need the anointing to be a worship leader, but because <u>we are all called to worship GOD, we may want a worship leader (who is *Anointed to worship)* laying hands on us to pray. Being prayed over can strengthen the Anointing on us to worship GOD, so it is always a good thing! In 1 Corinthians 12:31 (AMP), the Word tells us "But earnestly desire and zealously cultivate the greatest and best gifts and graces...</u>". So you see, we can never have too much of the Anointing of GOD! Hanging around others who operate in a stronger Anointing than you do is wisdom!

Jesus knew that the Anointing on His disciples would strengthen in accordance with their faith in GOD. The more time they spent in His presence, the stronger their Anointing. The Word says, "<u>Not forsaking or neglecting to assemble together [as believers]</u>, as is the habit of some people, <u>but admonishing (warning, urging, and encouraging) one another, and all the more faithfully as you see the day approaching</u>" (Hebrews 10:25 AMP). So, you see, it is the Holy Word of GOD that we Christians <u>hang out together</u>! As we are also commanded (ordered, instructed, directed), "therefore encourage (admonish, exhort) one another and edify (strengthen and build up) one another, just as you are doing" (1 Thessalonians 5:11 AMP). This tells us just what our conversations are to be about while we are together. We are to come together as a family and encourage one another! The world will use any excuse to get together and party. As Christians, we don't need an excuse, *our command is to celebrate the love of GOD with one another. The Holy Spirit is the new wine whose effects are far better than any Earthly wine. His effects are life, liberty, and love! All of which are necessary for an abundant (satisfying, full of hope) life!* **All** <u>that those walking in the darkness of this world (the shadow death) are needing is the love of GOD (to be) shed abroad in their hearts!</u> Unless we tell them about Jesus and the love of GOD, they will continue to walk on in darkness (the shadow of death). A good portion of the Church has reliably given the idea for centuries that the Body of Christ is a dead body when it comes to hope and joy. Why would the world desire to become part of a family that shows constant fighting and division, finger-pointing, backbiting and accusations; also, belief in glorifying GOD through sickness, disease or infirmity and extreme poverty when it comes to loving one another? What kind of a person would want that kind of a relationship with GOD? Only a martyr of self.

As Revival has swept the World in various places in recent years, what as a whole have we, the Church Body, done to keep it going? Would you say that mostly we have talked about it? It's a sad truth that this also accounts for the rate of revival growth. *When we learn to worship GOD in Spirit and in Truth, by yielding all of our heart and all of our self to His Spirit, only then will revival break forth where we are*! We need to do it corporately, together as a Body; one or two people in church worshiping the LORD is not going to get us where GOD desires us to be unless others join in and we begin worshiping as a whole.

He desires our worship. Jesus declared, "GOD is Spirit, and those who worship Him must worship in spirit and truth" (John 4:24 NKJV). Jesus lived the example in this. It is to our benefit to worship Him, not because He is some insatiable creature with a lust for all people to do nothing except stand in awe and warped (craven) fear of Him, but because *He knows that in worshiping Him, we come toward the fullness of the understanding of Who He is and in that comes the fullness of understanding who we are in Him*. **With this understanding of Who He is comes safety, health, and freedom from sin, sickness, disease, and despair as we learn to walk in His [complete] love and faith!**

"I and My Father are One" (John 10:30 KJV). "I am the vine, ye are the branches: He that abideth in Me, and I in him, the same bringeth forth much fruit: for without Me ye can do nothing" (John 15:5 KJV). The Holy Spirit of GOD is the Holy Spirit of Jesus Christ, which is the Holy Spirit! Real worship will always lead us into reverential awe of [understanding] Who He is, <u>which in turn delivers us from the bondage of (craven) fear</u>; which *includes* deliverance from infirmities of the (once enslaved) mind. It is written, "For GOD did not give us a spirit of timidity (of cowardice, of craven and cringing and fawning fear), but [He has given us a spirit] of power and of love and of calm and well-balanced mind and discipline and self-control" (2 Timothy 1:7 AMP). Jesus said, "*I am the Door*; anyone who enters in through Me will be saved (will live). He will come in and he will go out [freely], and will find pasture. The thief comes only in order to steal and kill and destroy. **I came that they may have and enjoy life, and have it in abundance (to the full, till it overflows)**" (John 10:9-10 AMP). *How did we get the opportunity to go through this Door?* "For GOD so greatly loved and dearly prized the world that He [even] gave up His only begotten (unique) Son, so that whoever believes in (trusts in, clings to, relies on) Him shall not perish (come to destruction, be lost) but have eternal (everlasting) life" (John 3:16 AMP). Jesus in agreement with the Father told us, "I am the Good Shepherd. The Good Shepherd risks and lays down His [own] life for the sheep" [Ps. 23] (John 10:11 AMP). *In worship comes knowing (GOD), abiding (in GOD), healing (from GOD) and restoration of our whole man through the Holy Spirit because of the price that Jesus paid and all this a [completely] free gift from GOD.* Out of this comes the fullness of our salvation; wholeness of mind, body, and spirit! When the (whole) Church worships Him in Spirit and in truth, then this will bring Revival of proportions we have not yet known before! "that they all may be one, as You, Father, are in Me, and I in You; that they also may be one in Us, that the world may believe that You sent Me" (John 17:21 NKJV). When this happens, revival will come and others will want a part of what we have!

As the Church, and the example of the living Body of Christ to the World, it is our <u>calling</u> to live in the <u>fullness</u> of Him. To live in the fullness of His joy! This can be done by worshiping GOD together: through our testimonies, through our prayer, through the encouraging and enlightening Words of GOD we give (share with) one another called *Word of Knowledge and Word of Wisdom*, through our faith [(in action) bringing about the manifestation of healing and miracles] and anything else that GOD chooses to do through us!

The Bible says that *an unbelieving spouse may be won over, without words, by a believing spouse just by living the example!* (See 1 Peter 3:1). If someone were to ask you how many people you feel will be won over to Christ during this year just because of your example in Christ
de(at home and at work), how many do you think that would be?
"THEREFORE BE imitators of GOD [copy Him and follow His example], as well-beloved children [imitate their father]" (Ephesians 5:1 AMP).

Jesus Healed the Breach!

Let's bring some things that we have learned together with clearer understanding. At no other time in history has it been as easy to worship GOD as it is now! GOD so loved us that He sent Jesus to heal the breach between GOD and Man. Not only is Jesus our way to salvation, but Jesus is also our bridge to communing with GOD. Yes, there were accounts of Saints worshiping GOD in the Old Testament, but all under the Anointed covering of the Holy Spirit. At that time, the Holy Spirit would overshadow them, but He did not indwell them as He does us. He *visited them* but didn't take up residence. Although GOD was with His people, He did not (permanently) indwell His people and make them one (heart, Spirit) with Him until Jesus. (John the Baptist was filled with the Holy Spirit from the womb as a prophetic act of GOD. "For he shall be great in the sight of the Lord, and he shall drink no wine nor strong drink; and he shall be filled with the Holy Spirit, even from his mother's womb." "And it came to pass, when Elisabeth heard the salutation of Mary, the babe leaped in her womb; and Elisabeth was filled with the Holy Spirit; and she lifted up her voice with a loud cry, and said, Blessed art thou among women, and blessed is the fruit of thy womb. And whence is this to me, that the mother of my Lord should come unto me? For behold, when the voice of thy salutation came into mine ears, the babe leaped in my womb for joy. And blessed is she that believed; for there shall be a fulfilment of the things which have been spoken to her from the Lord" (Luke 1:15, 41-45 ASV).) <u>Jesus Christ was created as GOD and man</u> when the Holy Spirit came upon Mary, his Mother, and the power of the Highest overshadowed her (see Luke 1:26-38). Then, at Jesus' baptism, it was <u>Jesus, GOD in man, indwelt by the Spirit of GOD</u>, which is the Holy Spirit. (See Luke 3). After Jesus, it was the one hundred and twenty gathered in the upper room on the day of Pentecost. (See Acts 1 and 2). All accounts of the people who worshiped in the Old Testament gave prophetic utterances. We have recorded not only prophetic utterances and worship regarding the coming Messiah (Christ), but there are also prophetic utterances about other important events in history as well! The Old Testament books of Daniel, Ezekiel, Isaiah, and Jeremiah, to name a few, are prophetically accurate and in-line with the New Testament book of Revelation as it describes Last Days events. And all of the examples we read in the Old Testament about worshiping GOD are meant to act as guides and references to our worship of GOD. All worship recorded in the Bible was GOD inspired.

In many churches today, it is not uncommon to hear someone singing in the Holy Spirit. When an interpretation is made by the Spirit, they are not only praise-filled, but often prophetic. We are living in the most exciting and Spiritually-Knowledgeable time in history! At no other time have we had so many prophets walking the earth. At no other time have we understood the Bible with the clarity that we have today. The book of Daniel prophesied about today. (See the Book of Daniel in the Old Testament, Chapters 7–12). The visions took Daniel through the End Times with all of its ferocity. Daniel was so terrified by what he had seen that it says...well, let's read what it says together. "The vision of the evenings and the mornings which has been told you is true. But seal up the vision, for it has to do with and belongs to the [now] distant future. And I, Daniel, fainted and was sick [for several] days. Afterward I rose up and did the king's business; and I wondered at the vision, but there was no one who understood it or could make it understood" (Daniel 8:26-27 AMP). There was absolutely no way that Daniel could have understood the technology that he had experienced seeing in his vision. How would a man of his era describe a computer, a jet, or even the Euro Rail? In the final verse of the final chapter of Daniel, he is comforted by the angel who tells him, "But you [Daniel, who was now over ninety years of age], go your way until the end; for you shall rest and shall stand [fast] in your allotted place at the end of the days" [Heb. 11:32-40] (Daniel 12:13 AMP). How amazed Daniel must have been to have seen all of those things. There wasn't any way he could pass it off as being his wild imagination because they didn't have technology even remotely similar to what he saw. How he must have prayed for us (GOD's people) all! How he must have praised a GOD that was so awesome as to have made mankind with the ability to learn and create as he did! How he must have marveled at the bridges and buildings. How he must have wondered at the foolish acts of man. How sad he must have felt. With all of man's great jumps in inventions, he still hadn't learned how to conquer greed. Daniel still saw the ugly face of war in his people's future.

As we have spoken of throughout the Old Testament in the books of the Prophets, there is great revelation to be had by us about our lifetime. This is that 'tick in time' that was foretold so long ago. We are going to worship Him through it!

"Are you ready for an outpouring of My Revelation so great that it floods the earth?" Holy Spirit

The Anointed Worship of King David
Psalms in Hebrew is Tehillim, which translates Praises!

King David loved the LORD GOD with all of his heart. He was from the direct lineage of Abraham, Isaac, Jacob and Joseph. He grew up a humble shepherd boy guarding, guiding and keeping his father's flock by day and by night. David was a psalmist, that means he wrote songs. David was the inspired author of many of the songs in the Book of Psalms. David, who grew up as the little shepherd boy tending his Father's flock, praising and worshipping GOD out beneath the open heavens, was chosen by GOD to become the leader of Israel.

When Samuel was sent to anoint David as the future King of Israel, David was just a youth. Having had 7 sons of Jesse walk before Samuel, "... he asked Jesse, "Are these all the sons you have?" "There is still the youngest," Jesse answered. "He is tending the sheep." Samuel said, "Send for him; we will not sit down until he arrives." So he sent for him and had him brought in. He was glowing with health and had a fine appearance and handsome features. Then the Lord said, "Rise and anoint him; this is the one. So Samuel took the horn of oil and anointed him in the presence of his brothers, **and from that day on the Spirit of the Lord came powerfully upon David**. Samuel then went to Ramah." (1 Samuel 16:11-13 NIV) We see two distinct things here in verse 13. *And from that day on the Spirit of the Lord came powerfully upon David*. GOD could trust David with His Holy Anointing. *Samuel then went to Ramah*. After anointing David, Samuel left. David went back out to care for his father's flock because that's just the way GOD wanted it. GOD had been training David out in the wilderness with the flock while he cared for the lambs and fought off the lion and the bear. He was training David to take care of His flock, the children of Israel. GOD knew His children (the children of Israel) could be a handful, but He loved them. David would go through years of being tried in the fire as Saul relentlessly persecuted and pursued David as over and over again he sought ways to kill him (David). As this happened, David continued to pray, praise, and to worship GOD for his deliverance. David would be betrayed by close friends and family. Again, David pressed in and stayed close to GOD. Through it all GOD would continue in relationship with David creating in him a great shepherd and thus a great and much beloved King. Although David was King over all of GOD's People, Israel, he remained humble and loyal to GOD. When David did sin, he was quick to repent. Honesty caused David to pen many a song under the Anointing of the Holy Spirit. GOD loved His servant, David, and David loved, *Jehovah Rohi, the LORD my Shepherd*. (See Psalm 23:1)

2 Samuel 6 shows two good examples of David worshipping the LORD GOD. "David and all Israel were celebrating with all their might before the Lord, with castanets, harps, lyres, timbrels, sistrums and cymbals." and (2 Samuel 6:5 NIV) "When those who were carrying the Ark of the Lord had taken six steps, he sacrificed a bull and a fattened calf. Wearing a linen ephod, David was dancing before the Lord with all his might, while he and all Israel were bringing up the Ark of the Lord with shouts and the sound of trumpets." (2 Samuel 6:13-15 NIV) David gave his all in dance before Him in praise and worship that day. It is easy to see that David was a man after GOD's own heart! Above all else, King David loved the LORD GOD. David leaves us with a legacy of pure and unadulterated Worship. If you want to know how to worship, David is an excellent example to follow. You will fall more in love with GOD as you read the Psalms that David wrote. Yes, he was a man with faults, but he was a man that was zealous about his GOD.

The whole Book of Psalms is a great place to go to for great praise and worship songs! Psalm 119 is not only the longest chapter in the Bible but within it, there is help for any situation. Psalm 91 is a great song to pray over yourself and your family. The Lord is leading me to share an encounter that I had with him; I believe that this occurred in October 1995.

"The Vision"

In relating this vision to the few that I have shared it with, I have usually referred to it as "My David Vision." It all happened on an early October morning. Our five boys were attending a small private Christian school in Kentucky and I had just dropped them off at school. Upon arriving back home, I went into my bedroom to spend my morning quiet time with the Lord. As I came over to the side of my bed where I often read the Word, a tiredness started to come upon me. I lay on the bed to read feeling its effects and I remember saying something to the effect of, "Oh, Lord I am just sooo tired. Is it alright if I lay down and take a nap for a little while or so?" I remember crawling beneath the covers and trying to read the Bible at least a little while. Within moments, the Bible fell on my chest where I found it when I woke up, for I had fallen into a deep sleep. Or so I thought...

My Arrival into Heaven

I was in a bright valley standing beside a man that I had no memory of ever having met before. He seemed familiar to me. He asked me, "*Do you know who I am?*" I remember shaking my head no with my mouth hanging wide open. When you are in Heaven, there is simply no denying it.

He told me, "*I am David.*" I had no words to say. This man was the man who was once the King of Israel. He asked me, "*Do you know why you are here?*" I felt like I should have known. If you have ever felt like that, then you understand. I wondered fleetingly, "*Should I know?*" I shook my head no again. He was still smiling when he asked me if I knew my name. Inside, I was talking to myself. "Come on, Jean, you know your name! ..." I managed to say, "Jean." and then close my mouth. Part of my soul felt really afraid, but there was this pervading peace that was all around us... that was working on my soul, training it, teaching it. I know now that peace was GOD's Presence and His Presence is peace, real peace, perfect peace. (See: Isaiah 26:3) My soul was afraid only because it was not wholly renewed to the mind of Christ, the Anointing (Holy Spirit) Who lives within me. To those who can receive, Holy Spirit is the mind of Christ. Christ is the Prince of Peace just as GOD is Love; He desires to be King over every part of us because He loves us, He designed us, and because of this He knows what is best for us. During my trip to Heaven, it was made evident that He needed to rule and reign in all of me. I needed *Him* to be seated on the Throne in my soul. I also learned that in order to do that someone had to be deposed. It was me.

David now gave me a look that showed me the import of him having my full attention. He said, "*You have been brought here to learn how to worship GOD.*" I instantly thought, "Why me?" "Oh, GOD, You've *got the wrong person!"* Don't misunderstand, I loved GOD with all of my heart and I loved to *worship Him in spirit and in truth*, but I was so far from perfect! *Why would GOD want to use someone like me? And how could GOD use someone like me?* There had to be far better candidates than myself to bring up to Heaven and to learn to do something as important as worshipping GOD. My mind kept telling me that David had been stuck with someone as imperfect as me and that it would soon be obvious to him...as if it wasn't already. Apparently, that's not what GOD was thinking and that's not what GOD was seeing. *Man looks at the outward appearance, but GOD looks upon the heart,* and God was seeing my heart. He was seeing the heart of a true worshipper. Yes, a woman who still made mistakes and was far from walking a perfect Jesus walk, but one who was hungry for more of His Presence, humble before Him, and one who knew how to love on Him like crazy! He saw someone who was willing to do anything to get closer to Him; get up at all hours of the night and early morning to sneak outside and worship and talk to Him beneath the stars. Someone who had a flashlight on under the covers so that she could read the Word while her husband slept. GOD, who is the revealer of hearts made it clear to me at a later date that *I was willing.* That's why He chose me. He also spoke to my heart, *David was willing.* If I wasn't humble enough before, when He spoke those last words to me I was then.

We began walking through the most glorious valley! *Everything around us was alive and if you can believe it or even if you can't, everything was praising GOD; every plant, every grass blade, everything!* You could feel them and I don't mean that you can reach down and touch them, which you can, but you can actually *feel them, they're alive and vibrating with life.* Perhaps to understand this you need to be there, but you can.

The fragrances of Heaven are perfect and fitting. We do not have the ingredients for any perfumer on earth to create such lovely and exquisite fragrances. I was in awe of the perfection of the grass beneath us. My senses were captivated by its beauty and I was studying it intensely. As we walked I admired how each perfect blade is exactly the right size, shape, thickness and texture. Its brilliant emerald* hue seemed to call out to me to come walk through it and enjoy myself.

"But as it is written: "Eye has not seen, nor ear heard, Nor have entered into the heart of man The things which God has prepared for those who love Him.""
I Corinthians 2:9 NKJV

GOD has such an incomprehensible (and limitless) supply of creativity that just taking in the sights, scents and sounds of one Heavenly Valley could take you all of eternity. Because His Creativity never ends, you would never stop discovering!

My head was turning this way and that as I tried to take it all in. Every single creation was so amazing! The exquisite flowers that grew on both sides of the valley, as well as on the valley floor, were the first flowers that I was to see in Heaven. Ethereal and beautiful, they were stunning little gems with their exquisite centers. GOD had set them like small jewels amidst the emerald grass covering the valley floor and over most of the slopes past which we walked. Thinking of them reminds me of stars set in a velvety night sky. I remember one section of the valley where more tropical, rain forest type foliage lives up on the flowy, slopping valley walls. There are flowers and plants there that I have never seen before that day. When we walked out of the valley there before us were rolling green hills and a body of still beautiful water. There was a stream winding through a beautiful meadow like a shiny ribbon. It wound its way amongst the gently rolling hills *and* through the little undulating hills that look like beautiful ripples of green. The stream has a peek-a-boo effect as it moves happily along through those ripples. The gentle hills seem to roll on endlessly, yet there is varying landscape dotted here and there. It is everything that you would expect the Heavenly land of King David to be... And much more! Oh, so much more!

Heaven is an amazing place. GOD is everywhere there! Once you have been, you realize that leaving this planet is a very wonderful thing for a child of the GOD!

"Harvest as if you go home tomorrow."
Holy Spirit

The Tour

There in front of us, seated atop a low hill, was a brilliant palace which fairly dazzled the eye! Behind this palace, set amongst the rolling hills, is a beautiful forest complete with fir trees, deer, birds, squirrels and other little creatures. They live in harmony with one another. It is a serene, happy, tranquil place. It looks like a perfect place to walk around and commune with GOD. It looks like an ideal place to worship the LORD. This is David's. This is all David's.

When he offered me a tour of his home I was surprised and very excited! Out front were steps; long, low, wide, beautiful white stone steps leading up to the main level. They ran the entire length of the palace. At the top of the stairs there were columns supporting the structure covering the outside area. The temperature outdoors was, as with everything else, absolutely perfect. We walked up to doors of extraordinary size and beauty leading into one very large rectangular room. There are large vases in that room among the other pieces. Beautiful. Everything in that room was perfectly placed and although I do not remember seeing a lot of things in the large room, it was perfect, just perfect.

Nearly straight across from the doors through which we entered this main room were large open doorways through which I could view a bit of a lovely courtyard. I longed to go out into that courtyard. As we passed by the open doorways I gazed outside and saw that the courtyard is surrounded by the palace on three sides. We walked up a straight staircase that shares the same wall, but to the right; it's beautiful white stone abutting the wall. I don't remember the stair railing in detail, but gold and exquisite have come to mind.

Once upstairs, there is a long hallway with many doors. Room after room is filled with beautiful and amazing things. You would recognize the similarity in the furnishings. David is an excellent tour guide. My senses were reeling by the beauty I was experiencing within each room and as we toured he did his best to make me feel comfortable. I started to relax more after we had toured the first (guessing) 8-15 rooms or so. As we continued to go into room after room, I was better able to walk around and take my time in admiring everything. The furnishings and beautiful objects in Heaven have a pure beauty and perfection of craftsmanship and material that the things on earth cannot compare to. People have asked me, "*Were there beds?*" I believe there were, yes, and the scripture that comes immediately to mind is in Psalms.

When I remember You on my bed, I meditate on You in the night watches. Because You have been my help, Therefore in the shadow of Your wings I will rejoice.
(Psalm 63:6,7 NKJV)

Did you know that the shadow of His wings is His Glory? It's impenetrable and impregnable, satan and his cohorts cannot touch us as long as we dwell in His shadow. We can lay down our life for Christ, but satan cannot touch us.

Therefore My Father loves Me, because I lay down My life that I may take it again. No one takes it from Me, but I lay it down of Myself. I have power to lay it down, and I have power to take it again. This command I have received from My Father. (John 10:17-18 NKJV)

Jesus received the command from the Father to lay down His life and He chose to obey in accord (unity) with the Father's will for *in all things He submitted unto the will of the Father.*

WHAT JESUS BELIEVES

When they came to arrest Jesus in the Garden and Peter stretched out his hand and drew his sword... Jesus said,

Or do you think that I cannot now pray to My Father, and He will provide Me with more than twelve legions of angels? How then could the Scriptures be fulfilled, that it must happen thus?
Matthew 26:53-54 NKJV

If we belong to GOD and are following Him as Jesus did, GOD keeps us safely in *the* shadow *of His wings, His glory. We can remain safely in that place* according to Psalm 91. We can choose to lay down our lives from inside that place in accordance with the Father's will, just as Jesus did. If we are His, we will follow Him, even to being martyred, if that is His will. And much to satan's chagrin, it will bring GOD Glory if that is our course as we go trusting in our Heavenly Father Who will be there with us. His Holy Spirit remains with us on earth and sees that we go safely home into His Heavenly Kingdom! So we can see that satan cannot touch us.

When you stay in Me, My child,
To be absent from your body is to be present with Me.
Holy Spirit of Jesus Christ

In Heaven, Glory is evident everywhere. No matter where you go in Heaven, you will experience it! Glory is the atmosphere of Heaven!
Jean

(My recommendation to *anyone* who has a dream or a vision is to write down your dream or vision immediately and note every detail, even those that seem insignificant to you at the time. Later you may find those seemingly insignificant details have real meaning and are an important piece of the what you have been shown. GOD doesn't make mistakes. If He has given you a dream or a vision, there is purpose in it, so write it down even if you do not understand it and even if you do not remember it all. Trust GOD to reveal to you what He wants you to know and trust Him to do it in His timing. GOD can hold back from our memory the full vision if He desires it. Perhaps He desires to wait for an appointed time to bring the fullness of it back to you. So there are always going to be exceptions to writing down full dreams or visions. I have heard someone say that if we receive a vision from GOD, then we will remember it in detail, but I have not found that to be true in my experiences. Just as neither have I found it true in this, my trip to Heaven).

The Teaching

After my grand tour and I do mean *Grand Tour*, we went out into the courtyard to begin my lessons. Scrolls were brought to us. We sat at a table made of stone, not one that was not polished, but cut with the kind of a tool which gave it a large, sort of chiseled look around the edges. The benches matched it in style. It was really lovely. I was excited about being able to sit down at that table on one of its benches. I remember two stone tables, one out front and one out back. I do not remember which table was in the courtyard, but it might have been the round table in the courtyard. The courtyard is where I was first taught about the Psalms. The other table was rectangular and it was really lovely too. David is a good teacher. I knew to pay attention, although I found it hard to always concentrate due to where I was. After a while we changed location and sat at the table out front which was placed on the lush grass. The table was absolutely perfect! As David taught me on the Psalms he penned, I learned when, where and why he had written each one. It was very interesting to hear his reasons for writing each of them and feeling the way that he had. I kept thinking to myself, *you did that?!* And as embarrassing as it was, he would often answer me by saying, "Jean, I was just a man." I kept thinking, "Oh, ya. I forgot!" In Heaven they can hear our mind speaking just as clearly as the mouth. *Because David was as human as you and I, we can relate to David's trouble with the people he loved in his life, He had good relationships with those that he loved and later turned to become his enemies. How he hurt when they deceived him! He showed me which Psalms would help me in certain types of crisis situations.*

When he first began to teach me from the table outside, I didn't ask any questions, but when he asked if I had any questions, I remember having lots of them. It was always okay; he had plenty of answers. I remember him pausing at times to speak to the Father in prayer and receive help in answering something that I had asked. After lots of teaching on the Psalms at both tables he stopped and asked me if I was hungry, and something was brought for us to eat. I believe we were served by the angel that had been his original guardian angel on Earth, but I am not certain. I hope I have this part of the vision correct, I am doing my best. As the angel walked out toward us carrying our food, he smiled at me. I was so awed by the glory of the angel and so in awe at everything that I just looked away at first. When I smiled at the angel, I took a quick look at him again, and then quickly averted my eyes. They are glorious creatures, absolutely glorious! Heaven is a perfect surrounding for them. They seem to be males, but there is no feeling about sexuality towards them whatsoever. Your feelings toward them are completely pure (as are your feelings toward everyone there). He was a delight. I remember David speaking with him, and me saying something to him in reply to a question of his, but I was still so awed at being in the presence of and served by this glorious angelic creature, that I found it difficult to speak! I feel sure a barrage of questions must have hurled through my mind as he was walking away and then finally out of view.

David was very candid during his telling of why he had written each Psalms and whom they were about. I remember him telling me that he had written a particular one after either he had hurt his wife, Abigail(?), or did he say, she had hurt him. Obviously, he did have a recollection of his time on Earth. (I have to say for myself that I hope we don't remember all the wrong we have done forever! Seriously, I trust that GOD's Word is truth, "And GOD will wipe away every tear from their eyes; there shall be no more death, nor sorrow, nor crying. There shall be no more pain, for the former things have passed away." Then He who sat on the throne said, "Behold, I make all things new." And He said to me, "Write, for these words are true and faithful" (Revelation 21:4-5 NKJV). "And the ransomed of the Lord shall return and come to Zion with singing, and everlasting joy shall be upon their heads; they shall obtain joy and gladness, and sorrow and sighing shall flee away" (Isaiah 35:10 AMP). Those are promises I hold onto! Now back to David.) We spoke of those friends who had betrayed him and how he had gotten through those difficult times. It was all he could take when Jonathan died. He knew what it was like to lose the closest person in the world to him. The Bible tells us that he loved him more deeply than any woman. Now that's a special friendship! With GOD, he made it through. **He told me that there is much healing in *praises*. He said that people <u>can</u> worship their way well!**

If you stay in the Anointing long enough, sickness, which is a sidekick of death, has to leave. It simply cannot survive very long in the presence of GOD). So for anyone who is sick, worship till the glory falls on you and then keep at it as long and as often as you can until you get well. You will find that in worship you start to desire the Word and that causes a real hunger to know GOD to grow within you! The more you worship, the more you desire to know GOD, and the more you read His Word and get to know Him, the more your faith grows! The more your faith grows, the more Anointing is poured out through you and not only will you get healed, but others will be drawn to you and they will get healed too!

David's Worship

Finally, David and I walked back to the valley where I had first arrived, only this time we stopped in a section that was fairly narrow and the verdant plants that grew on its walls seemed to drip down its sides in luxuriant greens with splashes of color. It was breathtaking to see, but that was nothing in comparison to what I was about to witness. David said, "*This is how you WORSHIP the LORD! Watch me and never forget! This is how you WORSHIP the LORD!* " As he had repeated,

"*This is how you WORSHIP the LORD*" for the second time, his hands had gone up, palms upturned, and his elbows had raised to about shoulder level. It was then that *he turned his face upwards* and started to sing. He sang a song that I recognized as being in the Book of Psalms! I stood transfixed. *His whole countenance had changed. There was glory all over his face!* He was completely enraptured in worshiping GOD and *I was completely enraptured by the purity and beauty of perfect worship!* His whole being sang to the LORD.

This was what GOD was talking about in the Bible. This is what He desired His Church Body to be partakers of. Worship wasn't a one-sided affair. I understood now; it was pure communion with our most HOLY GOD! That was worship, you gave and GOD gave, you gave and GOD gave, it was a continual giving one to the other! It was beautiful! It was alive with Life! Like David said, "This is how you WORSHIP the LORD!" I wanted to WORSHIP like that with all of my being! I have never wanted anything as much as I wanted that in my whole life! When he finished he said, "*Never forget what you have learned today.*" Then he paused before adding, "*Teach others what you have been taught here!*" Each word was full of import, the depth of which I am sure I will only fully comprehend when I am someday in Heaven for my reward. David then told me it was time for me to go back. I started to say, "*No!*" And then in an instant, I was back in my bed.

The David that we referred to in the Bible as King David, but who now resides in the presence of a more glorious King, King Jesus, has instructed me according to the will of our Most Holy GOD to teach others to worship. I have taught a few people to worship the LORD, but I feel that I have many, many more to teach. I feel in need of a refresher course according to my natural mind, but it all comes back to you when you raise your hands in worship! Your being will cry out in worship and desire for worship, once you have had a taste of it! You can never get enough of it and yet it is sooooooo satisfying that you can *never* get too much of it! How could anyone get too much of pure Life? They can't! It is impossible! As we spend time in the Presence of GOD, life is restored to our natural body. Are you sick?

Praise your way into Worship. Are you discouraged? Praise your way into Worship. Are you lonely? Praise your way into Worship. You won't be lonely anymore. His Presence is Life and it cures all. Yes, all.

Won't you stop for just a little while, or longer and begin to praise and worship the LORD right there where you are? If you are in your home, why don't you find a quiet place with a door you can lock, just so you won't be interrupted? Worship can carry all your fears away as you spend time with the LORD. A spirit of fear will not linger in His Presence. Your mind is renewed in His Presence. You will be amazed to find the faith to believe that everything will turn out fine because you have laid all your cares in His hands. You will know that they are safe there. You will know that you can trust Him with your deepest secret. You will know that He loves you unconditionally and without measure. You will know what it is to be in the healing presence of the LORD. You will know the sound of His voice, the feel of his Spirit as He caresses your very heart and soul with a love so deep and so pure, no human love could ever compare! You will know where to go in the Word to get your answer. You will know what it is to be a child of the King! The more often that you get alone to worship, the more consistent will be your faith in your GOD and King! He is the LORD and no other is like Him, no other can be compared to Him! Come away with Him now, He is calling you! (To those of you in office buildings, it is alright to have silent worship, GOD is well able to hear your heart cries right where you are. He knows when you can't come away from your desk to be alone with Him)! Do you hear Him? He's calling you...*Come away with me! Even now, come away!*

> "I am waiting to bring you into new levels of Worship and Revelation. In My Presence is fullness of Joy!
> Your heart's deepest desire has always been for Me.
> My deepest desire has always been for you."
> **Holy Spirit of GOD**
>
> **The Helper**

WHAT JESUS BELIEVES

Today, as Holy Ghost filled Christians, we are all blessed with the Anointing to worship GOD. GOD loves us so much that He sent us His Son, Jesus. Jesus loves us so much that He gave His life in exchange for ours. The Bible teaches us that He loved us ere (before) we knew him. "But GOD demonstrates His own love toward us, in that while we were still sinners, Christ died for us" (Romans 5:8 NKJV). "For GOD so loved the world that He gave His only begotten Son, that whoever believes in Him should not perish but have everlasting life" (John 3:16 NKJV). "Simon, to whom He gave the name Peter;" (Mark 3:16 NKJV); Peter means rock. Every time Jesus called Peter's name, he was being strengthened in who he was! "Rock. Rock. Rock." Jesus loved him and Jesus prayed for him. In the end, (Peter) *Rock was solid for the Lord, his Rock!* (see Isaiah 32:1-2)

Jesus first poured out His love for all of mankind and was then loved in return by those with yielding hearts. He sent His Holy Spirit to abide in Temples made by the heart of GOD. As we read before, the first Temples to be resided in down here, after Jesus and John the Baptist, were the one hundred and twenty followers of Jesus who were waiting in that upper room for the dissension of someone called the Holy Spirit. They had never been filled with the Holy Spirit before and so they did not know what to expect. The way Holy Spirit came into the room with them was amazing and breathtaking. Just imagine yourself there on that day. It's a beautiful morning and the birds are singing outside. You've been waiting and praying and fellowshipping with the rest of the 120 in that upper room for 40 days ..."And in the day of the Pentecost being fulfilled, they were all with one accord at the same place, and there came suddenly out of the Heaven a sound as of a bearing violent breath, and it filled all the house where they were sitting, and there appeared to them divided tongues, as it were of fire; it sat also upon each one of them, and they were all filled with the Holy Spirit, and began to speak with other tongues, according as the Spirit was giving them to declare" (Acts 2:1-4 YLT98).

Can you imagine praying and praying for this Power, this Holy Spirit to be sent down, praying for you to do all of GOD's will and mostly asking GOD to help you to serve Him with all of your heart? All the while you are wondering and wondering what it will be like for all of you when GOD's Holy Spirit is on earth abiding with you. What will it be like when His Power shows up? What will happen? "Am I ready for this, GOD? Oh, GOD! Make me ready! Please make this human heart ready for what's coming!" I want to make Jesus smile when He looks on my heart and actions. Oh, how I miss Jesus! "Father, how will Your Holy Spirit arrive? How soon shall He..." *ROAR ...Whoosh... ROAR... The sound of mighty rushing wind that your mind compares to 100 storms all puts together can be heard RUSHING INTO THE ROOM! And this loud breath from Heaven is all around you and in you and all through you and over you as tongues of fire on your heads*; and then in an instant, you yourself and all in the room, once mere humans, are suddenly changed from the inside out and speaking in languages that you never learned to speak! Some around you are singing in beautiful languages that you cannot understand, but you KNOW that *it is the Promise! He has come! He has come!* This Holy Power of Heaven has arrived! Oh, praise GOD, He is here! He is Here and *He is in you now! He's taken residence in all of you!* Each face is shining with the radiance of a new love and fire is upon each of your heads...it's so much to take in! It's glorious! It's so glorious! You have never felt such Peace! You have never felt such Power! You want to go out and shout it from the rooftops that Jesus your King is risen and He IS the Savior of the World! Grace! You feel Grace like you have never experienced Grace before! This is what your Jesus felt! The feelings flooding you are beyond description! They are absolutely amazing and wonderful beyond adequate description! No wonder Jesus could love and give Himself so freely as He served the lost lambs of Israel. You feel like your feet are 10 feet off the ground and you have never Worshiped GOD or desired to Worship GOD like you do now! Everything in you is keyed in to Him! You understand His calling for you. It's all so clear now! You have eyes of love to see and ears to hear with now in a whole new way! It's like the Fire of GOD was just dropped into you. Oh, wait, that's right! He just moved in! The Fire of Heaven! You are one of those now carrying the Fire of Heaven! For a moment you stand quietly. You are in awe. Complete awe. The Breath (of Heaven) is so Holy that you have to fall prostrate on the ground. You are utterly undone. Oh, LORD, how majestic is Your name in all the earth! You abound in Grace and Mercy! Oh, Father, Father, Father! Oh, Jesus, Jesus, Jesus! Holy Spirit! Oh, H O L Y S P I R I T!!!

Everyone is laughing and crying and calling out upon the Name of the LORD as all extol His endless virtues! "Oh, Father GOD, You are Holy! You are so Holy! You are greatly to be praised! Let every creature great and small praise You, Father GOD!!! I love you more than I ever knew that it was possible to love anyone! This love...this love...*you know* this love! Jesus! Jesus walked down here in this love! No wonder He went away every night to pray! He wasn't just going away to pray, He was going to spend time with You, Father! You fall prostrate on the floor and continue to worship and laugh and cry. There's a puddle below your face of tears and snot and you don't care! I love You, Father! Jesus, oh, Jesus, I love you more today than I have ever been capable of! I'm not alone! He's here! You're here! Oh, Holy Spirit, how I love you! Thank You! Thank You! Thank You! The room is filled with beautiful songs and beautiful words, but best of all it's filled and you are filled with the most beautiful Person on earth, Holy Spirit... Now that's POWER! That's Love!

Jesus loves us so much and GOD loves us so much and the Holy Spirit loves us so much that even before They had created the Earth, They had a plan ready for our redemption and empowerment! HalleluYAH! Now that's "GOD!"

It is the same way with Him today. If we are to come to GOD, we must come to Him with yielded hearts, ready to love and be loved. He will give us the ability and He will show us the way! His love (agape: unconditional love) is the purest kind of love there is. It is perfect love. Don't be afraid, little lamb, and allow yourself be put off by fear. Remember, *your Shepherd has not given you unto a spirit of fear, but unto a Spirit, His precious Holy Spirit of POWER, LOVE, and a SOUND MIND!* (Ref. 2 Timothy 1:7). Allow the LORD to teach you today through His Word, including the *Song of Songs*, of His great love for you!

"When you focus on Truth, the lies are exposed and destroyed. My Word is Truth."
Holy Spirit

One of the Reasons That Jesus Is Called the Rose of Sharon
"Oh, What a Fragrance!"

Song of Songs 1:3 (AMP) [And she continues,] "The odor of your ointments is fragrant; your name is like perfume poured out. Therefore do the maidens love You." Did you know that the fragrance of GOD can be smelled in the natural? It's true! It is far more wonderful than any earthly flower or perfume I have ever experienced! In the above verse from Song of Songs where the bride says to her groom, '*the odor of your ointments is fragrant,*' this is in reference to the sweetness of GOD's manifest presence. He is indeed purely (wholly and completely) wonderful! This beautiful presence of the Holy Spirit ushers us into the manifest presence of GOD, where we want to fall to our knees and cry out *Abba, Father!* And the sweet name of *Jesus!*

"*Your name is like perfume poured out.*" Feeling a great surge of love for Him, "*Therefore do the maidens love You.*" We cry out from the depths of our spirit to Him (vs. 4). "Draw me! We will run after you!" Hearing your cries, the Lord will draw you even closer to Him, "The king brings me into his apartments!" Drawing us ever closer in His sweet presence, we give our declaration, 'We will be glad and rejoice in you!' Oh, the joy of being in His presence! Oh, the ecstasy of it all! "We will recall [when we were favored with] your love, more fragrant than wine. The upright [are not offended at your choice, but sincerely] love you." Oh, yes how we love you! You have given us Your New Wine, Your Holy Anointing and you have placed it in new wineskins, which are us, Your Holy Temples! We are filled to the brim with Your New Wine! We are filled to overflowing as Your sweet presence flows out of us and onto others! Your presence residing within us causes us to rejoice in great celebration! Once you have experienced being this close to GOD, you will <u>ever desire it</u> and nothing else can hold a candle to it! This is worship! This is Love in the purest sense!

"My beloved [shepherd] is to me like a [scent] bag of myrrh that lies in my bosom" (SS 1:13 AMP). The love we are experiencing at this moment in worship is like the headiest perfume and we keep it clutched to our breast (heart) because we cherish it so! When we get a really cherished gift at Christmas time or on some other special occasion, we will cry out in delight as we clutch our cherished possession to our bosom. That is how GOD desires that we love Him. He never asks from us, but what He is willing and able to help us to do. And no matter how much love we give Him, He will assuredly give us *more* back in return!

"Will you take time for Me, My Beloved?" Holy Spirit of GOD

Now, let's experience a few of the verses from his GOD's perspective. "Come away with me from Lebanon, my [promised] bride, come with me from Lebanon. Depart from the top of Amana, from the peak of Senir and Hermon, from the lions' dens, from the mountains of the leopards" [2 Cor. 11:2-3] (SS 4:8 AMP). Here, the Lord is calling us, His beloved, away from the world and all of its dangers, pains, and entrapments. He is calling us to come (apart) to Him! "You have ravished my heart *and* given me courage, my sister, my [promised] bride; you have ravished my heart *and* given me courage with one look from your eyes..." (SS 4:9). My heart is so captured by the words of the Lord to us here, "you have ravished my heart." Oh, to be so cherished and loved by someone that we are able to do that to their heart, and yet it is *His* heart we have done it to! "You have...given me courage with one look from your eyes..." Our eyes are mirrors of our hearts. When GOD looks in our eyes, He is looking into our hearts. To think that GOD receives courage (encouragement) from us, to pour out more of His love upon us, is too incredible for comprehension!

"How beautiful is your love, my sister, my [promised] bride! How much better is your love than wine! And the fragrance of your ointments than all spices!" [John 15:9; Rom. 8:35] (SS 4:10 AMP). Jesus finds our love [His promised Bride and sister] beautiful! He finds us more intoxicating than the finest wine! He finds the fragrance of our love more fragrant than all spices! We are on His mind and in His heart at all times. No one can ever love us the way our GOD can!

"You are My sweet desire. I have eternity for you."
Holy Spirit

"I am the good shepherd; and I know My sheep, and am known by My own." (John 10:14 NKJV)

WHAT JESUS BELIEVES

His Love...

His love is closer than a whisper.
His love is sweeter than the next breath I take.
His love is more satisfying than a stream in the desert.
His love is purer than the driven snow.
His love is more ageless than eternity.
It can span the whole Universe
His Love...

Jean V. Fahey
Inspired by the Holy Spirit
December 28, 1998

In His Presence

Jesus knew that there was healing in GOD's presence. He knew that there was strength to be had in GOD's presence, He knew there was fresh infilling of power in His Father's presence, but He also knew the joy of the awesome oneness they shared together as He worshiped His Father! When people stood around Jesus, it was the *Power* that we refer to as *the Anointing of GOD* that they experienced. It is what drew people to Him. His words were Life and they were Power. His words were GOD's Words and that made them completely Spiritual. They (the people) came again and again and again, not even knowing why. *He's interesting!* they'd say. *He speaks like no other we have ever heard. What is it about him? What is it about this man?*

What they did not understand is that they came because their spirit man was fed each time Jesus taught. He did nothing and said nothing except according to the will of the Father, and since *They* (GOD the Father, Son, and Holy Spirit) created each human being with an eternal spirit (from an eternal Spirit), He was communing with them Spirit to spirit. Sadly, hardheartedness has always been a problem for mankind and the human soul often gets in the way of eternal life with GOD. Many a person has gone to Hell because his head kept getting in the way of his heart by trying to analyze GOD and His free plan of salvation.

In order to continue to walk in victory, we must continually follow and obey GOD in all things. Just as Paul describes beating his body into submission in order to win, so must we. Paul didn't allow his human desires to dictate what he did. He compared it to a race that we must run as if to win the prize. He taught this in hopes that none would be snared by the things of the flesh and in so doing lose the prize that they had obtained in Christ Jesus. "Am I not an apostle? Am I not free? Have I not seen Jesus Christ our Lord? Are you not my work in the Lord? If I am not an apostle to others, yet doubtless I am to you. For you are the seal of my apostleship in the Lord. My defense to those who examine me is this: Do we have no right to eat and drink? Do we have no right to take along a believing wife, as do also the other apostles, the brothers of the Lord, and Cephas? Or is it only Barnabas and I who have no right to refrain from working? Who ever goes to war at his own expense? Who plants a vineyard and does not eat of its fruit? Or who tends a flock and does not drink of the milk of the flock? Do I say these things as a mere man? Or does not the law say the same also? For it is written in the law of Moses, "You shall not muzzle an ox while it treads out the grain." Is it oxen God is concerned about? Or does He say it altogether for our sakes? For our sakes, no doubt, this is written, that he who plows should plow in hope, and he who threshes in hope should be partaker of his hope. If we have sown spiritual things for you, is it a great thing if we reap your material things? If others are partakers of this right over you, are we not even more? Nevertheless we have not used this right, but endure all things lest we hinder the gospel of Christ. Do you not know that those who minister the holy things eat of the things of the temple, and those who serve at the altar partake of the offerings of the altar? Even so the Lord has commanded that those who preach the gospel should live from the gospel. But I have used none of these things, nor have I written these things that it should be done so to me; for it would be better for me to die than that anyone should make my boasting void. For if I preach the gospel, I have nothing to boast of, for necessity is laid upon me; yes, woe is me if I do not preach the gospel! For if I do this willingly, I have a reward; but if against my will, I have been entrusted with a stewardship. What is my reward then? That when I preach the gospel, I may present the gospel of Christ without charge, that I may not abuse my authority in the gospel. For though I am free from all men, I have made myself a servant to all, that I might win the more; and to the Jews I became as a Jew, that I might win Jews; to those who are under the law, as under the law, that I might win those who are under the law; to those who are without law, as without law (not being without law toward God, but under law toward Christ), that I might win those who are without law; to the weak I became as weak, that I might win the weak. I have become all things to all men, that I might by all means save some. Now this I do for the gospel's sake, that I may be partaker of it with you. Do you not know that those who run in a race all run, but one receives the prize? Run in such a way that you may obtain it. And everyone who competes for the prize is temperate in all things. Now they do it to obtain a perishable crown, but we for an imperishable crown. Therefore I run thus: not with uncertainty. Thus I fight: not as one who beats the air. But I discipline my body and bring it into subjection, lest, when I have preached to others, I myself should become disqualified." (1 Corinthians 27 NKJV)

In this race, the fight is truly on as we discipline our bodies and bring them into subjection, so that, when we have preached to others, we ourselves should not become disqualified. When we run the race, we run to win the prize! Part of this winning is the win over our flesh nature. It isn't called flesh for nothing! It is totally fleshy in attitude.

Getting our flesh to sit down so that we can worship the Lord can be a real fight. <u>Our spirit, which is now saved, wants to commune with GOD, our flesh, which will never be saved, wants to do the things that serve self.</u> Starting off with praise lifts our spirits and ushers us into worship; staying in worship ushers us into deeper worship; staying in deeper worship ushers us into deep worship. Deep worship is that place where our spirit most longs to be. Deep worship is that place where our spirit communes with GOD and receives deep revelation from His heart. As you begin to praise, you may find that your busy day is talking to you and your mind is a million miles away from worship. This can lead to frustration, which is an open door for discouragement and self-pity (all actions and traits of our *flesh*). Don't give up! Making a little mental list of things that you are truly thankful to GOD for can help you get over the roadblock of flesh. Fortunately for us, when we are beginners at worshiping GOD, He often graces us with His presence just because we took the time to show up. <u>Don't get discouraged</u>, with consistent training, our flesh goes under quite easily.

The Word declares in Nehemiah 8:10, "...for the joy of the LORD is your strength."

GOD taught David to rejoice before the LORD with psalms and hymns and spiritual songs. Let's let ourselves imagine for a bit and go back in time, back to the time of shepherds on a lonely hillside when King David was a boy...

"Go to sleep little lamb," David says, gently stroking the fur of the little creature he cradles tenderly within his slender boyish arms. The lamb softly bleats a reply of submission and lays its little head down trustingly against its small shepherd. Smiling, the boy looks up to the starry sky and once again he tries to count them. Giving up in awe a short time later, a quiet song of praise bursts from his youthful lips.

"Behold, bless the Lord, All you servants of the Lord, Who by night stand in the house of the Lord! Lift up your hands in the sanctuary, and bless the Lord. The Lord who made Heaven and Earth Bless you from Zion!" (Psalm 134 NKJV). [Maybe this was written in the man-made sanctuary or maybe it really was written in a GOD built sanctuary under the stars!]

[Imagine] Tenderly, he lays the little lamb down by the base of an old Olive tree. He will sleep close by the little lamb to ensure its protection. He doesn't worry about protection for himself. Kneeling down on his bed, he lifts his hands Heavenward and as his eyes again span the Heavens, he prays in faith, "The Lord is my shepherd; I shall not want. He makes me to lie down in green pastures; He leads me beside the still waters. He restores my soul; He leads me in the paths of righteousness for His name's sake. Yea, though I walk through the valley of the shadow of death, I will fear no evil; <u>for You are with me</u>; Your rod and Your staff, they comfort me. You prepare a table before me in the presence of my enemies; You anoint my head with oil; My cup runs over. Surely goodness and mercy shall follow me All the days of my life; and I will dwell in the house of the Lord Forever" (Psalms 23:1-6 NKJV). Can you hear the voice of the young David as he prayed?

"The Lord said to my Lord, "Sit at My right hand, till I make Your enemies Your footstool" " (Psalms 110:1 NKJV). David knew that his help was in the LORD and only in the LORD. He learned not to make the mistake of trusting in the arm of flesh! Although many of his lessons seemed hard, some were the reality of the consequences of the choices that he chose to make. GOD, in His infinite mercy and wisdom, has written them down, so that you and I can *learn from them* instead of *repeating them.* David also penned songs of deliverance. His heart was thankful for the deliverances he received as time and time again as the LORD GOD delivered him from his enemies. Can you imagine him bursting out in song after escaping King Saul? How his heart must have rejoiced in the GOD of his Salvation. David, the man, ever grateful for the mercy of the LORD, in that He didn't punish him as he deserved, according to the sins he committed. Even his wife, Bathsheba, the woman who was in an adulterous relationship with King David (prior to becoming his wife after the death of her husband, Uriah), is shown to have acquired Wisdom. Read Proverbs 31, the letter that she wrote to their son, King Solomon! Isn't it incredible to see that GOD can so change a heart that the same person isn't really the same person at all! Now, that's reason to worship!

"Wisdom is the gateway to joy."
Holy Spirit

7

Sharing the Vision

"...I am the Root and Offspring of David, the Bright and Morning Star." (Revelation 22:16) "And the Spirit and the bride say, "Come!" And let him who hears say, "Come!" And let him who thirsts come. Whoever desires, let him take the water of life freely." (Revelation 22:17)

Jesus is coming back for one Bride, not many Brides. GOD is calling the Church to lay down denominations and pick up unity of Spirit. We are one in GOD. One Body of Christ and as such we need to all share the same vision. Many parts, sharing and working together to complete the (One) vision. "Sharing the vision" means that the Church is sharing in the same vision that Jesus has for this world. It doesn't mean that we backbite one another for <u>Love doesn't backbite and Love doesn't have a critical spirit</u>. "You know, *they're Methodist!*" Or "Well, *those Baptists* don't believe the way we do!" Or "They are Catholics and you know what *they* believe!" It matters not the denominational name, division is division and Jesus said, *a house divided cannot stand.* We see Jesus' heart for us in this beautiful and powerful prayer to the Father, "I do not pray for these alone, but also for those who will believe in Me through their word; **that they all may be one**, as You, Father, are in Me, and I in You; **that they also may be one in Us**, that the world may believe that You sent Me. And the glory which You gave Me I have given them, **that they may be one just as We are One**:" *We will never be walking as one with GOD and shining with His glory (glorious love) if we are lots of little separates running around with different beliefs. As separates we cannot operate in the fullness of the power GOD has planned for the*

Church in the end time. In order to walk in the fullness of His Power (His Anointing), we must be One Body with One Head. We cannot serve 33,000 different Shepherds. There is only One and He is Jehovah Rohi (The LORD is my Shepherd). To walk as ONE, we must have the same beliefs that Jesus has. "**I in them, and You in Me; that they may be made perfect in one, and that the world may know that You have sent Me, and have loved them as You have loved Me**" (John 17:20-23 NKJV). How will the world know that He has loved us as He has loved Jesus if it doesn't show? GOD is powerful. Jesus showed that by example. How powerful does the Church look to the world right now?

Now that the *Light of the World* is seated in Heaven at the right hand of the Father and Holy Spirit has been sent down to earth to *us,* it becomes the responsibility of the Church to be peacekeepers within the body of Christ by living the example and by speaking out and up when necessary. There is no special seating or category in Heaven for Baptist, Methodist, Lutheran, Assembly of GOD or any other denomination. There is only one Body, of One Spirit, United in Love. This Love enables us to be a 'bright light' like the city on the hill that could not be hidden. "You are the Light of the world. A city that is set on a hill cannot be hidden" (Matthew 5:14 NKJV). Jesus has made a way for His Light to shine through us into the darkness of this world for all of mankind to see. He wants us to light the way for others to find eternal salvation through His love and sacrifice. *He wants His love story to be told* over every airwave, through every communication device, and wherever mankind dwells upon this Earth. We need to get this message into the densest jungles and into the darkest boardrooms! It is a beacon of hope to a lost and dying world. Why is it that it is usually *much* easier to convert a poor man in the jungle than a rich man in the boardroom? It's simple. While the jungle man sees the vulnerability of his own soul, the man in the boardroom often sees the ability of himself to supply his own wants and needs. The wealthy man in that well-lit boardroom is in as much darkness as that native jungle man was *before* he gave his life to Jesus. He just cannot see it yet, for in the natural he does not want for anything in his life. When the jungle man gets sick with a disease that the world says is incurable, he knows where to go! He believes with simple faith that the same great GOD Who created him is well able to remove the disease that is plaguing him! While the man in the boardroom, who has just received the prognosis for a similarly incurable disease, runs to all the doctors that he can afford! What is he going to do when all that money he has earned has run out and the disease is still plaguing him? He is left hopeless. Money *cannot* buy everything. This man needs Jesus.

We need to shout it from the housetops and from the mountain tops! *We need to share His love in the alleys of the ghettos and in the apartment complexes of the rich and famous!* There isn't anyone, not anyone at all, who doesn't need Jesus and His love. If we don't share the message of life that Jesus had somebody share with us, then when we stand in front of the Throne of GOD, what will we give in answer to GOD? There won't be any excuse at all for us not having spread the good news. It is a story of love, so simple, that even a child can understand it and be saved; and yet it is a story so profound that the wisest of men could never get to the end of all of the profound wisdom and knowledge it contains!

The Bible is a story about life and love, and who we are and can be. It is a story that never grows old because it is *LIFE* and everlastingly *ALIVE* with it! He is the giver of *LIFE*. *LIFE* is the Word of GOD. He [LIFE] cares about our tomorrows and todays. He cares about the tomorrows and todays of every lost sinner too! His mission on Earth was to spread the unconditional love of GOD, His Father. His mission was to tell them that there IS a way of escape from eternal damnation for them; there is a way to get out from under the heavy bondage of sin and shame! His mission was to show them His Father, which was to show them...love, love, love, unmerited grace, and favor. Remember earlier when we read in the Word where Jesus answers Philip, *'He who has seen Me has seen the Father?'* (Ref. John 14:9 NKJV). Can the world say the same thing about you and me? Can our family's say the same thing about you and me? When they see us, do they see Jesus and the love of the Father? If not, right now is the perfect time to confess it to GOD and get a fresh start. "There is therefore now no condemnation to those who are in Christ Jesus, who do not walk according to the flesh, but according to the Spirit" (Romans 8:1 NKJV). Ask GOD to not only forgive you for not being a good example of His love but *ask Him to help you to be a good example of His love, ask Him to fill you anew with the Holy Spirit!* You will feel refreshed in your heart and ready to take on the world again!

If you have never received the Baptism of the Holy Spirit, read Acts 2 and ask GOD to fill you with the Holy Spirit with the evidence of tongues. Remember, Jesus told His own disciples not to go out of Jerusalem, but to wait until the Holy Spirit had descended from on high and filled them with POWER! " `And, lo, I do send the promise of My Father upon you, but ye -- abide ye in the city of Jerusalem till **ye be clothed with Power from on high.**' And He led them forth without -- unto Bethany, and having lifted up his hands He did bless them, and it came to pass, in his blessing them, He was parted from them, and was borne up to the Heaven; and they, having bowed before him, did turn back to Jerusalem with great joy, and were continually in the temple, praising and blessing GOD. Amen" (Luke 24:49-53 YLT98). If Jesus told his disciples not to go out without the Holy Spirit, then you and I need to be clothed with power too! The Holy Spirit is *our* **Power *(dunamis)*.** The word for power in the Greek that is used here is **dunamis**. We've looked at it before, but let's take another look.

Dunamis (doo'-nam-is) is: from force (lit. or fig.); special miraculous power (usually by implication a miracle itself); ability, abundance, meaning, might (-ily, -y, -y deed), (worker of) miracle(-s), power, strength, violence, mighty (wonderful) work. [See the New Strong's Complete Dictionary of Bible Words].

The **dunamis** of the Holy Spirit can be said to be: <u>a force of special miraculous power, the ability of abundant meaningful mighty deeds, a worker of miraculous power in strength and violent mighty wonderful works!</u> (No commas!) Therefore, we have ***dunamis*** <u>***by the Holy Spirit*** *to the pulling down of strongholds!*</u> Conclusively, if we have been baptized into Holy Spirit, we have **dunamis**. If we have **dunamis**...we have a force of special miraculous power, the ability of abundant meaningful mighty deeds, a worker of miraculous power in strength and violent mighty wonderful works!

"For the weapons of our warfare are not physical [weapons of flesh and blood], but they are mighty before GOD for the overthrow and destruction of strongholds" (2 Corinthians 10:4 AMP). "Put on GOD's whole armor [the armor of a heavy-armed soldier which GOD supplies], that you may be able successfully to stand up against [all] the strategies and the deceits of the devil. For we are not wrestling with flesh and blood [contending only with physical opponents], but against the despotisms, against the powers, against [the master spirits who are] the world rulers of this present darkness, against the spirit forces of wickedness in the heavenly (supernatural) sphere. Therefore put on GOD's complete armor, that you may be able to resist and stand your ground on the evil day [of danger], and, having done all [the crisis demands], to stand [firmly in your place]. Stand therefore [hold your ground], having tightened the belt of truth around your loins and having put on the breastplate of integrity and of moral rectitude and right standing with GOD, and having shod your feet in preparation [to face the enemy with the firm-footed stability, the promptness, and the readiness produced by the good news] of the Gospel of peace [Isa. 52:7]. Lift up over all the [covering] shield of saving faith, upon which you can quench all the flaming missiles of the wicked [one]. And take the helmet of salvation and the sword that the Spirit wields, which is the Word of GOD. Pray at all times (on every occasion, in every season) in the Spirit, with all [manner of] prayer and entreaty. To that end keep alert and watch with strong purpose and perseverance, interceding in behalf of all the saints (GOD's consecrated people)" (Ephesians 6:11-18 AMP).

Let's read 2 Corinthians 10:4 AMP with this helpful definition included just for clarity. "For the weapons of our warfare are not physical [weapons of flesh and blood], but they are mighty {a force of special miraculous power, the ability of abundant meaningful mighty deeds, a worker of miraculous power in strength and violent mighty wonderful work, which is the Holy Spirit in us!} before GOD for the overthrow and destruction of strongholds."

Jesus said, "And from the days of John the Baptist until now the Kingdom of Heaven suffers violence, and the violent take it by force" (Matthew 11:12 NKJV). Let's read another translation of this verse. "From the time of John the Baptizer until now, the Kingdom of Heaven has been forcefully advancing, and forceful people have been seizing it" (Matthew 11:12 GW). GOD has called each of us as faithful soldiers to forcefully advance the Kingdom by seizing the opportunity and bring in His harvest! satan comes at the lost as a wolf, bear and lion would at a flock without a shepherd. This is why *GOD wants us to forcefully advance and bring in the harvest as quickly as possible!* The quicker we bring in the harvest, the more souls that are saved. **We can be forceful** (violent) **by the Holy Spirit** to the pulling down of spiritual strongholds. It isn't as if satan is going to willingly give us anything! In using the Word of GOD and the name of Jesus, we are told that he (satan) must let go of those things we tell him to let go of. Remember the following Scripture? "Most certainly I tell you, whatever things you bind on earth will have been bound in Heaven, and whatever things you release on earth will have been released in Heaven" (Matthew 18:18 WEB). This verse shows the parameters to our legal rights as GOD's children. It lines up perfectly with Jesus and how He taught His disciples to pray. "In this manner, therefore, pray: <u>Our Father in Heaven, Hallowed be Your name. Your Kingdom come. Your will be done on Earth as it is in Heaven</u>. Give us this day our daily bread. And forgive us our debts, as we forgive our debtors. And do not lead us into temptation, but deliver us from the evil one. For Yours is the Kingdom and the Power and the Glory forever. Amen. For if you forgive men their trespasses, your Heavenly Father will also forgive you. But if you do not forgive men their trespasses, neither will your Father forgive your trespasses" (Matthew 6:9-15 NKJV). A clearly-defined perimeter leaves no room for guessing. GOD's Word is our clearly-defined perimeter.

WHAT JESUS BELIEVES

We need to know the Word in order to be able to operate victoriously in spiritual matters. We need to know what our rights and weapons are: He's given us His authority to go and do as He did and **we use the same weapons that Jesus used** while He walked on the Earth. We need to enforce our rights and it will take using GOD's spiritual weaponry to do so. Remember, *satan only comes to kill, steal and destroy.* **By operating in faith and speaking the word (GOD's Truth), you become equipped to handle anything that the enemy can throw at you; death, sickness, disease, poverty, oppression of any kind, addictions, anything and everything satan can throw at you, you can defeat. The Word belongs to every Christian, but like a military arsenal of weaponry (on earth), you need to go inside the arsenal of the Word and get your spiritual weapons out in order to prevail over the adversary. We don't go swinging around an invisible sword, we speak the Word (see Psalm 103:20) and angels step in and complete our spiritual battle. Truth always prevails. Being in relationship with GOD makes you undefeatable as long as you follow His directions. GOD is a perfect Commander. <u>satan</u> is not going to back off if you don't use your spiritual weapons.** I heard a man of GOD say something to the effect of, "Can you imagine satan coming to you to attack you and you saying, "satan, the Word of GOD says that...wait just a minute while I look that up! But you really can't do what you were doing because...it says right here...just a minute...Well, I know it's in here somewhere!" *He is not going to hold off the attack while you hunt down that Scripture in the Bible to fight him with! You need to be armed and dangerous. You need to already have the Word inside of you when satan comes at you* and *you'll be ready with the Sword!* "<u>satan! It is written, No weapon that is formed against me will prosper</u>! (Ref. Isaiah 54:17).
Jesus already defeated you and you have to go now!"

As good soldiers of the Kingdom of GOD, we must stay close to our Commander-in -Chief, and follow His every leading as if lives depended on it, for they do. Lives and souls are at stake here. *We must keep advancing at all times bringing in the harvest and keeping on the Armor of GOD!* We know that it isn't as if satan is going to

WHAT JESUS BELIEVES

willingly fall back or let go of anyone! *In using the Word of GOD and the name of Jesus, satan must let go of those things we command him to let go of, but <u>we need to know and understand how to use the keys of the Kingdom, and what they are in order for us to operate in the full authority and power of GOD as Jesus did. That all comes with relationship. The better we know GOD and Jesus, the better we will operate in our spiritual weaponry and gifts.</u>*

What are the keys of the Kingdom of Heaven? The keys of the Kingdom of Heaven are the Word(s) of GOD. Utilizing the *Keys of the Kingdom* is utilizing GOD's authority; and <u>ALL of His Power is in that AUTHORITY</u>. To the mortal mind, that is impossible to grasp. To the one that has the mind of Christ, it becomes perfectly clear that as a child of GOD and a joint heir with Christ Jesus, OUR FATHER IN HEAVEN IS <u>ALL</u> POWERFUL AND HE <u>IS</u> AUTHORITY. HIS POWER CANNOT BE SEPARATED FROM HIS AUTHORITY AND HIS AUTHORITY CANNOT BE SEPARATED FROM HIS POWER. THEY ARE ONE AND THE SAME. THEY ARE FATHER GOD, LORD OF ALL CREATION! *TO HAVE HIS WORD IS TO HAVE HIS WORD.* TO HAVE HIS WORD IS TO HAVE HIS AUTHORITY. TO HAVE HIS AUTHORITY IS TO HAVE HIS POWER. HIS WORD, HIS AUTHORITY, HIS POWER ARE ONE AND THE SAME. THEY ARE THE KEYS TO THE KINGDOM.

WHAT WE NEED TO LEARN IS HOW TO UTILIZE THESE KEYS. THERE ISN'T ANY SCHOOL THAT CAN TEACH THAT OTHER THAN THE SCHOOL OF THE HOLY SPIRIT AND THIS REQUIRES TIME IN THE CLASSROOM WITH THE HOLY SPIRIT IN THE WORD OF GOD. Again, Jesus said, "**I will give you the keys of the Kingdom of Heaven; and whatever you bind (declare to be improper and unlawful) on earth must be what is already bound in Heaven; and whatever you loose (declare lawful) on earth must be what is already loosed in Heaven**" [Isa. 22:22] (Matthew 16:19 AMP). THEREFORE WE KNOW THAT IF IT IS ALREADY IN ACTION BY GOD IN HEAVEN, WE HAVE THE AUTHORITY TO UTILIZE THE KEYS OF THE KINGDOM, THE WORD OF GOD, TO BRING IT INTO ACTION ON EARTH BECAUSE GOD HAS AUTHORIZED IT!

WHAT JESUS BELIEVES

Know the Word of GOD. Knowing what the *keys* are IS KNOWING IN WHOM WE LIVE AND MOVE AND HAVE OUR BEING. WE BECOME BEAUTIFUL REFLECTIONS OF WHO HE IS, LIGHTHOUSES UPON A HILL! WE KNOW OUR AUTHORITY, AND WE LIVE AND MOVE AND HAVE OUR BEING IN THAT AUTHORITY, IN HIM, THE LIVING WORD! THIS AUTHORITY IS WHAT GAVE JESUS THE RIGHT TO SAY AND DO THE THINGS THAT HE DID WHILE HE WALKED THIS EARTH. satan KNEW JESUS HAD GOD'S AUTHORITY AND he HAD TO BOW TO THE LIVING WORD OF GOD, THE AUTHORITY AND ALL RIGHTEOUS POWER, EVERY TIME. When Jesus could do no mighty works in a place, it was because of their lack of faith, their lack of believing, thus their not receiving the power of the Almighty GOD to perform healing, miracles, and deliverance for them. *They had more faith in their sicknesses, diseases, and demons than they did in Almighty GOD!* That's sad. Therefore, satan continued to rule and reign as a thief and a murderer in their lives [inclusive of their minds and bodies].

Negative faith works the same as positive faith. **Jesus said**, "The thief comes only in order to steal and kill and destroy. I came that they may have and enjoy life, and have it in abundance (to the full, till it overflows)" (John 10:10 AMP). Only by acting on FAITH IN OUR FATHER'S WORD, WHICH IS HIS AUTHORITY AND HIS RIGHTEOUS POWER, AS WE SPEAK, LIVE, MOVE AND HAVE OUR BEING; FAITH BUILT UP READING THE WORD, SPENDING TIME IN PRAYER WITH THE LORD, SPEAKING AND LISTENING TO HIM, AND OBEYING HIS DIRECTIVES (His official and authoritative instruction, His moral and ethical directives; because He, our Commander, is confident, able to be trusted, accurate, true and reliable; for whom we should *always* have great respect, complete trust, and prompt obedience!) THEN AND ONLY THEN CAN WE LIVE OUR LIVES AS JESUS DID.

Why is it the Bible says, "So then faith comes by hearing, and hearing by the Word of GOD?" (Romans 10:17 NKJV). Why? Because we come to know Who He is and who we are in Him as we incorporate and absorb the Word, which will always take us to a higher level of understanding the pure and perfect truth of all things. It's all accomplished in Holy Spirit School. "But the anointing which you have received from Him abides in you, and you do not need that anyone teach you; but as the same anointing teaches you concerning all things, and is true, and is not a lie, and just as it has taught you, you will abide in Him" (1 John 2:27 NKJV). "Therefore I make known to you that no one speaking by the Spirit of GOD calls Jesus accursed, and no one can say that Jesus is Lord except by the Holy Spirit" (1 Corinthians 12:3 NKJV). The Holy Spirit made known, revealed to us, GOD as our LORD and Savior (revealed the Father and His Son, Jesus Christ, to us). Not a one of us came to know and accept Jesus as our LORD AND SAVIOR without direct drawing and revelation by the precious Holy Spirit of GOD. "However, when He, the Spirit of truth, has come, He will guide you into all truth; for He will not speak on His own authority, but whatever He hears He will speak; and He will tell you things to come" (John 16:13 NKJV). As the Holy Spirit gives us the message that has been given to Him by the Father, "...He, the Spirit of Truth...He will announce and declare to you the things that are to come [that will happen in the future]" (John 16:13 AMP).

It is vital that we know the Word of GOD, in which we live and move and have our being. It isn't about memorization. It's about knowing the Word. It's about living the Living Word, which in Itself is in constant action (He is a continually creative Zoe (life) force, which is always in complete agreement with the Father and the Son, as it is GOD and it is His power. As said, he (satan) is not going to hold off an attack while we hunt down *our key Scriptures* in the Bible to fight him with. If we are not armed with the Word, satan is still going to proceed forward with his evil plan. <u>We need to have the Word already inside of us</u>. That way, when he (the thief, murderer, and destroyer) comes, we'll be ready with the *Sword of the Spirit!*

"Miracles are Love in action!"
Holy Spirit

Where are the miracles? *Lack of time spent in the GOD's Holy Word and prayer accounts for the lack of real miracles abounding throughout the Church Body today.* There isn't any sickness or any disease in Heaven. The Word (GOD'S AUTHORITY) declares *by His stripes we are healed* and *Jesus took away our sins and gave us His righteousness* [Ref Isaiah 53:5-2 Corinthians 5:21]; therefore, everyone in the Kingdom of GOD has the right to be healed and walk in perfect health, and everyone has the right to be completely cleansed and forgiven of every sin. **It should be the 'norm' in the Church to see people get saved, healed, and delivered each time we open the doors! Miracles should abound!** It shouldn't be the accepted way of things for us to limp around smiling and grimacing, "Oh, I am just glorifying GOD by my silent suffering."

Hogwash!!! And *No! No! No!* Jesus already went like a lamb to the slaughter, so you and I can be free of sickness and disease! Glorifying GOD by staying sick and suffering is just another of *satan's lies* to keep the Church ineffective. satan knows that the second that we as a (unified and complete) Body of Christ get the revelation that GOD is Who He says He is and will do for us all that He has promised to do for us, that he, satan, is completely through. (It's his death knell that the end is upon him!) *He (satan) won't have a way in as we stand united.* "But the Pharisees, hearing it, said, This Man drives out demons only by and with the help of Beelzebub, the prince of demons. And knowing their thoughts, He said to them, any kingdom that is divided against itself is being brought to desolation and laid waste, and no city or house divided against itself will last or continue to stand. And if satan drives out satan, he has become divided against himself and disunified; how then will his kingdom last or continue to stand? And if I drive out the demons by [help of] Beelzebub, by whose [help] do your sons drive them out? For this reason they shall be your judges. But if it is by the Spirit of GOD that I drive out the demons, then the Kingdom of GOD has come upon you [before you expected it]" (Matthew 12:24-28 AMP). satan's time on Earth will be through before he expects it! *United we stand, divided they fall!*

Hogwash *[hog·wash (hôgwôsh, -wsh, hg-) n. 1. Worthless, false, or ridiculous speech or writing; nonsense. 2. Garbage fed to hogs; swill (as defined by* thefreedictionary.com *)].*

WHAT JESUS BELIEVES

GOD has commissioned me to write this book because <u>He has commissioned you and me, as Christians, to get the Word out, His Word. Jesus saves! Jesus heals! Jesus delivers</u>! If He changes His mind, which He won't, He'll let you know! He taught you how to do it by not only infilling you with Himself but by a perfect manual too. It's called the Bible! People are literally *dying* to know what you know. Meaning, of course, that they are dying *because they don't know what you know!* <u>We need to get out the message today!</u> <u>The message that tells the World that Jesus is a Savior who loves them</u>! *That GOD is not looking for a reason to "thump" them over the head!* **And that the Holy Spirit is here for <u>everybody</u> who wants Him!**

Again, Jesus loves! Jesus saves! Jesus forgives! And that is just the beginning of a life with Jesus! Let's get out there to the highways and byways and tell this old world that WE'VE GOT THE ANSWER! We've got the answer <u>for peace of mind</u>. We've got the answer for <u>perfect health</u>. We've got the answer to <u>prospering at all that we put our hands to do</u>. We've got the answer to <u>the future and what it holds</u>. We've got their answer to <u>a sound mind</u>. We have every answer for <u>every problem they have had, could have and will have! And His name is Jesus and He is the WORD</u>! We've got to get the Word out, His WORD! His Truth will save their life...eternally!

Note: to those looking for world peace, there isn't going to be any real and lasting world peace until Jesus wipes away every tear...Jesus is the Prince of Peace and our constant peace. It says "GOD will wipe away every tear from their eyes; and death shall be no more, neither shall there be anguish (sorrow and mourning) nor grief nor pain any more, for the old conditions and the former order of things have passed away" [Isa. 25:8; 35:10] (Revelation 21:4 AMP).

"Now I saw a new Heaven and a new Earth, for the first Heaven and the first Earth had passed away. Also there was no more sea. Then I, John, saw the holy city, New Jerusalem, coming down out of Heaven from GOD, prepared as a bride adorned for her husband. And I heard a loud voice from Heaven saying, "Behold, the tabernacle of GOD is with men, and He will dwell with them, and they shall be His people. GOD Himself will be with them and be their GOD. And GOD will wipe away every tear from their eyes; there shall be no more death, nor sorrow, nor crying. There shall be no more pain, for the former things have passed away." Then He Who sat on the throne said, "Behold, I make all things new." And He said to me, "Write, for these words are true and faithful." And He said to me, "It is done! I am the Alpha and the Omega, the Beginning and the End. I will give of the fountain of the water of life freely to him who thirsts. He who overcomes shall inherit all things, and I will be his GOD and he shall be My son" (Revelation 21:1-7 NKJV).

"Abide in Me, and I in you. As the branch cannot bear fruit of itself, unless it abides in the vine, neither can you, unless you abide in Me. I am the vine, you are the branches. He who abides in Me, and I in him, bears much fruit; for without Me you can do nothing" (John 15:4-5 NKJV). One of the fruits that abiding in Jesus provides is peace, as He is Peace.

GOD has called us to be overcomers. He is well able to keep us in perfect peace through every trial and tribulation, without exception.

- "You will keep him in perfect peace, whose mind is stayed on You, because he trusts in You" (Isaiah 26:3 NKJV). He is Zoe (Life) and He is Peace; He is Zoe Peace.
- "Peace I leave with you, My peace I give to you; not as the world gives do I give to you. Let not your heart be troubled, neither let it be afraid" (John 14:27 NKJV).
- "For GOD has not given us a spirit of fear, but of power and of love and of a sound mind" (2 Timothy 1:7 NKJV).
- "He who does not love does not know GOD, for GOD is love" (1 John 4:8 NKJV).
- "There is no fear in love [dread does not exist], but full-grown (complete, perfect) love turns fear out of doors and expels every

trace of terror! For fear brings with it the thought of punishment, and [so] he who is afraid has not reached the full maturity of love [is not yet grown into love's complete perfection]. We love Him, because He first loved us" (1 John 4:18, 19 AMP).

- "There is no fear in love; but perfect love casts out fear, because fear involves torment. But he who fears has not been made perfect in love. We love Him because He first loved us" (1 John 4:18, 19 NKJV).
- "Being confident of this very thing, that He who has begun a good work in you will complete it until the day of Jesus Christ" (Philippians 1:6 NKJV).
- Whether we live or die, He is able to bring us out victorious!
- "And they overcame him by the blood of the Lamb and by the word of their testimony, and they did not love their lives to the death" (Revelation 12:11 NKJV).
- **"Beloved, let us love one another, for love is of GOD; and everyone who loves is born of GOD and knows GOD. He who does not love does not know GOD, for GOD is love"** (1 John 4:7-8 NKJV)

"Stay inside My Spirit of Grace
And I will let you see My face.
And yet My face you have already seen
For when you see My Beloved
You see Me!"
Holy Spirit of Jesus

What Are We Eating?

"But he said to them, "I have food to eat that you know nothing about." "My food," said Jesus, "is to do the will of Him who sent me and to finish His work." (John 4:32, 34 NIV)

"And He said to them, be careful what you are hearing. The measure [of thought and study] you give [to the truth you hear] will be the measure [of virtue and knowledge] that comes back to you – and more [besides] will be given to you who hear" (Mark 4:24 AMP).

Good or bad, what we continually feed ourselves is what we will eventually become. "For out of the abundance of the heart the mouth speaks. A good man out of the good treasure of his heart brings forth good things, and an evil man out of the evil treasure brings forth evil things" (Matthew 12:34-35 NKJV). We can hear it in the office, can't we? We can hear it on the street. We can hear it on television and on the radio. Sadly, though, too often we can hear it in our homes and in our churches. We need to each ask ourselves, "What is it that others hear from the abundance of my heart?" Do they hear us lifting up others? Or do they hear us bad mouthing somebody? If we are going to be a part of **the** Church that Jesus has promised to come back for, the Church *without spot or wrinkle*, then we had better ask the LORD GOD to look inside of our heart and tell us what He sees. Then and only then can we truly repent, receive forgiveness and be changed. How can we be changed after repentance? Simple, *with the washing of water by the Word*. GOD needs to do it. Just like GOD did when He came in and cleansed us from all of our old sins and made us a dwelling place for His Holy Spirit when we received Jesus as our Lord. He will cleanse us again, over and over, each time we ask Him to. This is not a license to sin, this is an entitlement to our salvation! As heirs of salvation and joint heirs with Christ, we can come over and over and over to the LORD GOD in order to receive forgiveness. The blood is always there to wash away our sins!

Why did Jesus come and what does He desire for us; "that He might sanctify and cleanse her with the washing of water by the Word, that He might present her to Himself a glorious Church, not having spot or wrinkle or any such thing, but that she should be holy and without blemish" (Ephesians 5:26-27 NKJV). Now that's *love*!

WHAT JESUS BELIEVES

*GOD will **never never never** leave you or me.* (No commas!) His Word promises us that "GOD is our refuge and strength, an ever-present help in times of trouble" (Psalms 46:1 GW). How much trouble we get in often depends upon us. As easy as it seems to blame the devil, he just is not that big! Let's face it, a lot of our problems are brought on by u s, us! We know this is true by the list of regrets and mistakes that *we* play over and over for ourselves on that little tape player we have in our mind called *memory*. [Utilize Ephesians 5:25-26]. Those, *'if I could only go back's.'* Those, *'what if I had not decided to do that's.'* Those *'maybe if I had's...'* We could go on and on, but I don't believe we need to. What if instead of saying those *"What if's"* in past tense, we start seeing them in present and future tense? *Could we, can we, dare we?* Sure we do! We are enabled, empowered, and emboldened to do these things by the Holy Spirit. We give and we receive. We give and we receive. Seems kind of backward to the world's way of thinking, but *we are backward to the world's way of doing things!* And let us praise GOD for it! Since we don't have to rely on the world system, we are completely free to do things GOD's way! GOD is our source of income! Our job is not only a blessing of the LORD to us, but it is a source for giving to help others too. The apostle Paul was an excellent example of living this. Paul chose to work even as he ministered the Gospel of Grace. He explains why he provides for himself instead of having the body of Christ provide for him.

"and because of being of the same craft, he did remain with them, and was working, for they were tent-makers as to craft;"
Acts 18:3 YLT98

"After these things Paul departed from Athens and went to Corinth. And he found a certain Jew named <u>Aquila</u>, born in Pontus, who had recently come from Italy <u>with his wife Priscilla</u> (because Claudius had commanded all the Jews to depart from Rome); and he came to them. <u>So, because he was of the same trade, he stayed with them and worked; for by occupation they were tentmakers</u>. And he reasoned in the synagogue every Sabbath, and persuaded both Jews and Greeks. When Silas and Timothy had come from Macedonia, Paul was compelled by the Spirit, and testified to the Jews that Jesus is the Christ. But when they opposed him and blasphemed, he shook his garments and said to them, "Your blood be upon your own heads; I am clean. From now on I will go to the Gentiles." And he departed from there and entered the house of a certain man named Justus, one who worshiped GOD, whose house was next door to the synagogue. Then Crispus, the ruler of the synagogue, believed on the Lord with all his household. And many of the Corinthians, hearing, believed and were baptized. Now the Lord spoke to Paul in the night by a vision, "Do not be afraid, but speak, and do not keep silent; for I am with you, and no one will attack you to hurt you; for I have many people in this city." And he continued there a year and six months, teaching the Word of GOD among them. When Gallio was proconsul of Achaia, the Jews with one accord rose up against Paul and brought him to the judgment seat, saying, "This fellow persuades men to worship GOD contrary to the Law." And when Paul was about to open his mouth, Gallio said to the Jews, "If it were a matter of wrongdoing or wicked crimes, O Jews, there would be reason why I should bear with you. But if it is a question of words and names and your own law, look to it yourselves; for I do not want to be a judge of such matters." And he drove them from the judgment seat. Then all the Greeks took Sosthenes, the ruler of the synagogue, and beat him before the judgment seat. But Gallio took no notice of these things. So Paul still remained a good while. <u>Then he took leave of the brethren and sailed for Syria, and Priscilla and Aquila were with him</u>. He had his hair cut off at Cenchrea, for he had taken a vow. And he came to Ephesus, and left them there; but he himself entered the synagogue and reasoned with the Jews. When they asked him to stay a longer time with them, he did not consent, but took leave of them, saying, "I must by all means keep this coming feast in Jerusalem; but I will return again to you, GOD willing." And he sailed from Ephesus. And when he had landed at Caesarea, and gone up and greeted the Church, he went down to Antioch. After he had spent some time there, he departed and went over the region of Galatia and Phrygia in order, strengthening all the disciples" (Acts 18:1-23 NKJV).

WHAT JESUS BELIEVES

Paul does not have to work, <u>but</u> chooses the higher road in hopes of gaining more souls. "<u>Am I not an apostle? Am I not free? Have I not seen Jesus Christ our Lord? Are you not my work in the Lord? If I am not an apostle to others, yet doubtless I am to you. For you are the seal of my apostleship in the Lord. My defense to those who examine me is this: Do we have no right to eat and drink? Do we have no right to take along a believing wife, as do also the other apostles, the brothers of the Lord, and Cephas? Or is it only Barnabas and I who have no right to refrain from working?</u> Whoever goes to war at his own expense? Who plants a vineyard and does not eat of its fruit? Or who tends a flock and does not drink of the milk of the flock? Do I say these things as a mere man? Or does not the Law say the same also? For it is written in the Law of Moses, "You shall not muzzle an ox while it treads out the grain." Is it oxen GOD is concerned about? Or does He say it altogether for our sakes? For our sakes, no doubt, this is written, that he who plows should plow in hope, and he who threshes in hope should be partaker of his hope. If we have sown spiritual things for you, is it a great thing if we reap your material things? If others are partakers of this right over you, are we not even more? Nevertheless, we have not used this right, but endure all things lest we hinder the Gospel of Christ. <u>Do you not know that those who minister the holy things eat of the things of the temple, and those who serve at the altar partake of the offerings of the altar? Even so the Lord has commanded that those who preach the Gospel should live from the Gospel. But I have used none of these things, nor have I written these things that it should be done so to me; for it would be better for me to die than that anyone should make my boasting void</u>. For if I preach the Gospel, I have nothing to boast of, for necessity is laid upon me; yes, woe is me if I do not preach the Gospel! For if I do this willingly, I have a reward; but if against my will, I have been entrusted with a stewardship. What is my reward then? <u>That when I preach the Gospel, I may present the Gospel of Christ without charge, that I may not abuse my authority in the Gospel. For though I am free from all men, I have made myself a servant to all, that I might win the more; and to the Jews I became as a Jew, that I might win Jews; to those who are under the Law, as</u>

under the Law, that I might win those who are under the Law; to those who are without law, as without law (not being without law toward GOD, but under law toward Christ), that I might win those who are without law; to the weak I became as weak, that I might win the weak. I have become all things to all men, that I might by all means save some. Now this I do for the Gospel's sake, that I may be partaker of it with you. Do you not know that those who run in a race all run, but one receives the prize? Run in such a way that you may obtain it. And everyone who competes for the prize is temperate in all things. Now they do it to obtain a perishable crown, but we for an imperishable crown. Therefore I run thus: not with uncertainty. Thus I fight: not as one who beats the air. But I discipline my body and bring it into subjection, lest, when I have preached to others, I myself should become disqualified" (1 Corinthians 9:1-27 NKJV).

"Finally, brethren, pray for us, that the Word of the Lord may run swiftly and be glorified, just as it is with you, and that we may be delivered from unreasonable and wicked men; for not all have faith. But the Lord is faithful, who will establish you and guard you from the evil one. And we have confidence in the Lord concerning you, both that you do and will do the things we command you. Now may the Lord direct your hearts into the love of GOD and into the patience of Christ. But we command you, brethren, in the name of our Lord Jesus Christ, that you withdraw from every brother who walks disorderly and not according to the tradition which he received from us. For you yourselves know how you ought to follow us, for we were not disorderly among you; *nor did we eat anyone's bread free of charge, but worked with labor and toil night and day, that we might not be a burden to any of you, not because we do not have authority, but to make ourselves an example of how you should follow us.* For even when we were with you, we commanded you this: If anyone will not work, neither shall he eat. For we hear that there are some who walk among you in a disorderly manner, not working at all, but are busybodies. Now those who are such we command and exhort through our Lord Jesus Christ that they work in quietness and eat their own bread. But as for you, brethren, do not grow weary in doing good. And if anyone does not obey our word in this epistle, note that person and do not keep company with him, that he may be ashamed. Yet do not count him as an enemy, but admonish him as a brother. Now may the Lord of peace Himself give you peace always in every way. The Lord be with you all. The salutation of Paul with my own hand, which is a sign in every epistle; so I write. The grace of our Lord Jesus Christ be with you all. Amen" (2 Thessalonians 3:1-18 NKJV).

Try taking a small percentage of your paycheck to *start off* and helping others with it. Trust the Holy Spirit to lead you into this and watch what happens! GOD's love is shown to others in a tangible way when we give to them! Jesus was the perfect example of giving; everything He did was giving to others; everywhere He went, He was going to be a blessing to others, and **He did it all in obedience to His Father in Heaven**. When He sent out His disciples (including Judas, who held the money box) to give to the poor, the widowed, the orphaned, etc., He (Jesus) did this according to the will and command of the Father. We see an example of this on the night Jesus was betrayed by Judas. Jesus sent Judas out to go and fulfill Scripture that night, but the disciples thought Jesus had sent Judas on assignment to utilize the money as he normally did, being the keeper of the money for Jesus. "Now after the piece of bread, satan entered him. Then, Jesus said to him, 'What you do, do quickly.' But no one at the table knew for what reason He said this to him. For some thought, because Judas had the money box, that Jesus had said to him, 'Buy those things we need for the feast, or that he should give something to the poor'" (John 13:27-29 NKJV).

If you will plant where the Holy Spirit of GOD tells you to, He'll bring it back to you thirty, sixty, and one-hundred fold! By using it as seed, it will come back to you just as it would if you planted a kernel of corn. You will harvest a lot more kernels than your original one. The laws of sowing and reaping in the spiritual realm are identical to those in the natural. In fact, not only are they the same, but they are affected by one another. What it all comes down to is the simple reality that if you don't plant, then you won't harvest. Meaning, if you don't give, then you won't get what you could have received if you had given. So, if you are perfectly content with your life, don't give, but I have yet to meet anybody who was perfectly content with their life who didn't give. You must do it in faith and you must not destroy your harvest by giving the devourer access by your words. (Don't speak what you don't want to harvest!)

GOD is the giver of every good gift, yes! But don't forget, He loves to give and knows the benefits of giving and He wants you to know and receive too by following in His footsteps. (Ref. James 1:18)

"Watch therefore [give strict attention and be cautious and active], for you know neither the day nor the hour when the Son of Man will come. For it is like a man who was about to take a long journey, and he called his servants together and entrusted them with his property. To one he gave five talents [probably about $5,000], to another two, to another one – to each in proportion to his own personal ability. Then he departed and left the country. He who had received the five talents went at once and traded with them, and he gained five talents more. And likewise he who had received the two talents – he also gained two talents more. But he who had received the one talent went and dug a hole in the ground and hid his master's money. Now after a long time the master of those servants returned and settled accounts with them. And he who had received the five talents came and brought him five more, saying, Master, you entrusted to me five talents; see, here I have gained five talents more. His master said to him, Well done, you upright (honorable, admirable) and faithful servant! You have been faithful and trustworthy over a little; I will put you in charge of much. Enter into and share the joy (the delight, the blessedness) which your master enjoys. And he also who had the two talents came forward, saying, Master, you entrusted two talents to me; here I have gained two talents more. His master said to him, Well done, you upright (honorable, admirable) and faithful servant! You have been faithful and trustworthy over a little; I will put you in charge of much. Enter into and share the joy (the delight, the blessedness) which your master enjoys. He who had received one talent also came forward, saying, Master, I knew you to be a harsh and hard man, reaping where you did not sow, and gathering where you had not winnowed [the grain]. So I was afraid, and I went and hid your talent in the ground. Here you have what is your own. But his master answered him, you wicked and lazy and idle servant! Did you indeed know that I reap where I have not sowed and gather [grain] where I have not winnowed? Then you should have invested my money with the bankers, and at my coming I would have received what was my own with interest. So take the talent away from him and give it to the one who has the ten talents. For to everyone who has will more be given, and he will be furnished richly so that he will have an abundance; but from the one who does not have, even what he does have will be taken away. And throw the good-for-nothing servant into the outer darkness; there will be weeping and grinding of teeth. When the Son of Man comes in His glory (His majesty and splendor), and all the holy angels with Him, then He will sit on the throne of His glory. All nations will be gathered before Him, and He will separate them [the people] from one another as a shepherd separates his sheep from the goats; [Ezek. 34:17] And He will cause the sheep to stand at His right hand, but the goats at His left. Then the King will say to those at His right hand, Come, you blessed of My Father [you favored of GOD and appointed to eternal salvation], inherit (receive as your own) the Kingdom prepared for you from the foundation of the world. For I was hungry and you gave Me food, I was thirsty and you gave Me something to drink, I was a stranger and you brought Me together with yourselves and welcomed and entertained and lodged Me, I was naked and you clothed Me, I was sick and you visited Me with help and ministering care, I was in prison and you came to see Me [Isa. 58:7]. Then the just and upright will answer Him, Lord, when did we see You hungry and gave You food, or thirsty and gave You something to drink? And when did we see You a stranger and welcomed and entertained You, or naked and clothed You? And when did we see You sick or in prison and came to visit You? And the King will reply to them, Truly I tell you, in so far as you did it for one of the least [in the estimation of men] of these My brethren, you did it for Me [Prov. 19:17]. Then He will say to those at

His left hand, be gone from Me, you cursed, into the eternal fire prepared for the devil and his angels! For I was hungry and you gave Me no food, I was thirsty and you gave Me nothing to drink, I was a stranger and you did not welcome Me and entertain Me, I was naked and you did not clothe Me, I was sick and in prison and you did not visit Me with help and ministering care. Then they also [in their turn] will answer, Lord, when did we see You hungry or thirsty or a stranger or naked or sick or in prison, and did not minister to You? And He will reply to them, Solemnly I declare to you, in so far as you failed to do it for the least [in the estimation of men] of these, you failed to do it for Me [Prov. 14:31; 17:5]. Then they will go away into eternal punishment, but those who are just and upright and in right standing with GOD into eternal life" [Dan. 12:2] (Matthew 25:13-46 AMP).

When you read this next story, which do you think Paul reaped? Do you think he reaped thirty fold, sixty fold or one hundred fold?

"AGAIN JESUS began to teach beside the lake. And a very great crowd gathered about Him, so that He got into a ship in order to sit in it on the sea, and the whole crowd was at the lakeside on the shore. And He taught them many things in parables (illustrations or comparisons put beside truths to explain them), and in His teaching He said to them: Give attention to this! Behold, a sower went out to sow. And as he was sowing, some seed fell along the path, and the birds came and ate it up. Other seed [of the same kind] fell on ground full of rocks, where it had not much soil; and at once it sprang up, because it had no depth of soil; And when the sun came up, it was scorched, and because it had not taken root, it withered away. Other seed [of the same kind] fell among thorn plants, and the thistles grew and pressed together and utterly choked and suffocated it, and it yielded no grain. And other seed [of the same kind] fell into good (well-adapted) soil and brought forth grain, growing up and increasing, and yielded up to thirty times as much, and sixty times as much, and even a hundred times as much as had been sown. And He said, He who has ears to hear, let him be hearing [and let him consider, and comprehend]. And as soon as He was alone, those who were around Him, with the

WHAT JESUS BELIEVES

Twelve [apostles], began to ask Him about the parables. And He said to them, To you has been entrusted the mystery of the Kingdom of GOD [that is, the secret counsels of GOD which are hidden from the ungodly]; but for those outside [of our circle] everything becomes a parable, in order that they may [indeed] look and look but not see and perceive, and may hear and hear but not grasp and comprehend, lest haply they should turn again, and it [their willful rejection of the truth] should be forgiven them [Isa. 6:9, 10; Matt. 13:13-15]. And He said to them, do you not discern and understand this parable? How then is it possible for you to discern and understand all the parables? The sower sows the Word. The ones along the path are those who have the Word sown [in their hearts], but when they hear, satan comes at once and [by force] takes away the message which is sown in them. And in the same way the ones sown upon stony ground are those who, when they hear the Word, at once receive and accept and welcome it with joy; And they have no real root in themselves, and so they endure for a little while; then when trouble or persecution arises on account of the Word, they immediately are offended (become displeased, indignant, resentful) and they stumble and fall away. And the ones sown among the thorns are others who hear the Word; Then the cares and anxieties of the world and distractions of the age, and the pleasure and delight and false glamour and deceitfulness of riches, and the craving and passionate desire for other things creep in and choke and suffocate the Word, and it becomes fruitless. And those sown on the good (well-adapted) soil are the ones who hear the Word and receive and accept and welcome it and bear fruit – some thirty times as much as was sown, some sixty times as much, and some [even] a hundred times as much. And He said to them, is the lamp brought in to be put under a peck measure or under a bed, and not [to be put] on the lampstand? [Things are hidden temporarily only as a means to revelation]. For there is nothing hidden except to be revealed, nor is anything [temporarily] kept secret except in order that it may be made known. If any man has ears to hear, let him be listening and let him perceive and comprehend. And He said to them, be careful what you are hearing. The measure [of thought and study] you give [to the truth you hear] will be the measure [of virtue and knowledge] that comes back to you–and more [besides] will be given to you who hear. For to him who has will more be given; and from him who has nothing, even what he has will be taken away [by force]" (Mark 4:1-25 AMP).

Jesus tells us that if we give even a cup of cold water to one of these little ones in His name, we will not go without our reward! Can you imagine receiving a reward for giving someone a cup of cold water? What a mighty GOD we serve! As we read earlier, Jesus set the perfect example of living the life of a servant. Everywhere He went, everything He did, revolved around serving mankind in obedience to His Father. Even to the laying down of His life at the cross. You cannot serve any more completely than He did. As we read the Bible Scriptures again and again, we will understand how much better we can live a life of service.

He (Jesus) cares about this world today, just as much as He did when He created it, and just as much as He did when He walked the Earth as a man. He taught His disciples clearly and He was completely devoted to teaching them and to loving them. He is just as committed to teaching us and loving us! The Word of GOD tells us that "Jesus Christ is the same yesterday, today, and forever" (Hebrews 13:8 NKJV). He loved us knowing that we would *all sin and come short of the glory of GOD* (Ref. Romans 3:23). There is not anything we could ever do or say that would make Him love us any less, or any more. His love is unconditional and eternal! "For GOD so loved the world that He gave His only begotten Son, that whoever believes in Him should not perish but have everlasting life. For GOD did not send His Son into the world to condemn the world, but that the world through Him might be saved" (John 3:16, 17 NKJV). I hope this for you and I because we are so loved!

"To love My Word is to love Wisdom."
Holy Spirit of Jesus Christ

Let's read some [basic training] words of wisdom in Proverbs, "Train up a child in the way he should go, and when he is old he will not depart from it. The rich rules over the poor, and the borrower is servant to the lender. He who sows iniquity will reap sorrow, and the rod of his anger will fail. He who has a generous eye will be blessed, for he gives of his bread to the poor. Cast out the scoffer, and contention will leave; yes, strife and reproach will cease. He who loves purity of heart and has grace on his lips, the king will be his friend. The eyes of the Lord preserve knowledge, but He overthrows the words of the faithless" (Proverbs 22:6-12 NKJV). As we have learned, he (the LORD) has a **Word system** that works! We know that whatever seed we plant with our mouth is what we will eventually be reaping. What we sow, we will reap. Just as you would not go out to a field to pick watermelons when you had planted pumpkin seeds, neither would you go out to harvest wheat from your field knowing that you had not planted any seeds whatsoever! Again, the same principle of sowing and reaping in the natural works in the spiritual. *You have a bad marriage*, you say? That co-worker of yours is *just such a "know it all!?"* Well, what kind of seeds have you been planting all this time? Have you been planting the good seeds of 1 Corinthians 13 into the soil of those relationships or some *other* kind of seed? To know the kind of seed we have planted, we have only to look at the kind of harvest we are reaping. If you feel you do not see any harvest in that soul and it is bad soil, that doesn't mean there hasn't been any effect, and it certainly doesn't mean that there hasn't been any effect on others who have been listening. There are, after all, different types of soil in others around your sphere of influence. Jesus spoke to certain individuals and they rejected Him, but others were listening (to those conversations), weren't they? And because of it, they chose to follow Jesus and found eternal life! Having said that, never, never, never give up on your family. Take as example the father of the prodigal son, wait on that road (of hope, faith and prayer) for your prodigal. (See Luke 15:11-24)

None of this is meant to condemn you; rather it is meant to convict you because you are greatly loved of the LORD. People with low self-esteem will often think that someone is *coming down* on them or *judging* them. That is simply not true here. This is said with love and at the leading of Christ (the Anointed one and the Anointing). He wants you to know that He *really cares about you!* He wants you to know that there is a change coming to world order. It's His change. We are coming into the possessing of great amounts of wealth, but we will need the wisdom and the discernment to know what to do with all that wealth. Some of it is for us to enjoy because as a Father, He likes to give good gifts to us, but most of it is to reach the world with the good news and to help others.

"But this I say: He who sows sparingly will also reap sparingly, and he who sows bountifully will also reap bountifully. So let each one give as he purposes in his heart, not grudgingly or of necessity; for GOD loves a cheerful giver. And GOD is able to make all grace abound toward you, that you, always having all sufficiency in all things, may have an abundance for every good work. As it is written: "He has dispersed abroad, He has given to the poor; His righteousness endures forever." Now may He who supplies seed to the sower, and bread for food, supply and multiply the seed you have sown and increase the fruits of your righteousness, while you are enriched in everything for all liberality, which causes thanksgiving through us to GOD" (2 Corinthians 9:6-11 NKJV). By our giving, in His love, this world will see Jesus! This world will see the heart of love of the Father! The Word says, "... the goodness of GOD leads you to repentance" (Romans 2:4 NKJV). What a small price to pay, what a simple thing to do, to pour out GOD's love in the form of something tangible by sharing with others what we have! Oh, how wonderful to be able to love others in this way!

Let's read more of Romans 2, to better understand (by the Holy Spirit) what He is teaching us here. "Therefore you are inexcusable, O man, whoever you are who judge, for in whatever you judge another you condemn yourself; for you who judge practice the same things. But we know that the judgment of GOD is according to truth against those who practice such things. And do you think this, O man, you

WHAT JESUS BELIEVES

who judge those practicing such things, and doing the same, that you will escape the judgment of GOD? Or do you despise the riches of His goodness, forbearance, and longsuffering, not knowing that the goodness of GOD leads you to repentance? But in accordance with your hardness and your impenitent heart you are treasuring up for yourself wrath in the day of wrath and revelation of the righteous judgment of GOD, who "will render to each one according to his deeds": eternal life to those who by patient continuance in doing good seek for glory, honor, and immortality; but to those who are self-seeking and do not obey the truth, but obey unrighteousness—indignation and wrath, tribulation and anguish, on every soul of man who does evil, of the Jew first and also of the Greek; but glory, honor, and peace to everyone who works what is good, to the Jew first and also to the Greek. For there is no partiality with GOD (Romans 2:1-11 NKJV). Are we to judge another man's circumstances? We are to do all things in love! Is it not written, *GOD is love* and *in Him, we live and move and have our being; ... For we are also His offspring* (Ref 1 John 4:8 and Acts 17:28). If this is the case and GOD sent down His son to save each of us, not a one of whom was without sin, then is He not also desirous that we pour out this same (undeserved) love onto others, even in tangible form? "What good is it, my brothers and sisters, if someone claims to have faith but has no deeds? Can such faith save them? Suppose a brother or a sister is without clothes and daily food. If one of you says to them, "Go in peace; keep warm and well fed," but does nothing about their physical needs, what good is it? In the same way, faith by itself, if it is not accompanied by action, is dead. But someone will say, "You have faith; I have deeds." Show me your faith without deeds, and I will show you my faith by my deeds. You believe that there is one GOD. Good! Even the demons believe that — and shudder. You foolish person, do you want evidence that faith without deeds is useless? Was not our father Abraham considered righteous for what he did when he offered his son Isaac on the altar? You see that his faith and his actions were working together, and his faith was made complete by what he did. And the Scripture was fulfilled that says, "Abraham believed GOD, and it was credited to him as righteousness," and he was called GOD's friend. You see that a person is considered righteous by what they do and not by faith alone. In the same way, was not even Rahab the prostitute considered righteous for what she did when she gave lodging to the spies and sent them off in a different direction? As the body without the spirit is dead, so faith without deeds is dead" (James 2:14-26 NIV). Let us love not in word only, but also in deed! That they may know us by our fruit! True lighthouses upon a hill! This is faith in action and this is love!

Time is short and we are on the last minute hand of time before Jesus' return, let's get to it! Let's press in by prayer and thanksgiving, "Do not be anxious about anything, but in every situation, by prayer and petition, with thanksgiving, present your requests to GOD" (Philippians 4:6 NIV), and let's get the job done! At Judgment Day, it will be too late for regrets. The people we see separated from us then will stay separated from us for all eternity. No amount of our tears of regret will save them then. Those faces so dearly loved will be lost to us forever! Is it worth any grudge you may be holding against someone now to not go and forgive them unconditionally? No, they may not deserve it, but neither did we! Friend neither did we... And yet He cried out from the cross while bearing all the agony of our sins and our curses, *Father, forgive them, for they do not know what they do!* (Ref. Luke 23:34 NKJV). Jesus is telling us the same thing today, **My children, forgive them, for they know not what they do!** Can you hear His voice? Can you feel His love and forgiveness pulling on your heartstrings? As the Word says, "For He is our GOD, and we are the people of His pasture, and the sheep of His hand." Today, if you will hear His voice: "Do not harden your hearts, as in the rebellion, as in the day of trial in the wilderness, when your fathers tested Me; they tried Me, though they saw My work. For forty years I was grieved with that generation, and said, 'It is a people who go astray in their hearts, and they do not know My ways' " (Psalms 95:7-10 NKJV). Have you been *feeling* like you are living in a wilderness, perhaps a wilderness devoid of love or health and prospering? Jesus was speaking of the literal wilderness the Israelites had gone through in this Scripture. He also spoke of them testing GOD even after they had been eyewitnesses to His miracles! They were forced to wander around in that wilderness as a group for forty years! A wilderness they could have made it across in only a matter of days! The Israelites who did make it into the Promised Land *knew* that they served a GOD of blessing and prosperity, but they also knew that they could get themselves under the curses by the sins of disobedience and lack of faith in Almighty GOD.

The Lord had sent scouts, from each of the 12 Tribes of Israel, to go and scout out the land that He was about to give them. Upon their return, all of the scouts greatly feared the coming invasion, with the exception of Joshua and Caleb. On the day of the Israelites' declaration, "There we saw the giants (the descendants of Anak came from the giants); and we were like grasshoppers in our own sight, and so we were in their sight" (Numbers 13:33 NKJV). GOD gave the news that anyone 21 and older would not enter the Promised Land. A land flowing with milk and honey is the description that the Bible gives of the Promised Land, and all those people 21 and older would never see it! Joshua and Caleb were the exceptions because when they had scouted the land, they came back and basically said, *'Let's do it!'* They put their faith not in the size of the giants in the land, but in their GOD! Even Moses lost entering the Promised Land. One simple act of disobedience did it for him. Thank GOD for the grace of his New Testament Covenant that covers over sin! Although we have been delivered from sin and the curses brought on by sin and all of its entailing bondage to satan, that doesn't mean that we don't open doors to him, again and again, through our sin. While he (satan) cannot keep us in bondage to him, our choice to hold on to sin can! Sound dangerous? It had better because it is! Many people have died blaming others or GOD or claiming, *'If it is His will, then I will die in this sickness for Him.'* What a (sad) waste! Ignorance and sin can both bring about death. That is why it is so important that we, "Train up a child in the way he should go, and when he is old he will not depart from it" (Proverbs 22:6 NKJV). No matter the age, even a young child knowing the truth of the Lord can share about Him and command sickness and disease to leave, in the name of Jesus!

WHAT JESUS BELIEVES

Doors to the enemy can be opened unintentionally through unbelief, lack of knowledge, coveting or unforgiveness. Doors can also be opened by the words we speak. We can give the enemy access through our words, so let us be wise about the words we speak. Are we opening the door of blessing with our words or the door of curses? Whatever the name of the door, if it has allowed satan access he will take every advantage of every open door that he can! We may find a situation in our lives that just *won't go away* no matter what we seem to do. We may feel like we are trapped in it as if we are out in a *wilderness.* That is the kind of situation that satan loves and works hard to see us in. He wants us sick, he wants us poor, and he wants us dead; and he will use any means that he can to get us into one or more of those conditions. Jesus set us free from the law of sin and death, let us *not* choose to go back! <u>Our words are a vehicle, let us steer our lives and the lives of others into blessing!</u>

If you have been feeling the Lord pulling on your heartstrings to forgive someone unconditionally, then why don't you get down on your knees right now and refuse, *yes refuse* to get up until the Lord has helped you to receive the forgiveness you need for that person. One more word on forgiveness and we'll move on. Have you ever been angry as a child and stomped off to your room in the middle of a family gathering, at say Christmas or some other holiday, and during the time you spent fuming angrily in your room, not a soul came to get you? Well, I have. I found out later that no one even knew that I had been upset and *went off to be alone with it.* Not one person at that gathering was affected by my anger, other than me. It can be the same with our heart. When we allow offense to get in, which put bluntly is "hurt pride," then we have allowed it access to our innermost being, our heart. Once there, if left alone, it would do what I would have done in that room if I hadn't come out when I did, it will get worse. Unfortunately, offense is a type of death. <u>*There is no unforgiveness in love.*</u> Jesus never walked in unforgiveness, not even when betrayed by Judas. As we read earlier, He asked GOD not to hold his nailing to the cross to mankind's account, stating that *we knew not what we were doing*. It is the same with our fellow man. They don't really know what they are doing when they offend us either. You may say, 'oh, yes, he (or she) did know what he was doing when he hurt me!' The truth is nobody, but GOD can fully know what is truly being done to another's heart. <u>Most human beings would not say the hurtful things they say, so easily, to others if they could feel the full impact of the pain the words they were speaking would bring to pass</u>. We as Christians do not have the excuse of saying, *I just can't forgive them!* The Word clearly tells us that not only can *we do all things through Christ Who strengthens us*, but also that *the love of GOD is shed abroad in our hearts* (Ref. Philippians 4:13 and Romans 5:5). For it is firmly stated that *we have the mind of Christ (The Anointed One and His Anointing)* (Ref 1 Corinthians 2:16). "Therefore if there is any consolation in Christ, if any comfort of love, if any fellowship of the Spirit, if any affection and mercy, fulfill my joy by being like-minded, having the same love, being of one accord, of one mind. Let nothing be done through selfish ambition or conceit, but in lowliness of mind let each esteem others better than himself. <u>Let each of you look out not only for his own interests, but also for the interests of others. Let this mind be in you which was also in Christ Jesus</u>, who, being in the form of GOD, did not consider it robbery to be equal with GOD, but made Himself of no reputation, taking the form of a bondservant, and coming in the likeness of men. And being found in appearance as a man, He humbled Himself and became obedient to the point of death, even the death of the cross. Therefore GOD also has highly exalted Him and given Him the name which is above every name, that at the name of Jesus every knee should bow, of those in Heaven, and of those on Earth, and of those under the Earth, and that every tongue should confess that Jesus Christ is Lord, to the glory of GOD the Father. Therefore, my beloved, as you have always obeyed, not as in my presence only, but now much more in my absence, work out your own salvation with fear and trembling; for it is GOD who works in you both to will and to do for His good pleasure. Do all things without complaining and disputing, that you may become blameless and harmless, children of GOD without fault in the midst of a crooked and perverse generation, among whom you shine as lights in the world, holding fast the Word of life..." (Philippians 2:1-16 NKJV). This mind, being made up of love, it is simply impossible for us to *not be able to forgive **any** of our fellow man no matter what they have done.* Saying that we cannot love someone or forgive someone would be lying against GOD because of the promises He has given us regarding His love (the Holy Spirit) indwelling us. *'Oh, I never meant to call GOD a liar!'* Of course you didn't, but it doesn't change the fact that we are every time we give the excuse, *I can't!* Just remind yourself that *you "can do all things through Christ who strengthens you"* the next time satan tries to get you to take on any kind of offense and that will send him packing because you have given him *no place, no place* to set himself up a throne in your heart and *no place* to root! You do have the victory! You do, you have Jesus!

> **"Get ready to pray like you have never prayed before!"**
> **Holy Spirit**
>
> **"Get ready to experience My Victories!"**
> **Holy Spirit**
>
> **"I, even I AM your Beloved. Let us share our love on a bed of purity. Have I not said, be ye Holy as I am Holy? Have I not given My life for yours? Have you not given your life to Me? You are My Beloved. I AM your Rock and your Strength, your Fortress and your Deliverer. I AM the Christ, the Living GOD and I gave My life that we might be together forever!**
> **I, even I AM your Beloved. You belong to Me.**
>
> **Do not listen to the voice of a stranger for he is an adulterer and the father of it, a destroyer and the father of it, a murderer and the father of it, a thief and the father of it, a liar and the father of it.**
>
> **I AM the One true Love for you. I have your back and I AM your Hero. I will come back for you mounted upon My white horse.**

WHAT JESUS BELIEVES

> Listen only to My voice. Come, My Beloved, come away with Me into our Secret Chambers for there I will tell you the secret things that your heart has so desired to hear
> For I AM your Beloved."
>
> **Spirit of Jesus Christ**

"I have strength for all things in Christ Who empowers me [I am ready for anything and equal to anything through Him Who infuses inner strength into me; I am self-sufficient in Christ's sufficiency]" (Philippians 4:13 AMP).

"And put on the new nature (the regenerate self) created in GOD's image, [GOD-like] in true righteousness and holiness. When angry, do not sin; do not ever let your wrath (your exasperation, your fury or indignation) last until the sun goes down. Leave no [such] room or foothold for the devil [give no opportunity to him]. Let no foul or polluting language, nor evil word nor unwholesome or worthless talk [ever] come out of your mouth, but only such [speech] as is good and beneficial to the spiritual progress of others, as is fitting to the need and the occasion, that it may be a blessing and give grace (GOD's favor) to those who hear it" (Ephesians 4:24, 26, 27, 29 AMP).

> "Spikes (nails) could never keep Jesus up on the cross.
> Only Love could do that."
> **Holy Spirit**

8

On Whom You Can Depend

"For GOD so loved the world that He gave His only begotten Son, that whoever believes in Him should not perish but have everlasting life" (John 3:16 NKJV).

Simple faith in GOD is a major part of our relationship with him. Hebrews 4 is one that we all need to read and meditate upon often. "THEREFORE, WHILE the promise of entering His rest still holds and is offered [today], let us be afraid [to distrust it], lest any of you should think he has come too late and has come short of [reaching] it. For indeed we have had the glad tidings [Gospel of GOD] proclaimed to us just as truly as they [the Israelites of old did when the good news of deliverance from bondage came to them]; but the message they heard did not benefit them, <u>because it was not mixed with faith (with the leaning of the entire personality on GOD in absolute trust and confidence in His power, wisdom, and goodness) by those who heard it; neither were they united in faith with the ones [Joshua and Caleb] who heard (did believe). For we who have believed (adhered to and trusted in and relied on GOD) do enter that rest, in accordance with His declaration that those [who did not believe] should not enter when He said, As I swore in My wrath, They shall not enter My rest; and this He said although [His] works had been completed and prepared [and waiting for all who would believe] from the foundation of the world</u> [Ps. 95:11]. For in a certain place He has said this about the seventh day: And GOD rested on the seventh day from all His works [Gen. 2:2]. And [they forfeited their part in it, for] in this [passage] He said, they shall not enter My rest [Ps. 95:11]. Seeing then that the promise remains over [from past times] for some to enter that rest, and that those who formerly were given the good news about it and the opportunity, failed to appropriate it and did not enter because of disobedience, Again He sets a definite day, [a new] Today, [and gives another opportunity of securing that rest] saying through David after so long a time in the words already quoted, Today, if you would hear His voice and when you hear it, do not harden your hearts [Ps. 95:7, 8]. [This mention of a rest was not a reference to their entering into Canaan.] For if Joshua had given them rest, He [GOD] would not speak afterward about another day. So then, there is still awaiting a full and complete Sabbath-rest reserved for the [true] people of GOD; for he who has once entered [GOD's] rest also has ceased from [the weariness and pain] of human labors, just as GOD rested from those labors peculiarly His own [Gen. 2:2]. Let us therefore be zealous and exert ourselves and strive diligently to enter that rest [of GOD, to know and experience it for ourselves], that no one may fall or perish by the same kind of unbelief and disobedience [into which those in the wilderness fell]. <u>For the Word that GOD speaks is alive and full of power [making it active, operative, energizing, and effective]; it is sharper than any two-edged sword, penetrating to the dividing line of the breath of life (soul) and [the immortal] spirit, and of joints and marrow [of the deepest parts of our nature], exposing and sifting and analyzing and judging the very thoughts and purposes of the heart.</u> And not a creature exists that is concealed from His sight, but all things are open and exposed, naked and defenseless to the eyes of Him with Whom we have to do. Inasmuch then as we have a great High Priest Who has [already] ascended and passed through the heavens, Jesus the Son of GOD, let us hold fast our confession [of faith in Him]. For we do not have a High Priest Who is unable to understand and sympathize and have a shared feeling with our weaknesses and infirmities and liability to the assaults of temptation, but One Who has been tempted in every respect as we are, yet without sinning. <u>Let us then fearlessly and confidently and boldly draw near to the throne of grace (the throne of GOD's unmerited favor to us sinners), that we may receive mercy [for our failures] and find grace to help in good time for every need</u>

[appropriate help and well-timed help, coming just when we need it]" (Hebrews 4:1-16 AMP).

In our reading of this book of the Bible, it is made clear to us that GOD wants us to enter into a rest, a rest (due to) in our faith in Him. Did you know that even while you are going through the trials of life that you can be in a rest in GOD? Is that to say that we don't care what happens in our life and we will just float along, so to speak, wherever our path may go? No. It is very important that we are involved in what is going on in our life, but our involvement still means <u>total reliance on GOD</u>. To be resting in our GOD is to yield and willingly go along where ever His Spirit takes us, doing whatever He tells us to do. Whether or not it is GOD's will that a situation in your life is there, is up to <u>you</u> to find out. Through GOD's direction and leading in His Word and in prayer (by the Holy Spirit), we can always find out if GOD has put us in a situation or not, and *what to do about it.* Sometimes what GOD will have us do is *absolutely nothing!* Believe it or not, doing absolutely nothing can be the hardest thing to do. We will try to get out our Bibles and *conjure* up some Scriptures regarding our situation and what to do. And it would be conjuring up Scripture for us to just go and get any Scripture that <u>we felt like using to make a situation turn out the way we desire</u>. GOD isn't mad at us when we do this, He is just hurt that we didn't trust Him. He is also hindered from bringing the correct outcome to our situation. Mankind has been blaming GOD for centuries for things that not He, but we ourselves have brought about. In the past people have assigned their answers to the problems (and situations) of others based on their own experiences and opinions. What may have seemed convenient to them <u>has cost those of us who have listened and followed their advice a lot of additional problems. Wrong teaching ushers in chaos and confusion</u>. Which all adds up to the same thing...lack of victory.

"Before you go to the phone, come to My Throne. I will answer."
Holy Spirit

If you feel like you have a lack of victory in your own life, your own situation, <u>don't wait on the rest of the body of Christ to solve your problems.</u> You can get them by going to the Word and letting the Holy Spirit connect the pieces for you. You really can, you know. **Going before the Throne of GOD and searching out the answers in His Word are a sure way to Victory!** The Word tells us *"<u>and you, the anointing that ye did receive from him, in you it doth remain, and ye have no need that any one may teach you, but as the same anointing doth teach you concerning all, and is true, and is not a lie, and even as was taught you, ye shall remain in him</u>" (1 John 2:27 YLT98)*. That doesn't mean that we are not seek wise council or not go to *church*, but rather that **we can learn on our own, at all times, with the Holy Spirit as our guide and mentor**. He will be the One Who gives us GOD's perfect answer every time. *Wouldn't you rather hear the answer from Him and be positive that it is the right answer?*

"may we hold fast the unwavering profession of the hope, (for faithful [is] He who did promise), and may we consider one another to provoke to love and to good works, not forsaking the assembling of ourselves together, as a custom of certain [is], but exhorting, and so much the more as ye see the day coming nigh" (Hebrews 10:23-25 YLT98).

> *"Soon. Soon. Soon. I will come for you."*
> ***Spirit of Jesus Christ***
>
> *"My Church is not a building.*
> *I dwell in living (human) temples."*
> ***Holy Spirit***

WHAT JESUS BELIEVES

"Going to Church:
Gathering together.
Having intentional godly fellowship
with sharing and praying.
Not neglecting to give praise to and worship the One true GOD Who made all things and
by Whom we have Life and have been given entrance into Life Eternal with Him!"
Holy Spirit

"Where two or more gather in My Name
I will be there in the midst of them
and fellowship with them."
Holy Spirit

"Whoever has ears, let them hear what the Spirit says to the churches."
(Revelation 2:7,11a,17a,29; 3:6,13,22)

[In Revelation Chapters 2 and 3, Jesus says this a total of 7 times while giving John messages to relay to the churches (His Church) in Ephesus, Smyrna, Pergamum, Thyatira, Sardis, Philadelphia and Laodicea. Do you think this is important to Jesus?]

What is Church and what is our reason for going to Church? If we are going to church just to receive, then we are missing out on a lot. We are part of a Body. We are a single part of a whole Body of Whom Jesus Christ is the Head and each of us is important. Can you imagine closing your eyes and driving? Can you imagine drinking water without a kidney or eating your food without a stomach or intestines? Each part is important. *"But in fact God has placed the parts in the body, every one of them, just as he wanted them to be."* **(1 Corinthians 12:18 Amp)**

"GOD is Love, In Him there is no darkness."
Holy Spirit

WHAT JESUS BELIEVES

"Anyone who loves their brother and sister lives in the light, and there is nothing in them to make them stumble."
(1 John 2:10 NIV)

You are a specific body part that I *cannot* be. I am a specific body part that you *cannot* be. We are both necessary. Let's read what the Word says about this. Since Jesus is the Living Word, this is what Jesus believes.

(1 Corinthians 124-31 NIV)

"There are different kinds of gifts, but the same Spirit distributes them. There are different kinds of service, but the same Lord. There are different kinds of working, but in all of them and in everyone it is the same God at work. Now to each one the manifestation of the Spirit is given for the common good. To one there is given through the Spirit a message of wisdom, to another a message of knowledge by means of the same Spirit, to another faith by the same Spirit, to another gifts of healing by that one Spirit, to another miraculous powers, to another prophecy, to another distinguishing between spirits, to another speaking in different kinds of tongues, and to still another the interpretation of tongues. All these are the work of one and the same Spirit, and he distributes them to each one, just as he determines. Just as a body, though one, has many parts, but all its many parts form one body, so it is with Christ. For we were all baptized by one Spirit so as to form one body—whether Jews or Gentiles, slave or free—and we were all given the one Spirit to drink. Even so the body is not made up of one part but of many. <u>Now if the foot should say, "Because I am not a hand, I do not belong to the body," it would not for that reason stop being part of the body. And if the ear should say, "Because I am not an eye, I do not belong to the body," it would not for that reason stop being part of the body. If the whole body were an eye, where would the sense of hearing be? If the whole body were an ear, where would the sense of smell be?</u> **But in fact God has placed the parts in the body, every one of them, just as he wanted them to be. If they were all one part, where would the**

body be? As it is, there are many parts, but one body. The eye cannot say to the hand, "I don't need you!" And the head cannot say to the feet, "I don't need you!" On the contrary, those parts of the body that seem to be weaker are indispensable, and the parts that we think are less honorable we treat with special honor. And the parts that are unpresentable are treated with special modesty, while our presentable parts need no special treatment. **But God has put the body together, giving greater honor to the parts that lacked it, so that there should be no division in the body, but that its parts should have equal concern for each other.** If one part suffers, every part suffers with it; if one part is honored, every part rejoices with it. **Now you are the body of Christ, and each one of you is a part of it.** And God has placed in the church first of all apostles, second prophets, third teachers, then miracles, then gifts of healing, of helping, of guidance, and of different kinds of tongues. Are all apostles? Are all prophets? Are all teachers? Do all work miracles? Do all have gifts of healing? Do all speak in tongues? Do all interpret? Now eagerly desire the greater gifts. And yet **I will show you the most excellent way.**"

GOD is securing His Church in His Love. In doing this, dissention between the Body parts (brethren) will stop and we will, at last, be unified and work together as a single Body. We cannot walk in the footsteps of Jesus if we do not walk in agreement with one another. If we do not walk in Love we do not really know the Father for *GOD is Love and there is no darkness in Him.* He will lead His whole Body into all Truth. As we spend time seeking GOD we will learn about our gifts and how we as a part of the Body of Christ are to utilize those GOD given gifts and operate as our uniquely specific and needed part of the Body of Christ. Truth is Light. GOD is Light and GOD is Love. Love lights the Way for the Body of Christ. Jesus could not stumble and fall because He submitted to His Father at all times *and walked in the Light of Truth which is Love. Jesus walked in the Father. They were One. We are One with them and we are learning to walk in the Light of Truth which is Love.* "This is the message we have heard from him and declare to you: GOD is light; in him there is not darkness at all."

WHAT JESUS BELIEVES

(1 John 1:5 NIV) *We can't fail when we are walking in His Light because we are submitted to Him.*

"Darkness runs from the Light."
Holy Spirit

Jesus said that He will never leave us or forsake us and He has told us that He will never leave us alone (to be alone). Holy Spirit is here to stay with us and lead us in the light (will) of GOD, just as He led Jesus.

"My little flock
Do not despair
I will be with you
Everywhere."
Spirit of Jesus Christ

We are in the End Times just before the Millennium and Jesus will soon return and reunite the Church still living on earth with those who have gone before us. As the close of this age is quickly approaching a growing urgency to get the Gospel out to all Nations takes precedence within the Church. We will know those in the true Church by their Love.

"The More Excellent Way:"
Holy Spirit
(I Corinthians 13:1-13 NIV)

"If I speak in the tongues of men or of angels, but do not have love, I am only a resounding gong or a clanging cymbal. If I have the gift of prophecy and can fathom all mysteries and all knowledge, and if I have a faith that can move mountains, but do not have love, I am nothing. If I give all I possess to the poor and give over my body to hardship that I may boast, but do not have love, I gain nothing. Love is patient, love is kind. It does not envy, it does not boast, it is not proud. It does not dishonor others, it is not self-seeking, it is not easily angered, it keeps no record of wrongs. Love does not delight in evil but rejoices with the truth. It always protects, always trusts, always hopes, always perseveres. Love never fails. But where there are prophecies, they will cease; where there are tongues, they will be stilled; where there is knowledge, it will pass away. For we know in part and we prophesy in part, but when completeness comes, what is in part disappears. When I was a child, I talked like a child, I thought like a child, I reasoned like a child. When I became a man, I put the ways of childhood behind me. For now we see only a reflection as in a mirror; then we shall see face to face. Now I know in part; then I shall know fully, even as I am fully known. And now these three remain: faith, hope and love. But the greatest of these is love."

"Follow the way of love and eagerly desire gifts of the Spirit, especially prophecy. For anyone who speaks in a tongue does not speak to people but to God. Indeed, no one understands them; they utter mysteries by the Spirit. But the one who prophesies speaks to people for their strengthening, encouraging and comfort." (1 Corinthians 14:1-3 NIV)

Romans 11:29 together in the Amplified Version. "For GOD's gifts and His call are irrevocable. [He never withdraws them when once they are given, and He does not change His mind about those to whom He gives His grace or to whom He sends His call]" (Romans 11:29 AMP)

> *"No matter who you are, you have a calling.*
> *No matter what you've done, it isn't too late."*
> ***Holy Spirit***

No matter who you are, you have a calling. "Now concerning the things of which you wrote to me: It is good for a man not to touch a woman. Nevertheless, because of sexual immorality, let each man have his own wife, and let each woman have her own husband. Let the husband render to his wife the affection due her, and likewise also the wife to her husband. The wife does not have authority over her own body, but the husband does. And likewise the husband does not have authority over his own body, but the wife does. Do not deprive one another except with consent for a time, that you may give yourselves to fasting and prayer; and come together again so that satan does not tempt you because of your lack of self-control. But I say this as a concession, not as a commandment. For I wish that all men were even as I myself. <u>But each one has his own gift from GOD, one in this manner and another in that.</u> But I say to the unmarried and to the widows: It is good for them if they remain even as I am; but if they cannot exercise self-control, let them marry. For it is better to marry than to burn with passion. Now to the married I command, yet not I but the Lord: A wife is not to depart from her husband. But even if she does depart, let her remain unmarried or be reconciled to her husband. And a husband is not to divorce his wife. But to the rest I, not the Lord, say: If any brother has a wife who does not believe, and she is willing to live with him, let him not divorce her. And a woman who has a husband who does not believe, if he is willing to live with her, let her not divorce him. For the unbelieving husband is sanctified by the wife, and the unbelieving wife is sanctified by the husband; otherwise your children would be unclean, but now they are holy. But if the unbeliever departs, let him depart; a brother or a sister is not under bondage in such cases. But GOD has called us to peace. For how do you know, O wife, whether you will save your husband? Or how do you know, O husband, whether you will save your wife? <u>But as GOD has distributed to each one, as the Lord has called each one, so let him walk</u>. And so I ordain in all the churches. Was anyone called while circumcised? Let him not become uncircumcised. Was anyone called while uncircumcised? Let him not be circumcised. Circumcision is nothing and uncircumcision is nothing, but keeping the commandments of GOD is what matters. <u>Let each one remain in the same calling in which he was called.</u> Were you called while a slave? Do not be concerned about it; but if you can be made free, rather use it. For he who is called in the Lord while a slave is the Lord's freedman. Likewise he who is called while free is Christ's slave. You were bought at a price; do not become slaves of men. Brethren, let each one remain with GOD in that state in which he was called. Now concerning virgins: I have no commandment from the Lord; yet I give judgment as one whom the Lord in His mercy has made trustworthy. I suppose therefore that this is good because of the present distress— that it is good for a man to remain as he is: Are you bound to a wife? Do not seek to be loosed. Are you loosed from a wife? Do not seek a wife. But even if you do marry, you have not sinned; and if a virgin marries, she has not sinned. Nevertheless such will have trouble in the flesh, but I would spare you. But this I say, brethren, the time is short, so that from now on even those who have wives should be as though they had none, those who weep as though they did not weep, those who rejoice as though they did not rejoice, those who buy as though they did not possess, and those who use this world as not misusing it. For the form of this world is passing away. But I want you to be without care. He who is unmarried cares for the things of the Lord—how he may please the Lord. But he who is married cares about the things of the world—how he may please his wife. There is a difference between a wife and a virgin. The unmarried woman cares about the things of the Lord, that she may be holy both in body and in spirit. But she who is married cares about the things of the world—how she may please her husband. And this I say for your own profit, not that I may put a leash on you, but for what is proper, and that you may serve the Lord without distraction. But if any man thinks he is behaving improperly toward his virgin, if she is past the flower of youth, and thus it must be, let him do what he wishes. He does not sin; let them marry. Nevertheless he who stands steadfast in his heart, having no necessity, but has power over his own will, and has so determined in his heart that he will keep his virgin, does well. So then he who gives her in marriage does well, but he who does not give her in marriage does better. A wife is bound by Law as long as her husband lives; but if her husband dies, she is at liberty to be married to whom she wishes, only in the Lord. But she is happier if she remains as she is, according to my judgment — and I think I also have the Spirit of GOD" (1 Corinthians 7:1-40 NKJV). GOD leaves no excuse to walk away from an unbelieving spouse. If this is our calling, let us work at it. Who knows, but that the unbelieving spouse might be saved! And, Praise GOD, the Word tells us the children are sanctified because of the believing spouse (parent).

WHAT JESUS BELIEVES

Regarding GOD's gifting's, each of us has a calling in this too. "<u>I beseech you therefore, brethren, by the mercies of GOD, that you present your bodies a living sacrifice, holy, acceptable to GOD, which is your reasonable service</u>. And do not be conformed to this world, but be transformed by the renewing of your mind, that you may prove what is that good and acceptable and perfect will of GOD. <u>For I say, through the grace given to me, to everyone who is among you, not to think of himself more highly than he ought to think, but to think soberly, as GOD has dealt to each one a measure of faith. For as we have many members in one body, but all the members do not have the same function, so we, being many, are one body in Christ, and individually members of one another. Having then gifts differing according to the grace that is given to us, let us use them: if prophecy, let us prophesy in proportion to our faith; or ministry, let us use it in our ministering; he who teaches, in teaching; he who exhorts, in exhortation; he who gives, with liberality; he who leads, with diligence; he who shows mercy, with cheerfulness. Let love be without hypocrisy. Abhor what is evil. Cling to what is good. Be kindly affectionate to one another with brotherly love, in honor giving preference to one another; not lagging in diligence, fervent in spirit, serving the Lord; rejoicing in hope, patient in tribulation, continuing steadfastly in prayer; distributing to the needs of the saints, given to hospitality</u>. Bless those who persecute you; bless and do not curse. Rejoice with those who rejoice, and weep with those who weep. Be of the same mind toward one another. Do not set your mind on high things, but associate with the humble. Do not be wise in your own opinion. Repay no one evil for evil. Have regard for good things in the sight of all men. If it is possible, as much as depends on you, live peaceably with all men. Beloved, do not avenge yourselves, but rather give place to wrath; for it is written, "Vengeance is Mine, I will repay," says the Lord. Therefore "If your enemy is hungry, feed him; if he is thirsty, give him a drink; for in so doing you will heap coals of fire on his head." Do not be overcome by evil, but overcome evil with good" (Romans 12:1-21 NKJV).

"I, therefore, the prisoner of the Lord, beseech you to walk worthy of the calling with which you were called, with all lowliness and gentleness, with longsuffering, bearing with one another in love, endeavoring to keep the unity of the Spirit in the bond of peace. One Lord, one faith, one baptism; one GOD and Father of all, who is above all, and through all, and in you all. But to each one of us grace was given according to the measure of Christ's gift. Therefore He says: "When He ascended on high, He led captivity captive, and gave gifts to men." (Now this, "He ascended"—what does it mean but that He also first descended into the lower parts of the earth? He who descended is also the One who ascended far above all the heavens, that He might fill all things). **And He Himself gave some to be apostles, some prophets, some evangelists, and some pastors and teachers, for the equipping of the saints for the work of ministry, for the edifying of the body of Christ**, till we all come to the unity of the faith and of the knowledge of the Son of GOD, to a perfect man, to the measure of the stature of the fullness of Christ; that we should no longer be children, tossed to and fro and carried about with every wind of doctrine, by the trickery of men, in the cunning craftiness of deceitful plotting, but, speaking the truth in love, may grow up in all things into Him who is the head — Christ — from Whom the whole body, joined and knit together by what every joint supplies, according to the effective working by which every part does its share, causes growth of the body for the edifying of itself in love" (Ephesians 4:1-3, 5-16 NKJV).

> *"You are My custom work, but I'm not finished with you.*
> *Would you please hold still?"*
> **Holy Spirit**
> [I saw His face smiling in Love when I heard Him say this.]

Holy Spirit is working to complete GOD's Perfect Will, GOD's Perfect Light, in us! **When He asks us to *hold still* He is telling us to *be still and know that He is* Lord, teaching us we can trust Him even as we are moving forward in Him (in Him) through our daily lives.** <u>Moving forward requires walking in faith.</u> **Walking in faith is trusting in GOD**

like a little child. Jesus said that we must come to Him like a little child.

"At that time the disciples came to Jesus and asked, "Who, then, is the greatest in the kingdom of heaven?" He called a little child to him, and placed the child among them. And he said: "Truly I tell you, unless you change and become like little children, you will never enter the kingdom of heaven. Therefore, whoever takes the lowly position of this child is the greatest in the kingdom of heaven." Matthew 18:1-4 NIV

When we come to GOD, <u>we must come to Him with the simple faith of a child</u>. *Feel like you can't do it?* Meditate on His promise that *you can do all things through Him* and then just ask Him to help you to use your measure of faith. *Isn't that sinning to ask for help with something He has already given us?* No. When you give a bicycle to a child, you don't just say, *'Here it is! It's yours! Now ride it!'* No, you help them to learn to ride it by holding onto the handlebars and the back of the bicycle and walking along beside it. Then, when that child is feeling a bit more confident, you pick up the pace. After a bit longer, you may be able to let go of the front of the bicycle and steady only the back as the child masters the balance of the front wheel with the handlebars. Finally, you let go and the child probably doesn't even know that you have. Eventually, with consistent practice, that child can ride like a Pro. That is how it is with GOD and us. We are his children and He works with us at the level of faith that we are at. Until finally, we too are operating in faith *like a Pro!* **Operating in the faith that we have causes our faith to grow.**

GOD so desires our success that He has made it simple (for us). "So Jesus answered and said to them, "Have faith in GOD. For assuredly, I say to you, whoever says to this mountain, 'Be removed and be cast into the sea,' and does not doubt in his heart, but believes that those things he says will be done, he will have whatever he says. Therefore I say to you, whatever things you ask when you pray, believe that you receive them, and you will have them" (Mark 11:22-24 NKJV).

WHAT JESUS BELIEVES

Ask the Lord to search your heart right now for any unbelief that you might be harboring there over a situation that didn't turn out as you had planned, and therefore blamed GOD for the outcome of. It's easy to do. I have done it many times. We all have, but now is the day of salvation, now is the time of the latter rain, and that means that we are growing up as a Church Body. It's time now to *get out* our misconceptions by asking GOD to show us our heart on all things. He desires to remove wrong teaching and misconceptions out of all of us. In other words, He is removing untruth from those who press into Him. If you feel like you've been shaken <u>a lot</u> lately, you have! It shows that you have been picked by the hand of GOD to have a part in the end time harvest. If you haven't been shaken, why don't you get before GOD and ask him, *'Why haven't You shaken me?' This is not a time that we can be lukewarm, this is a time to* **choose hot or cold.** To not hearken (listen) to the Spirit of the LORD can be both physical and spiritual death.

Revelation 3:14-22 NIV

""To the angel of the church in Laodicea write: These are the words of the Amen, the faithful and true witness, the ruler of God's creation. I know your deeds, that you are neither cold nor hot. I wish you were either one or the other! So, because you are lukewarm—neither hot nor cold—I am about to spit you out of my mouth. You say, 'I am rich; I have acquired wealth and do not need a thing.' But you do not realize that you are wretched, pitiful, poor, blind and naked. I counsel you to buy from me gold refined in the fire, so you can become rich; and white clothes to wear, so you can cover your shameful nakedness; and salve to put on your eyes, so you can see. **Those whom I love I rebuke and discipline. So be earnest and repent.** <u>Here I am! I stand at the door and knock. If anyone hears my voice and opens the door, I will come in and eat with that person, and they with me.</u> **To the one who is victorious, I will give the right to sit with me on my throne, just as I was victorious and sat down with my Father**

on his throne. <u>Whoever has ears, let them hear what the Spirit says to the churches."</u>"" (suggested reading: Revelation Chapters 2 and 3.)

The Word declares that *the hearts of many will wax cold*. "<u>And because lawlessness will abound, the love of many will grow cold.</u> **But he who endures to the end shall be saved.** <u>And this Gospel of the Kingdom will be preached in all the world as a witness to all the nations, and then the end will come</u>" (Matthew 24:12-14 NKJV). It will be <u>their</u> choice to stay close to GOD or leave GOD's ways and GOD. Those of us who are preparing ourselves *faithfully*, **by prayer and supplications**, before GOD, and by spending quality time with Him in the Word, will be the only ones left standing up. You can read about the truth of this in the book of Revelation. It is a prophetic book and very interesting! Be sure to go into it with the help of the Holy Spirit, as at all other times. GOD will help you to understand His Word if you ask Him. " "Ask, and it will be given to you; seek, and you will find; knock, and it will be opened to you" (Matthew 7:7 NKJV). Keep on asking and it will be given you; keep on seeking and you will find; keep on knocking [reverently] and [the door] will be opened to you. For everyone who keeps on asking receives; and he who keeps on seeking finds; and to him who keeps on knocking, [the door] will be opened" (Matthew 7:7-8 AMP).

GOD is about to release full power on the Earth because His children ask for it. *That simple?* Yes. *They have been praying and seeking GOD.* Doing this involves what is often referred to by pastors as *dying to self*. Jesus died to Himself every day. Meaning He gave over the will of His flesh every day to GOD. He knew that man's nature was evil and that to give into it just once would mean that death would be victorious and we wouldn't get to Heaven. Being the GOD that He was inside, He did not give in to that flesh nature. Instead, He followed GOD's will at all times. *"Well, I am not Jesus!"* The Bible says that *for me to live is Christ (Philippians 1:21)*. That isn't claiming that we are Christ, but that He lives within us, guiding, keeping, and helping us. He is our rootstock. He is the one that the world should see when they look at us. When they read the Bible for the first time, they should think, *'Hey, that's just what so and so does! That's just how he/she is!'* Now, that would be a living example of Jesus! Us, so submitted and committed to GOD that the world knows that we are different. If the world doesn't see us as different, then *this little light of ours (mine) must be under a bushel! Oh no!* Time is ticking and it isn't going to wait for us. It does take commitment and integrity to be a full-blown, mature, Field-Harvesting Christian! Eternity for so many depends on our obedience to GOD. Imagine yourself at a car wreck and the car is on fire. There are 2 adults and 5 children in that car. GOD is the only One Who knows the one way to get all 7 out of the car so that they don't burn alive. We need to listen and obey GOD's Word of Instruction in order to save people from spending an Eternity in the Lake of Fire, along with satan! We need to walk in the Light of Love and **forgive** others over and over, *seventy times seven*. We need to be willing go wherever we need to go and to do whatever it takes to help lost souls to understand GOD Loves them and wants to save them! *If you were still a sinner, how many chances would you hope GOD would give you to get saved?* Me too! So let's get into the Word, learn it (and appropriate it, take it in as ours which it is), grow in it, have faith in it, and believe it! And we will be able to *'Let it shine! Let it shine! Let it shine!'* showing others that this is What Jesus Believes!

"The Beginning
of your new beginning is now."
Holy Spirit

"Always remember I Love you."
Holy Spirit

"**Expect Nothing Less than God's Best!**"
Author – The Holy Spirit, of course!

Works Cited

With much thanks and appreciation.

*Portions of Scripture have been used and not always Scripture in its entirety; hence, i.e. (See John 21:13-25).

Although I have utilized my personal Bibles and other online sources during my research, in this, my final edit for this publication all scripture quotes are from the Bible app. I thank you all

AMP Bible. You Version Bible App.

ASV Bible. You Version Bible App.

ASV Bible. You Version Bible App.

ESV Bible. You Version Bible App.

GW Bible. You Version Bible App.

HCS Bible. You Version Bible App.

KJV Bible. You Version Bible App.

NIV Bible. You Version Bible App.

NKJV Bible You Version Bible App.

TLV Bible. You Version Bible App.

WEB Bible. You Version Bible App.

YLT98 Bible. You Version Bible

WHAT JESUS BELIEVES

***Jesus Loves the Little Children*, the Song and the Story**
Jesus Loves the Little Children fast became a favorite, especially among children. Composer Clare Herbert Woolston Writes *Jesus Loves the Little Children*. Clare Herbert Woolston (1856-1927) was a preacher in Chicago Illinois. He wrote the words for *Jesus Loves the Little Children*. The music was written by George F. Root (1820-1895), who wrote the words and music for several well-known hymns, including *Behold the Bridegroom Cometh*! Root originally wrote the tune for *Jesus Loves the Little Children* to accompany an American Civil War song called *Tramp, Tramp, Tramp*.

Jesus loves the little children,
Refrain
Jesus loves the little children,
All the children of the world.
Red and yellow, black and white,
All are precious in His sight,
Jesus loves the little children of the world.

Alternate Refrain:
Jesus died for all the children,
All the children of the world.
Red and yellow, black and white,
All are precious in His sight,
Jesus died for all the children of the world.

Jesus calls the children dear,
Come to me and never fear,
For I love the little children of the world;
I will take you by the hand,
Lead you to the better land,
For I love the little children of the world.

Refrain

Jesus is the Shepherd true,
And He'll always stand by you,
For He loves the little children of the world;
He's a Savior great and strong,
And He'll shield you from the wrong,

WHAT JESUS BELIEVES

For He loves the little children of the world.

Refrain

I am coming, Lord, to Thee,
And Your soldier I will be,
For You love the little children of the world;
And Your cross I'll always bear,
And for You I'll do and dare,
For You love the little children of the world.

Refrain

Nothing but the Blood
"Let the little children come to Me, and do not hinder them, for the Kingdom of Heaven belongs to such as these" (Matthew 19:14).
Nothing but the Blood was written by Pastor Robert Lowry; he was the pastor of the Park Avenue Baptist Church of Plainfield, New Jersey in the late 19th Century. He wrote both the words and the music for the hymn
Robert Lowry, pub.1876
Copyright: Public Domain

Nothing but the Blood
What can wash away my sin?
Nothing but the blood of Jesus;
What can make me whole again?
Nothing but the blood of Jesus.

Refrain:
Oh! Precious is the flow
That makes me white as snow;
No other fount I know,
Nothing but the blood of Jesus.
For my pardon, this I see,
Nothing but the blood of Jesus;
For my cleansing this my plea,
Nothing but the blood of Jesus.
Nothing can for sin atone,
Nothing but the blood of Jesus;

WHAT JESUS BELIEVES

Naught of good that I have done,
Nothing but the blood of Jesus.
This is all my hope and peace,
Nothing but the blood of Jesus;
This is all my righteousness,
Nothing but the blood of Jesus.
Now by this I'll overcome —
Nothing but the blood of Jesus;
Now by this I'll reach my home —
Nothing but the blood of Jesus.
Glory! Glory! This I sing —
Nothing but the blood of Jesus
All my praise for this I bring.
Nothing but the blood of Jesus.

This Little Light of Mine is a gospel children's song written by Harry Dixon Loes (1895-1965) in about 1920. Loes, who studied at the Moody Bible Institute and the American Conservatory of Music, was a musical composer, and teacher, who wrote, and co-wrote, several other gospel songs. The song has since entered the folk tradition, first being collected by John Lomax in 1939. Often thought of as a Negro spiritual, it does not, however, appear in any collection of jubilee or plantation songs from the nineteenth century (Wikipedia):

This Little Light of Mine

This little light of mine, I'm gonna let it shine
This little light of mine, I'm gonna let it shine,
This little light of mine, I'm gonna let it shine,
Let it shine, let it shine, let it shine
Hide it under a bushel, no!
I'm gonna let it shine
Hide it under a bushel, no!
I'm gonna let it shine,
Hide it under a bushel, no!
I'm gonna let it shine, let it shine,
Let it shine, let it shine
Don't let Satan blow it out
I'm gonna let it shine

WHAT JESUS BELIEVES

Don't let Satan blow it out
I'm gonna let it shine
Don't let Satan blow it out
I'm gonna let it shine,
Let it shine, let it shine, let it shine
Let it shine til Jesus comes
I'm gonna let it shine
Let it shine til Jesus comes
I'm gonna let it shine,
Let it shine til Jesus comes
I'm gonna let it shine
Let it shine, let it shine, let it shine
This little light of mine, I'm gonna let it shine
This little light of mine, I'm gonna let it shine,
This little light of mine, I'm gonna let it shine,
Let it shine, let it shine, let it shine
Let it shine, let it shine, let it shine

Depending on the source, the song may take its theme from Matthew 5:16, "Let your light shine before men, that they may see your fine works and give glory to your Father who is in the Heaven." Or, it may refer to the words of Jesus in Luke 11:33, where He said, "No man, when he hath lighted a candle, putteth it in a secret place, neither under a bushel, but on a candlestick, that they which come in may see the light." Or, it may be based on Matthew 5:14-15, where Jesus said, "Ye are the light of the world. A city that is set on an hill cannot be hid. Neither do men light a candle and put it under a bushel, but on a candlestick; and it giveth light unto all that are in the house.

New Strong's Complete Dictionary of Bible Words. Online.

*NOTE: I have taken the liberty of adding brackets [ ] and/or parentheses ( ) containing words to clarify, or definitions to help define or give explanation; and/or I have also utilized ALL CAPS, **bold**, *italics*, and/or <u>underlining</u> for emphasis].

WHAT JESUS BELIEVES

*"This book will take you on a journey into the past
To bring you into your future."*

I take no credit for writing this book, I am simply a pen of the LORD, and His humble servant.

*I love you all. Don't ever stop your amazing Journey.
Jean*

www.ingramcontent.com/pod-product-compliance
Lightning Source LLC
LaVergne TN
LVHW051552070426
835507LV00021B/2536